An Arcadian Vision
Giving Form to Faith

John W. Ekstedt

authorHOUSE®

AuthorHouse™
1663 Liberty Drive
Bloomington, IN 47403
www.authorhouse.com
Phone: 1-800-839-8640

© 2011 John W. Ekstedt. All rights reserved.

No part of this book may be reproduced, stored in a retrieval system, or transmitted by any means without the written permission of the author.

First published by AuthorHouse   11/23/2011

ISBN: 978-1-4670-9781-9 (sc)
ISBN: 978-1-4670-9780-2 (hc)
ISBN: 978-1-4670-9779-6 (e)
Library of Congress Control Number: 2011919619
Printed in the United States of America

Any people depicted in stock imagery provided by Thinkstock are models, and such images are being used for illustrative purposes only.
Certain stock imagery © Thinkstock.

This book is printed on acid-free paper.

Because of the dynamic nature of the Internet, any web addresses or links contained in this book may have changed since publication and may no longer be valid. The views expressed in this work are solely those of the author and do not necessarily reflect the views of the publisher, and the publisher hereby disclaims any responsibility for them.

No part of this book may be reproduced, stored in a retrieval system, or transmitted by any means without the written permission of the author, except in the case of brief quotations embodied in reviews.

Front cover photograph, Jasper Lutheran Church by Stephen A. Nelson © 2009, used with permission.

Back cover photographs, Jasper Wolf© 2007 and Pastor Ekstedt © 2008 by Henry Beckmann, used with permission.

This book is a production of Jasper Lutheran Church, Jasper, Alberta Canada.

All proceeds from the sale of this book are to be used in support of the ministry of Jasper Lutheran Church or for projects as approved by them.

Arcadian: From ancient Greek. It is the name of a specific place in Greece but has come to refer to ideas or ideals about life as imagined in any idyllic place. The word connotes pastoral simplicity or a vision of paradise taken from images found in human discourse or from places in the natural world. In this book, the word *Arcadian* refers to a place of rustic idealism and to the words spoken or written in that place.

Dedication

This book is an object arising from the worship of the members and friends of Jasper Lutheran Church. They wish that it be dedicated to the glory of God and to the memory of each other.

The author dedicates his work to all those named therein in memory of the Arcadian vision we shared in the Canadian Rocky Mountains

Contents

Dedication	vii
Forward	xiii
Author's Note	xv
Preface	xix
1. Introduction	1
2. Reflections on Church	5
The Church as a Human Construct	5
The Church in a Particular Place	6
The Church as a Particular People	8
The Church as a Divine Construct	11
Arcadian Meditations (Selected Sermons)	14
3. The High Festival of Christmas	17
Getting Ready for Christ's Birth (Advent and Christmas Eve)	17
Show Me Your Ways:	17
The Voice of One Calling	21
Living Good, Living Well	26
Making a Body for God	29
A Gift Waiting to Be Received	32
The Light Shines in the Darkness	34
With Wonder at the Birth of God	37
4. The Festival of Epiphany (Learning to Know the Child)	40
On Preaching	40
Of One Spirit	44
Made for a Purpose	48
Images on a Flannel Board	51
Love is an Adult Thing	55
At the Heart of the Matter	58

5. The High Festival of Easter 63
   Lessons of the Passion (Lent) 63
   Celebration or Sacrifice: a Petition for Lent 63
   To Die in Jerusalem 69
   It Just Isn't Fair! 73
   The Work of the Church 77
   It Is My Passion! 82
   Self-denial and Repentance 86
   Stay Together! Stay Awake! 90
   A New Day Coming 92
   From Death to New Life (the Easter message) 95
   They Have Taken Away My Lord 99
   Unless I See . . . I Will Not Believe 103
   Who Are You, Lord? 107
   How Long Will You Keep Us in Suspense? 112
   Everything Here Is New Again 116
   Death Will Be No More 119
   Great Grace 122
6. The Festival of Pentecost 128
   Becoming What We Were Meant to Be 128
   The Life of a Good Person 132
   Enhancing the Flavor of Life 136
   Esther 137
   The Christian community 138
   The stranger in the faith 138

7. Lessons in Ordinary Time	140
To Know the Mind of God	141
Swimming in the Ocean of God's Mystery	145
Parabolic Teaching	149
A New Curtain	152
The Power of a Woman and the Love of a Mother	155
On Being Spiritual	159
Identity Theft	163
Sacrifice: What Is it?	167
A Pioneer of Salvation	171
Finding Peace in the Whirlwind	175
Watch Your Mouth!	179
On Politics	184
Faith and Food – Life in Two Dimensions	188
Is Freedom Just Another Word?	193
We Are All Together in This!	197
Now That's What I'm Talking About!	201
8. Essays	205
The Church in the World	205
A Shadow of Plenty in a Diminished World	207
Afterward	212
Postscript	218

Forward

Like many people of my generation, I've often been seen as a Lone Wolf; or – at the very least – the Lone Wolf of the group.

Lone Wolves are by nature the kind of people who – although they may feel the need to be part of a group or pack – strongly feel the need for independence and autonomy. They hang out on the edges rather than join the inner circle.

The pack I've been running with lately is Jasper Lutheran Church, the congregation that is featured in this book.

Running with such a pack already marks you as "odd" because Jasper's earthly paradise is a place where people worship the Creation but have little use for the Creator. And if you talk about **Alpha and Omega** here – people won't immediately make the connection with the God who is "the Beginning and the End." They will probably think you're talking about an animated film starring an unlikely pair of wolves

But living in such a paradise lost, you can learn a great deal about "eccentric" lone wolves – the four-legged kind and the two-legged kind – that live outside the circle.

And probably the most important thing you can learn is that ***all lone wolves were once part of a pack before they left or were forced out.*** Many of them long to return to the pack from which they were ostracized. And the lone wolves who survive best are those that maintain a relationship – albeit a distant one – with the pack. Such relationships benefit the pack, too

The other thing you learn is that every pack needs a leader.

In churches we usually call such leaders **pastor,** which means "shepherd", or **minister**, which means "servant".

To me, John Ekstedt is more than a shepherd or a servant.

To me, John is The Old Wolf – what the Wolf Cubs in Canada (a.k.a. Cub Scouts in America) used to call "Akela": the symbol of wisdom, authority, and leadership. (Rudyard Kipling obtained the name Akela for the wolf featured in his Mowgli stories from Hindi, meaning "solitary" or "alone".)

And here – as he has done many times before – The Old Wolf offers us a meal, with juicy meat to be chewed and bones to be gnawed on.

Stephen A. Nelson
Jasper, 2011

Author's Note

A few years ago, I published a memoir titled *Shades of Northern Light* (AuthorHouse, 2006). I had decided to put together some reflections on my life because I was experiencing the vacuum that comes with any significant life change, especially one like retirement that can slow or even stop the driving forces that motivate a person through life. I was well into my seventh decade, experiencing various health problems (less than four months later I would suffer a massive heart attack), and feeling that I had pretty much done what I was placed here to do.

In that memoir, I tried to express my disappointments, along with all the things that have given me satisfaction. One of the areas of disappointment had to do with my religious experience. I had been raised in a sincere and dedicated religious community. Very early in my formal baccalaureate education I knew that, no matter what else I did, I would complete theological training and become a clergyman.

At the time of publishing my memoir, those days of aspiration were long gone. Much of the energy and many of the ideas that had motivated me through the long years of preparation to meet that particular goal were lost to me. In effect, I had spent my life wandering the world looking for a place to practice my skills and express my beliefs. I started out in organized religion but over time applied my craft in several of western society's other significant institutions. I met with some successes, experienced notable failures, and finished the day in a vacuum of depleted energy.

I do not mean to imply that I had been left depressed and bitter, or even unfulfilled. That is certainly not true. I had, to that moment, had a very good life as life among human beings goes. I just thought that my life was pretty much over as a positive and productive force. For the first time I could not see anything on the way ahead.

In a sense, *An Arcadian Vision* is about what happened next.

The primary subject of *An Arcadian Vision* is an exploration of the thing that I set out to do in the very beginning. That thing was my desire to give expression to my spirituality through the medium of organized religion. In preparation to do this, I had attached myself to a church, practiced its forms, learned its theology and developed some skills that I considered useful to practice faith in the mundane or temporal world. Those skills were developed through studies in practical theology, applied science, public administration and adult education. As the years progressed, I practiced these skills in institutions of organized religion, medicine and mental health, public education and criminal justice.

While *An Arcadian Vision* offers reflections on the role of church in spirituality and religion, it is not written as a study in theology, though the inclusion of a number of sermons presents some opportunity for comment in that area. Rather, it is intended as an essay on spirituality as a human attribute and the desire among many to give their spirituality formal expression. It is about the church as a human and divine institution established for the purpose of expressing spirituality, and why people may be drawn to it or away from it.

I write about the church from the perspective of the last parish that I served as a pastor or priest. I discuss lessons confirmed for me about the meaning of the church in the lives of people for whom religion is not a vocation. I conclude with some commentary on the nature of the church and theology in a world where these things do not appear as they did when I entered the seminary as a young man.

I wish to thank Warren Waxer (he will be surprised) for stimulating my return to the study of Hebrew texts. I will forever be grateful to Stephen A. Nelson, Heather Daw, Hans Intscher and Gertie Kofin (they shouldn't be surprised) for challenging many of my theological assumptions through their careful attention followed by persistent questions and comment. With these people, I was unable to hide or procrastinate since they heard my speaking and always confronted me in person at the time and in the place where the speaking occurred.

For any insights that I may have at the moment and certainly for the renewed hope that I have realized through my time in a little church in a far away place, I have many people to thank in addition to those mentioned above. These are not only people from the church that I served but of the town and region wherein it was located. Each one, of course, has a story to tell and I was lucky to learn some of each of their stories. They are Henry Beckmann, Vicki Beckmann, Carrie Berry, Leiselotte Brenne, Debbie Brill, Horst Bulda, Brigitte Bulda, Dong Han, Morley Fleming, Val Fleming, Alice Gerber, Debbie Gerber, Doug Heine, Donna Heine, Mark Hendricks, Doris Intscher, Gina Jabs, Fred Kofin, Komiko Kurosaki, Mike Moberly, David Prowse, Ken Rice, Bill Skene, Adela Torchia, and Nelda Wright.

Some members from the Anglican and United churches and a few members from the other churches in town shared ecumenical experiences with us and became our friends as did some regular visitors to Jasper National Park who were so faithful in their attendance at our little chapel. I am grateful for the time my wife Kay and I had as members of the Summit Singers (the Jasper community choir). We remember the welcoming hand of the management and staff at Jasper Park Lodge where I had the privilege to officiate at a candlelight service on Christmas Eve each of the years we were there. It was a joy for both of us to participate in the regular worship services for seniors at Alpine Summit Lodge.

I would be remiss not to mention with special thanksgiving Henry Beckmann, who provided the bridge between my first call to Jasper in 1966 when it was part of the Central Lutheran Parish and my last call in 2008 after it had become a parish in its own right. Henry and I are contemporaries and he was part of the welcoming committee on both occasions. His work and that of his wife Vicki in later years is, in my mind, the miracle of commitment that brought me the great gift to serve Jasper again. He carries the memory of this congregation, including the vision of those whose work brought this church into being, such as Louise and Bill Kronstedt, now departed.

There were others, of course, including our son, daughter-in-law and grandchildren from Edmonton, Alberta who cared for us in so many ways and kept us in the things we needed, especially in the beginning. We remember the attention and encouragement we received from our children and their spouses in Quebec and British Columbia, and our grandchildren in British Columbia.

While Kay and I both benefited from the love, kindness and generosity of all these people, in my case it was Kay, once again, who made it all work and whom I have most to thank for this opportunity.

Preface

Religion, it seems, has become a dirty word. When religion is discussed in the forum of journalism or politics it is often with reference to the influence of religion on unspeakable acts by human beings. Religion is juxtaposed with discrimination, misogyny, terrorism and war. It is viewed as the motivator behind oppression and the abuse of innocents.

Religion, of course, is about belief systems, especially belief systems that attribute the source and meaning of life to a god, a divine presence, or some other power greater than individual human beings. Depending on where people live and the belief system they follow, their religion is usually attached to an institution with a hierarchy and human authorities. This gives religion an aura of impenetrability in that its essence is seen to be mysterious and available for interpretation only by selected human beings. As a result, the keepers of religious knowledge can wield great power over the attitudes and actions of others.

Religion, as a location of human authority, may become a vehicle for exercising political influence or waging war. It may be seen as antithetical to individual freedom or social progress.

The world has changed dramatically in a very short time, within the lifetime of all adult persons currently living. Among the many and abrupt changes has been globalization. The globalization phenomenon means, in part, that cultures are merging and overlapping, triggering conflict and competition for resources. In this atmosphere, the potential for religious differences to assume importance in social and political conflicts is heightened.

Religion as an institutionalized belief system demands adherence in order to function. Many call this adherence faith. People talk about living their faith within the particular confines of their religion. Faith as a motivator is powerful and, often, unassailable. However, rather than being seen as an act of free will, faith is often taken as the force behind the loss of free will. Otherwise, critics say, how do we explain the atrocities performed by human beings in the name of their religion or their inability to see the obvious errors in some religious pronouncements or practices?

Yet every culture – every civilization – that the world has known has been built on religious principles, including the most advanced cultures of the contemporary world. Billions of people continue to express their faith in religious practices and find comfort in doing so. Yes, the world is changing. People are being dislocated. Secularism and humanism have gained force as ideologies people use to guide their actions and give order to their communities – if for no other reason than to blunt the edge of religious conflicts and disagreements. But is religion passe? Is faith no longer vital as a human attribute? Is it helpful to make a distinction between the institutions of religion and the nature, or essence, of faith?

An Arcadian Vision is about religion in the contemporary world from a Christian perspective. The larger questions of religion and faith mentioned above can probably not be addressed without some understanding of faith as expressed by a particular religion in a particular culture. Otherwise the discussion is simply too abstract to have any meaning.

Not knowing the meaning of faith or the purpose of religion makes it possible to use these things as the motivation for vicious prejudices and terrible acts. But, apart from that, it also makes it easy to treat a religious person or a "person of faith" without respect, thereby hindering any possibility for healing in a world so full of social and cultural competition and conflict.

Within western culture and specific to Christianity, there are two issues that seem to stand out among the many concerns related to the place of religion in modern life. The first is the connection between spirituality and organized religion. For many, this issue is about whether or not adherence to the teachings of a particular faith or religion is necessary to maintain a positive spirituality.

The second issue has to do with the relationship between faith and reason. This issue is often before the public in debates about whether or not scientific knowledge can be reconciled with the teachings of organized religion.

Central to both these issues is the existence of the church. It is the church that persons are often resisting when they argue for spirituality in the absence of religion. The church, it is said, is spirituality institutionalized into something rigid and unforgiving. Religion is described as the outcome of defining our spirituality according to rules or dogma devised by a paternalistic hierarchy called a church.

It is this idea of church that is also taken to be the authority standing in opposition to the findings of science. Churches are seen as places where an antiquated worldview is proclaimed, counter to the evolution of human knowledge in a rational and humanistic world.

While these issues, or the questions emerging from them, seem to arise from phenomena considered unique to modern western culture, such as secularism or humanism, they are in fact as old as human knowledge and human culture itself. Faith and reason have always been at each other's throats. As a result, the problem of understanding ourselves as spiritual creatures has been the inspiration for the highest level of human achievement in art, music and literature as well as the cause for great anxiety, depression and suffering. It is said, of course, that suffering and achievement often go together.

It is possible that these matters take on a different edge now that science, as an exercise in reason, has progressed so far and that the institutional church in modern western culture has declined as a popular expression of spirituality and community. But we should be careful not to think that the conflict between faith and reason has emerged as a *result* of scientific inquiry, humanistic philosophy, individualism or the failure of the institutional church to remain relevant. The struggle to understand the things of the world and to know the origin of life has always been with us, as any study of world history will affirm.

We should not be discouraged that these questions reemerge in every era or even in every generation. For those parents, of whom I have met many, that lament the falling away of their children either from the institutional church in which they were baptized or from other cultural and family traditions, I say be of good cheer. It has always been thus. If the thread woven in a child's rearing has sufficient strength and if the weavers are not too jealous of their weaving, the child will be held safe into adulthood.

This does not mean, however, that we should cease to try to get at the heart of the matter or be afraid to ask the difficult questions necessary to either find our faith or reaffirm it. It is true that sometimes questions about faith or about the church are not asked seriously. We may sometimes find ourselves confronted with arguments concerning the relevance of faith from persons whose real motive is to avoid any pressure to commit to public religious expression or who wish to belittle the commitment of others to any such enterprise.

But many people are genuine seekers who want to know who they are and the purpose of their being. They ask questions of life seriously and without prejudice toward others. I believe that this applies to most of us. We want to know the relationship between our reason and our spirituality. We want to know what faith is, and once we have found it we want to give form to it. However, we may not know how to begin.

As to the questions about the relationship between science, spirituality and religion, what follows will assume that:

1. There is no conflict between religion and science since there is no conflict between faith and reason. There are disagreements among people about these matters because we are all human and unlikely to see clearly regardless of which arguments we favor. The trouble comes when people on either side insist on the rightness of a particular point of view. We probably serve each other better if we begin these discussions by acknowledging that "the truth is not in us". This does not mean, of course, that we cannot know the truth. It just means that sometimes our egos and opinions get in the way of finding it.
2. We are spiritual creatures whether we are religious, in the institutional sense, or not. Being spiritual is an inherent part of our being. We come to the question of religion as beings of body, mind and spirit. How religion and science serve to improve or inhibit our growth as such beings is another matter.

This book is an attempt to address the problem of religion and spirituality, if only in a small way. What follows is an exploration of practices and beliefs that some use to give form to their faith. But perhaps more importantly, it is an effort to address the matter of faith itself.

1. Introduction

The various sections and chapters that comprise most of this book are notes, observations and sermons written during my tenure as the pastor of a small mountain parish in Alberta, Canada. The call to this parish was extended to me near the end of the first decade of the twenty-first century. As part of my call, I produced sermons for several congregations and contributed materials for church publications, newsletters, other print media and electronic media. Some of that work has influenced the writing for this book or is included within it.

The bulk of material in this book is selected sermons presented as part of the weekly worship experience at Jasper Lutheran Church, the church of my last call. Sermons are usually prepared and spoken by one person for the hearing of many persons. They are not written with an isolated reader in mind. Sermonizing does not just involve the reading of a text. It is the speaking of a text in a particular environment. The behavior of the speaker and the nature of the environment affect how the text is spoken and how it is heard. Much of this book has been spoken before gatherings of people. The numbers have varied from seven or eight to well over two hundred at a sitting.

There have been many recent changes in the ministry of the church resulting from the growth of information technology. This presents an interesting challenge for sermon writing. While all of the sermons included in this book have been spoken before an assembly of people, some have been posted for reading by persons using a computer, often on the same day or in the same hour that they were spoken. The ability to do this is considered a blessing by some pastors and priests as well as by those who are not willing or able to hear such messages in person or in a group setting. I have received comments from many people who have read one or more of these sermons on the church web page. These people usually communicated with me using the same technology they used to read the sermon. Often, they wanted to engage in a dialogue and ask questions for which they expected an answer or to provide suggestions for a follow-up sermon. On occasion, I have realized that more people had read one of these sermons via Internet than had heard it in church the week it was presented. But I must confess that I find greater satisfaction when receiving responses to a sermon in person after the service in the church at the hour it is spoken there.

When people read a sermon that was intended for speaking, the possibility exists that something might get lost as people try to make meaning from the written word. The same concern might be expressed about putting such sermons in a book. For that reason, these sermons have been edited somewhat so that they may be read a little more like written material and a little less like spoken material. Still, it is important to remember that most of this writing was meant for speaking.

I recognize in presenting these essays that within Christendom different words are used for similar concepts or practices depending, often, on history and tradition. For example, the titles that church officials use often indicate the general tradition of the church that they represent. I have chosen to use the words pastor and priest when referring to the primary church official in most congregations. Other words commonly used are minister, reverend or preacher. In some traditions the words deacon and deaconess are titles for full-time officials with high-level responsibilities in the Christian church.

The reader will also find references to "Jasper" and "the park" in the various articles and sermons. The town of Jasper, Alberta, Canada in Jasper National Park is the location within which these meditations and reflections were devised, and they were intended for the edification of the people who lived or visited there. However, while this work is an attempt to offer lessons on faith and spirituality that speak to a particular time in a specific place, they may have general application because they speak to the human condition that we all share in any time and in any place.

In the sermons, there are many references to "the readings". This is because the church in Jasper followed an order of scripture readings for the church year and the sermon was often based on one or more of them. The readings are usually arranged as a First Reading (usually from the Old Testament), a Psalm, a Second Reading (normally from the New

Testament) and the Gospel (usually from one of the four Gospels of the New Testament). The members of the congregation had these readings provided for them in the regular Sunday bulletin and were able to make reference to them while they were being read and during the sermon.

Another persistent reference in the sermons is to "the word and sacraments". While "the word" as used in the Bible has a more profound theological meaning, for our purposes here "the word" is taken to mean the word of God as found recorded in the Holy Bible of Christianity of which I have used several translations. The sacraments are taken to be the Eucharist (Holy Communion) and baptism. Sacraments are practices of the church, prescribed in the Holy Bible, that have high meaning. Here they are defined as the means by which God the Holy Spirit confers and maintains faith in believers. They are sometimes called "the means of grace".

Within Christendom, there is much controversy concerning the meaning and use of the word and sacraments. Nevertheless, it is rare within Christendom to attend a church where the use of the Bible and some form of communion or baptism ritual are absent.

While the meditations included here are biblically based, it might be said that they reflect a Reformation theology now considered somewhat more conservative than the liberal progressive theology in vogue today. As the author of these works, I do not think that this is the place for a discourse on the evolution of theology and religion in the modern era, though I will of necessity reference this issue in some of the sermons and other writings. Here it is sufficient to say that the sermons, especially, are my return to the study and presentation of God's word as found in the English Bible (using King James, Revised Standard and New International versions) with reference to original Greek, Hebrew and Aramaic texts wherever possible. As a concession to my Lutheran heritage, I have on occasion blown the dust off of my German Bible. I have used the tools of hermeneutics (biblical interpretation) and homiletics (the art of preaching) that were part of my early training.

Not everyone will agree with the theology present in some of this material. Many church teachings are controversial or involve elements allowing for more than one interpretation. The Bible itself is full of accounts of disagreement or uncertainty among people about what God has said and what they are expected to do about it. But I think we should find joy in the struggle to find meaning in scripture and in our lives. I have had opportunity for formal study in biological science, education, the humanities and theology. It has been in the study of theology that I have found the most controversy coupled with the greatest enlightenment. Being open to the views of people from other traditions that have a genuine interest in the study of God is a great blessing. It is in this context that I have discovered some of the most thoughtful people that I have ever met.

The theology of the church is learned sequentially or developmentally. It must be assimilated through applications in everyday life. Good sermons build on one another rather than existing as isolated facts or assumptions. Of course, most teachers and preachers of God's word understand that God works through His word when faithfully spoken to do things the speaker cannot anticipate. In this sense, the preacher is a conduit through which knowledge passes into the lives of hearers in all different stages of life experience. The speaker does not generate the power of the word spoken nor necessarily know the needs of the people who hear it. The priesthood is a high calling that requires the preacher to be faithful to the word (an exhausting discipline), in touch with the hearers to the greatest extent possible, and totally trusting in the power of God (the Holy Spirit) to make it work where it is needed.

2. Reflections on Church

The Church as a Human Construct

Some people have struggled valiantly to master the more esoteric meanings of church. The church, as both an ancient and modern phenomenon, has been studied by theologians, scientists and educators and written about by people from every walk of life in song, poetry and prose. Many of these efforts result in profound statements and expressions of deep meaning. But for most people, the church is simply a place or a venue for gathering. For them, the church is not otherworldly, a noble concept, a great idea or transcendent architecture – though clearly it can be all of those things. Instead, it is a building that must be supported and kept in repair. But for all the real world practicality of it, most churches do mirror in their architecture the ideals that brought the people together in the first place. The problem of its repair and upkeep may have as much to do with the replacement of a cross or of an ornate stained glass window as it would with the repair of broken plumbing or a worn out furnace. Churches are not like other buildings. Strangers may take pictures of them as souvenirs. These buildings are often named after people regarded as saints or great teachers. Their design and construction may express an image or understanding of God. A church can be picked out of a crowd of buildings. People can often find these places without being given direction or an address. They can identify with these buildings whether or not they belong to them. Even as strangers in a strange land, most have little fear of entering them.

While it is common to think of churches as merely buildings, albeit ones that may be unusual or extraordinary, on reflection most would agree that a church is more than a building. We all realize that the church is, first of all, a community of people. These are usually people who share a place of habitation and who with luck and limited resources obtain or construct a building for their use that, as much as possible, reflects their common vision about life and living.

The definition of church depends, of course, on who you are and where you are coming from. It may be one thing to a devout Catholic and another to a devout Baptist, though they may each come from a place of deep commitment to organized religious expression. Church may be experienced a totally different way by a secular humanist or someone without a background or interest in organized religion. In this book, the reader will find several essays on the meaning of church from a Christian perspective. But the reader will be aware that even this perspective on church is further honed and refined by the writer's background first in a form of evangelical Christianity and later in the Lutheran tradition. Like everything we experience, we know the church from the place where we stand. This book about church arises from a specific religion (Christianity), a specific tradition (Lutheranism) and a specific place (the mountains of northern Alberta, Canada).

The use of the word "church" comes to us from Christian literature and traditions. Other organized religions tend to use different words to define all or part of what Christians mean by church – words such as Mosque or Synagogue. In North America, we often relate the concept of church to European ideas and images, sometimes forgetting that Christianity is rooted in the near- and middle-Eastern cultures.

However, it remains true that most of us who are native North Americans understand the roots of our institutionalized church experience as coming from Europe. This is true of the Lutheran tradition and certainly true of the little place in the northern Rocky Mountains from which this book springs.

The Church in a Particular Place

After many years away, Kay and I entered the town of Jasper, Alberta by rail on a warmish spring day. For many, the railroad is the preferred method of travel to this little town. Jasper had been part of the first parish I was assigned to as a young clergyman in 1966. Now, forty-two years later, we were excited to once again observe the towering mountains looming overhead and smell the pine resin being warmed by the sun.

An Arcadian Vision

The church that I had served was still there and we were glad to see it. The building had been built in 1924 and was now considered a heritage building in a town that had been founded in 1911 and originally named Fitzhugh. The town was surveyed in 1913 and renamed Jasper after a fur trade post called Jasper House that had been established in the area in 1813 and operated by the North West Company and later by the Hudson's Bay Company. Jasper is situated in the northernmost national park in the Canadian Rocky Mountains and nestles between spectacular mountain ranges on the edge of a gorgeous valley. Through these ranges flows the Athabasca River served by several major tributaries. The valley is referred to as the Athabasca River Valley.

Jasper is a place of images. No one can go there and return without images, even if those images are only lodged in memory. The sights, smells and sounds of Jasper are unique to itself and quite extraordinary. Everyone has a particular image that defines Jasper National Park and the town of Jasper. My favorite image of the town is the railroad.

The town of Jasper largely exists in its present form because of the railroad. While the influence of the railroad on the town is declining, it is still an important visual aspect, with many of its residents being active or retired railroaders. The railroad is in large part the reason for the existence of people in this place where people are mostly an alien presence.

Every church is part of a particular place and it is important for the work of the church that the members know the place they are in, understand its character and sensitivities, and are cognizant of its needs in real time. The church must be ready to respond with the love of Christ and the application of the law and gospel to each specific situation as needed. It is my view that neither the regular membership of a church, nor its officials, can stand aloof from the community and its specific interests. Each town, city, or rural conclave has its own being of which the church is a part. The pastor must remember that the church is in the world (although not of it). Pastors or priests cannot know how to minister in a particular place until they touch the earth of that place and learn how to live in it.

The town of Jasper is in a place of great physical beauty and has unique character because it exists in a national park. There are almost always more temporary residents and visitors in town than the number of permanent residents. Much of the energy in the town is directed toward the preservation of the environment and to the care of the flora and fauna so unique to the area. The people who live in, work in or visit Jasper are always aware that they are in a unique habitat that has the potential to elevate and enhance their lives in ways not experienced in many other places.

Jasper as a particular place also demands much from the people who occupy it. The place seems to need more than the usual care, and its isolation can leave people feeling detached and lonely. It is, after all, largely a community of strangers and transients. The people of Jasper learned long ago of their responsibility to address the needs of their detached and sometimes rootless community members and have organized themselves in many ways to do just that.

Jasper National Park and the town of Jasper constitute the community of Jasper Lutheran Church. They are its parish. The gospel applies to the specific needs of a place like this as it does to every place and in every situation. But those who speak the gospel must know where they are if they are to address the people there with meaning. The church must be part of the ground on which the people walk to find their way and live their lives.

In this book, we acknowledge the comfort and stability that results when the ministry of the church is consistent wherever it is proclaimed. When the forms of worship are familiar and the words and music can be spoken or sung from memory, people are elevated and enriched no matter where they are. But when these things are done with true knowledge of the place where the words are spoken and the songs are sung, the entire community is uplifted and "even the stones cry out".

The Church as a Particular People

The church is a gathering of people. By its history and its presence, the little church in Jasper provides a good example of the power of the church as a gathering of people. It survived a very long time before it had a building to call its own.

The Jasper Lutheran church community began to gather in the middle of the twentieth century (1952). As is so often the case in North America, the early members were European immigrants, some of whom were refugees from the upheaval of the Second World War. They had strong roots in reformation theology as it had developed in northern Europe. They saw their faith as the source of the personal strength and social bonding necessary to forge the transition to a new land and culture.

For the first quarter century of its existence, Jasper Lutheran church was a mission within a larger parish served by pastors who were usually resident elsewhere in the parish or, in the earliest days, outside of the parish.

Travel was quite often prohibitive because of weather and distance. The parish stretched from the eastern edge of the Rocky Mountain foothills west into the center of the mountains themselves. This is a distance of over a hundred and fifty miles or two hundred and forty kilometers. Therefore, the worship times were not consistent and locations for meeting were sometimes unpredictable. But the community remained steadfast and the membership was able to grow.

In the mid-60s, the venerable Catholic Mission in Jasper decided to construct a new church building. Their original church building was, and is, one of the treasured structures in the Jasper townsite. After considerable negotiation, the Catholic Church building was purchased by the Synod (church administrative body) of which Jasper Lutheran Church was a member. I had become pastor of that parish a year earlier (1966) and the negotiation to obtain this building was among the first of my administrative duties as a new clergyman. The Jasper mission moved into the renovated building in June 1967 and remains there today.

All churches that I have known have been places where people seek spiritual solace. They often do it in a church building because that, for them, is where they can best identify their spiritual needs and give expression to them. It is where they "do religion", religion being the means by which they can exercise their spirit or faith. Churches are where spiritual knowledge is found and where the symbols of God's presence are kept. Churches are where people find voice to express their deepest sentiments and wrestle with their most profound difficulties. Churches are where the priests and pastors reside who have dedicated their lives to the provision of spiritual leadership. It can also be the place of false prophets, scoundrels, sorcerers and their apprentices.

It is important to see churches as places where people from a community reside and carry out their lives. If it is only seen as the place where the priests dwell, then when a priest (or pastor) leaves the church it becomes vacant. It is, in fact, common to describe churches without priests or pastors that way, and in my opinion this does terrible disservice to both the meaning and reality of church. Of course, when we say a church is vacant, we really mean that the *position* of priest or pastor has not been filled. The office of priest is a position within the church that, in one way or another, is governed or supervised by the church itself. The church does not stand empty when the priest is gone unless the people, who are the church, also go away. We read in the New Testament that the apostle Paul, in his work to help organize churches in various locations, constantly entreated

Christians in those places to understand that *they* were the church in that place and were able to act with power and authority in his absence.

The people need to remember, as does the priest or pastor, that the office of the priest is, by definition, transient. In practice this is a good thing, although at the time of vacancies it is usually experienced negatively. There are many reasons why it is a good thing for pastors and priests to live a transient life, but the main one is that the work of the church in a place must be in the hands of the people who are of that place. When the work of the church is seen to be in the hands of church "professionals" it becomes subject to distortion and abuse. The church is, among other things, a place of care and healing. People are vulnerable there. They may be willing to give themselves up to another, seemingly superior, human presence to find relief. Of course human beings help each other in all the houses of care and custody constructed for the welfare of people in the community. But the power of healing does not rest with superior human beings no matter what institution they represent or how well they are intentioned or trained. And to believe in other human beings that way is to become vulnerable to abuse and subject to fraud. For the sake of the people of the parish, as well as the priest, it is usually best that priests see their tenure as temporary, no matter how long they stay in a particular place.

I have attended churches and other houses of spiritual gathering in many locations, Christian and non-Christian. I have served in enough churches as an "official" to see the commonality of purpose people bring to them. Everyone has been wounded, some seriously. While it is true that most church members are or appear to be centered and confident in their everyday lives, one quickly learns of the effects on them of the consequences of sin. From the small uncertainties of daily living to the ravages of war and the experience of death, all are subjected to the pain and grief arising from their mortality. They come to church in the company of others to find hope. They want a place of solace and someone who will speak to their trouble. This is where the office of the priest comes in. It is why the people want a priest or pastor and why a vacancy is a troubling thing. But vacancy or not, the church remains and the source of hope remains – in the Word of God.

Defining hope has been the focus of centuries of theological study and debate. The search for the meaning and source of hope continues to occupy modern sciences such as psychology and sociology. The feeling of hope and the human longing for it have given us some of our greatest art, music and folk wisdom. It is the value that people ascribe to hope that makes it possible for the church to be populated by purveyors of false hope. People are willing to give almost anything for the promise of hope, and quite often equate this with the existence of a pastor or some other charismatic figure. A pastor or priest has failed if he or she moves on to another mission and the people left behind are confused about where hope resides.

The church is a conundrum in that it is both human and divine, spiritual and material. Its sins stand out in stark relief as blight on a perfect flower. Its goodness softens the hardest thing and brightens the darkest corner. Its guilt is a blood sacrifice. Its innocence is a newborn child.

Much has changed in the world just in my lifetime. In this book the dilemma these changes have created for the church is noted, as is the role of the church as a fixture in a changing world. But for those who know the church and for whom the church has been the institution wherein they have marked their lives, there is no need for analysis. The church is the place where the word transcendence means something, where we are all bigger and better than we would otherwise be. And no matter where we are, it is simply home.

The Church as a Divine Construct

But is the church anything else after the people gather and find a place? A better question might be "is the church anything *before* the people and the place"?

If the church is anything other than the tangibles that give it presence and make it visible, then that thing must be intangible and exist in the realm of ideas, mysticism or spirit. Christians argue that the church *is* more than an idea, a building, or a gathering of people. They assert that it has spiritual significance in that it is God present in the world. It is the place where God dwells. It is the body of Christ. Christ was the physical manifestation of God in the world and the one who commissioned the New Testament church to be the continuation of God's presence in the world.

This, of course, is mysticism at its highest level. The maker of all things, the source of life and being, the ultimate mystery, exists in the world. This Being can be known. While God is everywhere, it is in the church that the knowledge of God and the knowledge from God are expressed and, for many, it is where God is found.

But what if the church of place and community is false and its ideas corrupt? What if God is not present there? What if the knowledge of God is not expressed there? How does a person know that and what is to be done about it?

There are many controversies about religion and spirituality, the nature or existence of God, the possibility of absolute truth, the relevance of theology in the domain of science and other related matters. The Bible contains warnings and admonitions in both the Old and New Testaments about these types of controversies and the role of the church in confronting them. Most of these warnings focus on the need to assess the veracity of the information people are getting and who it is that is giving it to them. "Beware of false prophets, which come to you in sheep's clothing, but inwardly they are ravening wolves" (Matt. 7:15).

With regard to the church, the issue always seems to come down to the question of authority. Who speaks the truth? And where is it found? How do you tell a false prophet from a true one? This was another of the Apostle Paul's persistent warnings to the churches as he moved from place to place. In encouraging church members to assume authority for their own religion, he also worried about them being taken in by false prophets and teachers (see, for example, I Corinthians, chapter eleven).

There are many ways to address this question, but in its simplest form the answer is that true prophets speak for and from God and not for or from themselves. True prophets always place the interests of the ministry ahead of their own. True prophets always give credit or authority to God. A false prophet tends to assume personal authority or take personal credit for the ministry he or she is performing. False prophets seek support for the work they do by emphasizing *their* needs even though such requests may be couched in the language of self-sacrifice. You can tell by listening and watching. "By their fruits you will know them" (Matt. 7:20).

Members of a church have the responsibility to be diligent in the support of genuine servants of the Word who will faithfully minister to their needs. But as part of this responsibility the watcher or the listener also needs to be a genuine and honest seeker of the truth. Honest seekers are not just looking for something to make them feel better or that will give them more personal benefits. This, after all, is often the motive of the false prophet. An honest seeker is open to truth as it comes, no matter how inconvenient or disturbing.

It is very easy for people to convince themselves that the truth is a lie or that a lie is the truth, especially when the truth seems to require more than it gives back and a lie appears to make more sense. Sometimes falsehoods can seem more helpful or more immediately comforting. Scripture warns us about being deceived by others but we are also warned not to deceive ourselves ("Do not deceive yourselves . . ." Gal. 3:18). People can deceive themselves when they seek the truth by looking for a predetermined answer or an answer that will please them. People can allow themselves to be fooled by others when they rely only on the word of others to inform them. They must go to God's Word themselves with an open mind and seek the kind of enlightenment that allows them to distinguish between the truth and a falsehood. And it should be noted that this is not just good advice when seeking spiritual or divine knowledge; it is also necessary when seeking scientific or human knowledge.

Of course, there is always the problem of keeping the community church viable or reasonably successful so that it can accomplish its mission. What is the church to do when its members begin to fall away and it seems to fail in the eyes of the world or even in the eyes of its own members? Should it change its message to become more acceptable? Should it tell people what they want to hear? There are many ways that a church can adjust its forms and symbols as some of its historical or cultural practices become less relevant. But how far do you go before you begin to change the essence of what a church is and the truth becomes a lie? Christendom has always struggled with these questions.

Seekers need to know what they are looking for and not succumb to the desire just to be accepted or comforted or to preserve the things they are used to doing or having (as important as these things might be). In a changing world, we must all be wise enough to know what's worth saving and what can be given up. Nevertheless, as the pressures of a changing world close in on the church, it is easy to give away too much and become confused about what is important and what is not. As the young preacher Timothy was being ordained in the ministry, he was cautioned that "the time will come when men will not put up with sound doctrine. Instead, to suit their own desires, they will gather around them a great number of teachers to say what their itching ears want to hear" (2 Tim. 4:3).

The search for truth is a struggle for both the theologian and the scientist. And these are people who purport to make a career of searching for the truth. For the seeker who wishes to find the meaning of life and know the nature of things while managing the quotidian cares of family and occupation, it can be a discouraging struggle. This is why we often look for the easy way out by finding a supportive community group (sometimes a church) that does not demand more than we think we can bear.

The church needs to understand this problem and this need while remaining true to who and what she is. Maybe, in a small way, these notes from a mountain hideaway can be of help.

Arcadian Meditations (Selected Sermons)

I consider this the meat of the book. As Stephen A. Nelson observed in the Forward, this section is intended as "juicy meat to be chewed and bones to be gnawed on". You may want to start this part of the book by recalling the period of time within which most of it was written (2008-2010) and some aspects of the state of the world at that time.

The year 2008 was a year of economic disruption so profound it would change the course of the modern world. Some of the largest and most powerful financial institutions were threatened with collapse endangering the viability of many of the world's largest industrial corporations. Entire countries faced the specter of economic disaster in the years immediately following including, most notably, the United States, Greece, Ireland and Italy.

During this year and the several years following, catastrophic environmental events such as the earthquake in Haiti and the hurricane on the Gulf Coast of the United States wreaked considerable devastation in human suffering and environmental damage. Wars continued apace, with the conflicts in Pakistan and Afghanistan further weakening world economies and distorting international politics. And, of course, war itself had entered a new paradigm as a result of nearly a decade of focus by the world on the problem of terrorism. Diseases such as AIDS and malaria were plaguing entire regions and adding considerable distress to people in countries – many on the continent of Africa – already suffering from a history of poverty, war and dislocation.

This was also the year the first person of African-American descent was elected President of the United States, a change of huge importance to people all around the world.

These happenings affected every community no matter how small or isolated, including the little town of Jasper, Alberta. But each place has its own local issues as well and Jasper is no exception. Canada, as a whole, has been wrestling with problems associated with the status and well being of its indigenous or aboriginal peoples. Jasper National Park was formed, in part, through the dislocation of indigenous people in the early twentieth century. During the two years of these sermons, descendents of these original people began serious work to find some recompense for this dislocation. Events were held in Jasper and elsewhere in the park calling

An Arcadian Vision

attention to this issue and challenging a number of civic decisions on matters related to tourism, use of land, and the symbols or images used within the park.

In addition, Jasper experienced an important change in demographics during the first decade of the twenty-first century partially as a result of the need for workers to serve the leisure-time population so essential to the economy of the park. A large component of the temporary residents employed to service the paying visitors in the town and park arrived from places in Southeast Asia, the South Pacific and elsewhere, bringing a new mix of population to the town and resort locations. Incidents of vandalism, harassment and discrimination began to escalate as the town tried to adjust to this change.

Jasper is not particularly unique in the way local and world issues affect its population. Perhaps the fact that it exists within a National Park and is relatively isolated does add some characteristics not common to other places. But generally, as far as human nature goes, Jasper is a place like any other,

Much more could be said about the state of Jasper's affairs during this time and also that of the world as a whole. But these few notes will hopefully serve to remind us that the speaking of a sermon on a Sunday morning in any location is done in context. The context is not always specifically addressed, but often the direction of a sermon is influenced by the collapse of a major bank, a demonstration by aboriginal people in the town square, an earthquake in a far off country, or the killing of a world renowned terrorist. It's just something to keep in mind while reading the sermons.

These sermons are organized according to the church year. When they were written and delivered, the congregation in the town of Jasper was used to a fairly detailed ordering of the church year. Scripture readings for each Sunday were organized in three-year cycles and emphasized all the major and minor themes of the church year. It was a common practice to use one or more of these readings as the basis for each Sunday's sermon. The sermons that follow are presented with general reference to the time of the church year within which they were spoken. However, they will not necessarily flow in the exact sequence of their original presentation.

Within Christendom, there are many formats used for organizing the activities and messages of the church. Some of these are quite complex and involve the recognition of major and minor saints as well as high and low festivals. The days or seasons of the year may be assigned a color or a symbol. The organization of these things has evolved as a specialty within some churches. A few people have considerable knowledge and expertise in preparing the church for worship on special days or during specific seasons, including the decoration of church furniture, the dress of officials and the arrangement of materials and orders for worship.

However, regardless of the degree of complexity or adornment that may be preferred, all of Christendom recognizes and celebrates the major festivals of Christmas and Easter. The central teachings of Christianity focus on the birth, death and resurrection of Jesus Christ, and these teachings are highlighted no matter what the formalities of the worship experience might be in a particular church. The worship planning throughout the church year is used to organize the various teachings of the church related to these central themes. Several seasons follow on one another for this purpose. Thus Christmas is preceded by Advent and followed by Epiphany. Easter is preceded by Lent and followed by Pentecost. All, or only some, of these seasons may be highlighted for purposes of organizing the worship experience in a particular place. Many people prefer the high formality that some churches offer. Others prefer a less formal atmosphere. This is purely discretionary and, as with any good cuisine, may be done "to taste".

The church in Jasper has practiced several forms of worship over the years but always with attention to the basics of the church year as it flows from Lutheran tradition. I suppose that it is obvious to say that the church year is not the same as the calendar year in our western tradition. Thus, we start with Advent usually beginning in late November or early December and end with a period called Pentecost that usually is completed by late summer or early fall. There are also parts of the church year that are not considered to be in any of these seasons. Some call this Ordinary Time and calculate it as occurring between Epiphany and Lent and between Pentecost and Advent.

Note: The reader is reminded that the tone of the writing changes with the introduction of the sermons. The writing becomes less introspective and more outwardly directed. It may be helpful to try and imagine them as being presented in a place of worship.

3. The High Festival of Christmas

Christmas is one of the most commonly observed of the Christian church festivals. It is a high festival in many churches. This means that it is regarded as a remembrance of an event fundamental to the life of the church and its observance may involve high pomp and ceremony. As with all church observances, there are various understandings about how the date for Christmas has been determined and its relationship to other non-Christian festivals and rites.

Getting Ready for Christ's Birth (Advent and Christmas Eve)

Advent means *coming*. Many people think of Advent as the time leading up to Christmas and during which various traditions may be observed at home as well as at church. These may include the use of an Advent wreath, Advent candles and Advent calendars. Those who attend church in the western Christian tradition may be familiar with the use of some of these items in formal worship. There are four Sundays in Advent, during which the teachings focus on preparing for the Second Coming of Christ while commemorating the First Coming of Christ.

Show Me Your Ways:

(A meditation written for the First Sunday in Advent)
The days are surely coming (Jeremiah 33:14)

John W. Ekstedt

Be on guard (Luke 21:34*)*
There will be signs (Luke 21:25)
Show me your ways (Ps. 25:4)
How can we thank God enough? (I Thessalonians 3:9)

Curiosity, expectation – these are the attributes of an inquiring mind. We not only wonder about things, we expect to know about those things. A question requires an answer. A searching should result in a finding.

A few weeks ago, we reminded ourselves that we are creatures who can think about our own thoughts. We talked about what powers this ability gives us and how it is an aspect of our having been made in the image of God. (It was suggested after the service on that Sunday that this may be part of what we mean by "soul".) We also discussed how our sinfulness has perverted this ability, sometimes resulting in a storm of torment as we struggle with a vision that has been distorted and thoughts that have become twisted and confused. In another sermon we talked about finding "meaning in the whirlwind". The whirlwind was defined as the confusion of the mind.

Yet still we are curious. Still we seek the truth. And the questions that emerge from our seeking give evidence to our real nature as children of God. Who are we? Why are we here? What is the nature of life? What is the source of life? Do we have life after death?

We have also talked before about how this inquisitive energy expresses itself in a variety of creative acts. Art, literature and music are all expressions of our curiosity about life and living and the expectation that if we just keep trying we will finally see the truth revealed – even, possibly, in a work done by our own hands.

A couple of months ago, I read an article about some of the influences on the Group of Seven, that famous group of Canadian painters who, in the 1920s, are said to have set the standard for Canadian art. (A painting by one of their members recently sold for $3,000,000.) This article was written by a man named Brett Grainger who has specialized in writing about religion and politics, including a recent book titled *In the World but not of It*.

In his article about the Group of Seven, Mr. Grainger tries to show how their art was a reflection of their search for meaning, especially given the conditions of the time in which they lived. The First World War had resulted in a renewed search for philosophies or beliefs that would provide comfort in a war-torn and economically unstable world. It has been argued that, at least for some of these painters, their creativity was the result of their search to find a more satisfying way to view the world and to justify their own place in it. This is exactly what our gospel for today *(Luke 21:25-36)* is talking about – how to find redemption from "distress among nations", "people (fainting) from fear" and "foreboding of what is coming in the world".

My oldest son, a professional artist, has more than once encouraged me to try to understand the motivation and the resulting work of artists like those who were members of the Group of Seven. And we should all try to understand such things if we can. This is important to our education and, as all art must do, it helps us to define our own search for meaning.

But this is not a course in art or art history. I only mention these things to highlight the extent to which human beings will go in the search for meaning and in the expectation that they will find it.

Today is the first Sunday in a new church year. The first Sunday in Advent not only begins our time of waiting for the coming of the Messiah, but it is the first step in our journey through the church year. On this journey we seek to learn what we can about who we are, why we are here, the nature of life, the source of life and life after death. Human beings can try to express their curiosity and meet their expectations about these matters in many ways. We don't have to invent a church year to do it. Perhaps the Group of Seven painters tried a different way. Brett Grainger writes about how he had to leave the way of his grandparents and find his own way back to his faith. In a sense, we all have to find our own way to express our curiosity and meet our expectations about what we want from our life of faith in this world.

One of the popular debates these days is about the relationship between "spirituality" and "religion". This debate takes many forms but at its center are questions such as: 'Do we need organized religion to express our spiritual nature or to find our way to God?' 'Can I be spiritual without being religious?' or, 'Do I need to bind myself to the dogma of some organized church to find the truth that I seek?'

I have to tell you that I don't think this is a very important debate and it is certainly not a new one. But it is an indication that people are curious about the meaning of life and that, for some, the idea of organized religion as a way to know life's meaning is not satisfying and does not meet their expectations. Sometimes I hear people saying that if organized religion were the right way to go, it would be perfect in and of itself. There would be no use of war to further its ends, no violation by priests and ministers of the innocence of others, no fraud to deprive people of their wealth and no mistake or disagreement in the teaching of God's Word. The fact that all of these things exist in one form of religion or another makes the church suspect and drives some to seek the truth only in their knowledge of themselves.

Can a person know and worship God without a church? Well, if by church we mean a specific denomination or place of worship, then of course a person can know God outside of the church and no one requires a building of a certain type in order to pray. But if by the church we mean the bride of Christ, the body of believers who have come to Christ by faith and who recognize Him as God among us then, no, we cannot know God outside the church because when we know God, we are the church.

We who know God and are the church search for His truth and seek to worship Him in many ways. Sometimes we find a temple that pleases us and we worship Him there. Sometimes we join a specific denomination because their way of worship and their method of organizing biblical teachings help us to express our curiosity and meet our expectations. Sometimes the faith of our fathers is just fine for us. Sometimes we want to express ourselves a different way.

But whatever we do, as members of the body of Christ, as members of the church, we are bound to follow the guidance of the Holy Spirit and to seek the message of truth that comes from God's word. And the purpose of our earthly church, including the building or structure within which we worship, is to provide a means and a discipline for hearing the word of God and receiving the power of the Holy Spirit.

Yes, our earthly churches and religions are imperfect. This is because those who are involved are sinners, curious about who they are and why they are here but who do not always understand what they are hearing or even what they are seeking. The Group of Seven painters knew they were living in an imperfect world and were imperfect themselves. They had seen war and trouble on a scale not previously known and they wanted to find something better or at least know that this crazy world had not ruined their capacity to see and express beauty.

They used their art to accomplish this. Some of us also use art, or perhaps music, or maybe words – or any of the talents that God has granted us – to create beauty in a difficult and troubling world. Our efforts may be imperfect but we strive to develop our gifts to the highest level we can. And we all know that we cannot do that alone. The Group of Seven knew that. They needed and used each other in their quest to express their curiosity and meet their expectations. And from that has come a great, almost mystical, legacy.

We often feel this way about our church. It is not perfect. It is full of sinners. Sometimes its collective voice sounds like a gong or a clanging symbol. It just does not ring true. When we notice this, it saddens us and we fear for our church – and we pray for it.

But for all of this, it is our church, our religion, that consistently brings us back to the place of our curiosity and where we can begin once again to search out the great lessons that give us meaning in life.

The church year is something made up by people – it is an arbitrary thing, it is a human thing. It is their way of organizing themselves in the search for meaning and hope and love. People build and maintain their churches because they know that participating faithfully in *their* church will make them better members of *the* church.

Today we are starting a new season of inquiry within a church that we have made for ourselves. Hopefully we will find a new way to ask some of the old questions. We do this for the love of God and each other. So let us begin. Let us gird ourselves up for another year together, asking our questions and searching for the answers.

This is Advent. Christ is coming. In our lessons for today we read about Christ's first coming prophesied from antiquity. We also hear about the promised Second Coming when the work of the church will be finished in the world. In a spiritual sense, this is the beginning and the end of things. This is the alpha and omega of our spiritual journey. We are told that, as we near the end of our journey, there will be signs and wonders to behold. And we hear how people who are focussed too much on themselves and their worries may miss these moments of revelation and may fail to know or understand the truth of what God has prepared for us.

We are all spiritual, of course. But expressing this spirituality and growing in it is another thing. Especially since there are so many things that get in our way: the things that weigh us down, the worries of this life. Our religion is the way we express our faith, our spirituality. Our church is the place where many of us do that. Let us find comfort in this and, as we begin this church year, see if we can find new ways to apply old truths to the questions that we have about who we are and why we are here.

The Voice of One Calling

As is written in the book of the words of Isaiah the prophet: A voice of one calling in the desert, prepare the way for the Lord, make straight paths for him.

Every valley shall be filled in, every mountain and hill made low, the crooked roads shall become straight, the rough ways smooth. And all the people will see God's salvation (Luke 3:4-6).

Our meditation is taken from the gospel for today where, once again, we begin our preparation for the coming of the Christ Child by considering the life and work of John the Baptist.

John is a wonderful character in the saga of Jesus' coming. He is the perfect symbol of Advent. There are several reasons for this. One is that he so clearly represents the transition from Old Testament prophecy to New Testament fulfillment. He is a New Testament person with Old Testament parents who raised him in the old ways but who understood that their son had been chosen to prepare the way for a new era in the history of the world. Their son would announce the coming of the One through whom the promise of salvation would finally be realized.

Zechariah and Elizabeth, John's parents, were elderly when John was born. In this sense also, they were symbolic of the end of the old era. Today, in place of our usual Psalm, we read the prayer of Zechariah (Luke 1) offered up after the naming of his son. It is recorded in the New Testament but it is an Old Testament prayer. It sounds like a Psalm because much of it is taken from the Psalms and other Old Testament books. It is the last sound of the Old Testament voice before the new preaching begins about Christ's coming.

Mary, who became the mother of Christ, was Elizabeth's cousin. When they learned that each of their births was attended by a prophecy and that they were going to give birth at approximately the same time, they stayed with each other and rejoiced at the wonder of what was about to happen. Mary was young, just starting her adult life, and she represented the new era that would be announced by John, Elizabeth's son, and fulfilled by Jesus, her son.

John is the person in the middle. His is the voice of transition. Even his naming signals a new time and a break with tradition. It would have been proper in the ways of the Old Testament for Elizabeth's son to be named after his father, Zechariah. But Elizabeth would have none of it. She insisted that her son be named John. The temple elders protested this, pointing out that no one in her family had ever been named John. But she knew, and Zechariah confirmed, that this was a time to break from the old ways. John it would be, here *by the grace of God* (the name John is normally said to mean "by God's grace").

So John is an important biblical figure, the individual we associate with

An Arcadian Vision

Christ's coming. The person who was assigned the task of letting everyone know that there was a new day coming. He is our Advent personality.

John takes on this importance even though, in the literature of the Bible, he is a relatively minor character. The book of Matthew, for example, presents John in an interesting way. In Chapter 3, we are informed that John the Baptist is preaching in the desert at about the time Jesus was starting his ministry. Then we have ten chapters concentrating on Jesus' ministry. In Chapter 14, we have the record of John's beheading. And that seems to be the extent of it. The passages in Luke, from which some of today's readings are taken, place the emphasis more on John's parents and the events attending to his conception.

We know that John was an itinerant preacher for a very short time. We know that, as part of his ministry, he was an advisor to Herod the King. We do not know how he came to achieve this stature, but we do know that this was a dangerous role. It would eventually result in his death, thereby providing a lesson for all religious leaders who would seek to enter into the confidence of presidents and kings. John did not meet Jesus until he was an adult, almost at the end of his life, and when he met him he wasn't sure how he was supposed to behave.

John did not give us great sermons nor did he teach carefully constructed doctrine. His message was simple and straightforward "there is one better than me coming. Let me help you get ready for him".

But John did give to Christendom one of the singular sacraments in its theology – the sacrament of baptism. John was a baptizer. The rite of baptism was the way in which John could confirm an individual's commitment to the faith and signify the bond all believers have with each other. While he was baptizing, John would say "I baptize with water but the One who will come after me will baptize with the Holy Spirit". Little did John know that it would be through his baptism of Christ with water that the Holy Spirit would come and that the rite of baptism would thereafter be a means by which the Holy Spirit would descend on anyone receiving it in faith. This is a great mystery and one of the things that we should remember about John the Baptist.

John the Baptist has been one of my favorite biblical characters for as long as I can remember. As a child, the image of John as a kind of wild man living and preaching in the desert, wearing his coat of animal skins and eating locusts with honey was appealing to me. He was a kind of action hero in a world that was otherwise so removed from my experience that I had a hard time relating to it.

Even as an adult, my hero worship of John the Baptist didn't abate too much. For me, his life was the example of what a preacher should be and through him I was able to begin sorting out the various roles expected of me as I entered the ministry during the third decade of my life. (By the way, in my mind, my first call was literally to the wilderness. It was to the very large Central Lutheran Parish in north central Alberta. There were three churches and six communities to be served and the space between them was wilderness indeed. The idea that John the Baptist was a wilderness preacher was very comforting to me in these circumstances.)

John's example of a "voice crying in the wilderness" was most helpful as I tried to accomplish the task of preaching – because John was a preacher. He was called a prophet, but he was not a prophet, at least in the Old Testament sense of that. Even Jesus said (Matt. 11) that he was more than a prophet. He was not a pastor – he had no church. He was not a theologian – he did not even seem to fully understand the significance of the ritual of baptism he used so effectively and for which he finally became famous.

He was, through to his soul, a preacher of the Gospel – a teller of the Good News. As Jesus said, "he is my Father's messenger – preparing the way for me". And John's message was simple, as the message of the Gospel is – "believe me when I tell you", the preacher says, "I know of one greater than me who is coming soon. He is bringing salvation. Get ready".

The message of the Gospel, while simple, is difficult – partially because of its simplicity. It seems so unlikely. There really must be more to it than that. It requires nothing of me but faith and even that comes by the power of the Holy Spirit – that is, it is a gift of God. It seems so unbelievable and yet the preacher asks us to believe.

John's life is an example of how this preaching can be done and even what the price might be to do it. He lived for his preaching and died because of it. He was able to do this because it was God Himself who had called him to it. We learn in Luke 1 that John was called before he was conceived. He could preach this impossible message because it wasn't his message. It was God's message. And that's the way it is with all preachers of the Gospel.

It's interesting that, though John the Baptist is presented to us as something of a wild man – at least that's the way it appeared to me as a child – he is an example of the discipline required in a preacher's life. The angel Gabriel, when informing John's parents about their child to come, made it clear that they must raise their son to lead a disciplined life, avoiding strong drink and eating a careful diet. He was to take care of himself and do nothing to excess. It was this training that would allow him to withstand the difficulties of the life of a preacher and it is an example to all preachers.

Its important for us to remember – as we start another time of preparation for the coming of our Lord – that John was not sent to prepare people for the *birth* of Christ, he was sent to prepare them for the *ministry* of Christ. The relationship between John's ministry and Christ's ministry is wonderfully and dramatically presented in the prayer of Zechariah (Luke 1). In this prayer, Zechariah begins by remembering God's promise of a Savior, and that through this Savior salvation would come to all people. And in the prayer, he recognizes his own son as the fulfillment of the prophecy that a child will be born who "will go before the Lord to prepare the way".

John was a voice crying in the wilderness (or desert, which was the wilderness of Christ's world). There is a double meaning here. You will note that in our gospel (Luke 3:1-6) the word wilderness is used twice. In the original text, there are actually two different words used. The first wilderness is a place. It is the actual location where John received his commission to start preaching. The second wilderness is a condition. It is the state of a sinful world where things are rough and uncertain, where people face disappointment and confusion.

Similarly, "voice" refers to both a person and a task. The person in the narrow meaning is John; in the broader meaning it is everyone who proclaims God's word.

The task of the preacher is to give warning and provide promise. The purpose of the *warning* is to get the attention of people who may not understand what is happening to them in a world gone wrong. The purpose of the *promise* is to give people hope that salvation will come to them, that the crooked will be made straight, the valleys will be filled, the mountains made low and the rough places made smooth.

And so the ministry of John begins to prepare us for the ministry of Christ. As we begin our journey toward Bethlehem, this is worth thinking about. The birth of Jesus is not just a nice story or an excuse for a ritual of color in a faded and jaded world. It is about the coming of the person whose ministry will change everything. It is about God being with us. We are warned to prepare and be ready. We are promised light in a dark world with forgiveness and salvation for all.

Let us get ready to see this wondrous thing.

John W. Ekstedt

Living Good, Living Well

And the crowd asked him, "What then should we do?" (Luke 3:10)

Have you ever been in a place or in a situation where you were expected to pay a bribe? Places like this exist in many parts of the world. Even in developed democratic societies with political systems based on the rule of law, it is not uncommon to encounter situations where "something extra" is expected to expedite a transaction or guarantee a quality product. Recently, in Canada, there was a minor political scandal when it was discovered that some departments of the federal government had actually built bribe funds into their budgets in order to assure access to contracts in other countries or receive efficient delivery of products ordered. This has been a common practice with private companies as well. Of course, we don't always call a bribe a bribe. There are many euphemisms for the extra monies expected over and above the listed price of products or services.

While various forms of bribery occur in North America, most of us really don't know much about life in a society where bribery is a way of life. In places like that, almost every encounter with a public official involves some form of danger or threat that can be ameliorated only by some type of payoff, enticement, reward, hush money or inducement. In some places, demanding more than is actually due you is not only expected, it's the only way to make a decent living.

I used to belong to an organization that studied political corruption. Every year it would rank countries according to the level of corruption existing in the provision of public services such as infrastructure maintenance (roads, sewers, water supplies, etc.), law enforcement (police and courts) and administration (licenses, land titles, water and mineral rights, etc.). There was measurable corruption in every country studied but, as you might expect, it was most prominent in authoritarian or totalitarian regimes and in failed economies. Often both these conditions exist in the same place. A powerful authority tries to maintain rigid control over a population and, consequently, the economy may fail because people have little incentive to work. In addition, people living under these conditions have to spend considerable energy avoiding the demands of authorities as part of their survival strategy. This further weakens the overall social structure and adds to corruption.

I have often wondered why corruption is so wide spread, especially in places with relative political freedom, and why it takes so much of the resources of any society to deal with it. Even in a country such as ours, the effort in law making, regulation and enforcement to try and curb the tendency of individuals, corporations and political systems to demand more than is due them, is enormous.

And of course, corruption, where it occurs, becomes a way of life so insidious and commonplace that it often cannot be seen for what it is. How can it be stopped? Who will be the first to stop demanding bribes and try to live on totally inadequate wages? Where are the politicians that will give up bribery for honesty in the certain knowledge that they will lose power and be overtaken by their enemies?

It's interesting how many admonitions in scripture are directed to the common practice of bribery and extortion. In human affairs the nature of a social order reflects the heart and soul of its individual members. The fall into sin has resulted in considerable damage to the hearts and souls of people. Generosity has been replaced by greed. Kindness has been replaced by meanness. Peace has been given up for war. Enemies have become more numerous than friends.

In scripture, how often do God's people cry out against their enemies? The book of Psalms, for example, while usually identified with songs of praise for God's mercy and goodness, is largely about the problem of living with oppression, humiliation and constant threat from one's enemies. Being taken advantage of by others has been one of the great fears of human beings throughout recorded history. One of the great promises of scripture is that God's people will be held safe even when threats from their enemies seem overwhelming. For many, one of the elements of salvation is being free from the consequences of oppression by other human beings.

The truth of it is that the fall into sin has made bribery, extortion, meanness and war seem natural to people. It has become their way. Corruption is everywhere and constant because it's part of our nature as sinful beings. That's why corruption is so persistent and requires so much from us if we try to confront it. It is a problem reaching into the depths of the soul.

Have you ever wondered why those who try to act against the corruption of the human spirit are so badly treated? They killed John the Baptist and, of course, they killed Jesus. And the list is long of people, both ancient and contemporary, who have been imprisoned, flogged, tortured or killed because they spoke out about this problem.

All our readings for today (Third Sunday of Advent) address this issue, but especially the gospel (Luke 3:7-18). Actually, the gospel is a bit jolting. It seems, somehow, out of context for this run-up to the birth of Christ. John is doing his normal thing – offering the rite of baptism for all those who come to hear his teachings. But seemingly out of nowhere, he turns on them. "You brood of vipers!" he says, "who warned you to flee from the wrath to come?" In other words, he is saying *who told you to come to me and what do you expect to get here?* You get the feeling that John sees them looking for another advantage, a bribe of sorts, to use in their negotiations with God. In fact, he chides them for having tried that already. He says "Don't say to yourselves that you have Abraham as your ancestor and therefore deserve something special here – something more than is available to *other* people".

And, of course, they didn't get the point that John was trying to make. Corruption was in their hearts and John knew it. They had always thought that their heritage as children of Abraham was a trump card that could be used to get more than their due. They thought that their birthright could be used as a bribe – even in dealings with God. John saw this confusion in their souls and knew that he had to jump right on it before they also twisted baptism into some kind of leverage for personal gain.

In our theology, we talk a lot about the relationship between faith and works. Sometimes this can be confusing. Scripture teaches us that salvation comes by faith alone, not by any work that we do. Yet, over and over again, when people like John or even Christ are asked, "what do you want us to do?" there seems to be an expectation that some activity or work is required. There are indeed things people should or should not do. But these are things that come from faith. They are not done in order to *get* faith. It is this confusion in the people that has apparently frustrated John. Nevertheless, he answers their question in terms that might help them understand and hopefully realize that without faith the things Christ asks of them are undoable.

First, John says, you need to learn to share by learning how to give up some of what you have. Secondly, he says, you must not take from people things that are not owed you.

The problem is that these people, including tax collectors and other officials in their community, no doubt believed that they were living properly. This is also the case with so many people in the world of today who constantly engage in acts of corruption or selfishness. They just think that it is the way things are done.

In order to receive the gift of salvation, we need to repent of our sins. But how can we do that if we don't know what sin is or that it has taken over our lives?

This is why the response to "what should we do?" is so often an admonition to stop living the way we are living and learn how to live another way. We need to understand what a good life is. And once we understand that we will also know that a good life is possible only by God's grace. This realization makes us ready for the gift of salvation. It is not the work that saves us – it is the understanding that we are powerless to do the work apart from the grace and mercy of God.

In our gospel for today, John's use of this method to help people understand God's word seems to have worked. After he had finished with the harsh statement of rebuke and the demand of the law, they "were filled with expectation". They may not have known it but they were ready for the gospel. And John gave it to them. He pointed them to Christ who was coming and who would give them what they would require to "live good", that is, without corruption and to "live well" that is, with hope of salvation and a new relationship with God – no bribe required.

The power of John's preaching helps us to understand ourselves better and, therefore, more fully appreciate the purpose of Christ's coming. And this makes the Advent season a joy to us every time we experience it.

Making a Body for God

But a body you have prepared for me . . . (Hebrews 10:5b).

As we move closer to the moment of Christ's birth, the miracle and mystery of it take on greater dimension. In the gospel for today (Luke 1:39-55) we can begin to see the growing awareness within Mary about what this birth will mean. All the readings for today (Micah 5 – long before Christ's coming, Luke 1 – just before Christ's coming, and Hebrews 10 – after Christ's return to heaven), paint for us a portrait of the theology of Advent. The promise and eventual fulfillment of Christ's coming has sustained God's people from the fall into sin to the present day.

There is much that could be discussed from these readings, but it all seems to come together in the phrase from Hebrews that we have chosen for our text today, "but a body you have prepared for me".

This quote actually comes from the book of Psalms (40), and Paul is here reminding the Hebrew people that they have known all along about a great change coming, one that had been written about in a scroll long ago (Jeremiah 36). Paul is reminding them that their teachings had made clear that a day would come when old practices would be rejected and the people would prepare for a new era in their relationship with God. They would quit making sacrifices, that is, taking life in service to God, and they would begin the process of creating life, that is, making a body within which God would dwell.

A few weeks ago, we talked about this change in another way. When we dedicated our new chancel curtains, we were reminded that they signified a change that happened with the coming of Christ. The curtain in the temple no longer acted as a veil to hide God from us. Instead it has become a door through which we may enter into the presence of God.

We know that, before Christ, it was our sin that created the barrier between God and ourselves. The curtains in the temple symbolized this by literally blocking people from entering the Holy of Holies unless they had received the blessing or the anointing of the priesthood. People were told that it was dangerous to pass through the veil into the glory and brightness of God's presence. It would be too much for them and they could die from it. Human beings, in their sin, were not only blocked from passing through the veil, they could not even approach it or the altar before it without the making of a blood sacrifice. Blood had to be shed on the altar to appease the wrath of God and to allow those who had prepared the sacrifice a dispensation or a reprieve that would allow them to stand before God, even if at a distance.

From the moment of the fall into sin, it was blood that kept the people from being destroyed altogether. Blood is the essence of life and has always been the means by which life exists for human beings. God, who is the source of life, promised to always honor blood promises or blood sacrifices. This is the essence of Old Testament theology and this is why, when the plagues were put upon Pharaoh during the captivity in Egypt, the children of Israel put blood on their doorframes so that the angel of death would pass over them. This was called the Passover and it was a blood contract between God and His people.

The images of today's readings are about blood and the sacrifice required for men to be saved from the wrath of God. But these images and sayings are about the final blood sacrifice – the one that finally brings to an end the need for veils that block our way and the many sacrifices required to appease God's wrath. In this, the fourth Sunday in Advent, the time has come to prepare for a final sacrifice.

An important part of our Advent observance is learning about the sacrifice that would finally fulfill the longstanding Old Testament promise. And it is interesting that, while we rarely think about Advent this way, this is a time when we also observe how one human being was chosen among many to prepare this last sacrifice. This person, of course, was Mary.

An Arcadian Vision

We need to understand this. God had made clear to his people from antiquity that the only way sin could finally be forgiven and human beings reestablished in a right relationship with God was for God, Himself, to be sacrificed. And God would have to be sacrificed by human beings, just as human beings had always been responsible for making the blood sacrifices that gave them hope that God would forgive them and that the angel of death would pass by.

But in order for God to be able to be sacrificed by men, He had to take on a tangible form and become a man Himself. So already in the book of Psalms, David recognizes that he has a responsibility to begin to prepare a body for God. It is from David's lineage that the Son of God will be born. It is first of all to David that Christ refers in the quote from Hebrews. Paul is reminding the Jews that they are the ones, through David and finally through Mary, who will make ready the final sacrifice by making a body for God. God must have a body so that He may die. The old sacrifices and offerings aren't satisfying anymore to either the people or God. In spite of the old sacrifices, the veil or curtain remains closed. Something must happen so that it will be opened and all people will be able to see God's glory and receive His forgiveness.

In the scripture from Hebrews, Paul refers to this as "abolishing the first in order to establish the second". The first order of relationship between God and men based on blood sacrifices is over. With Christ, a new order of relationship is begun. In the new order, Christ's sacrifice has made possible the coming of the Holy Spirit to bring faith and forgiveness into the world. God's wrath is no more.

This is the awareness that Elizabeth and Mary have with each other as they meet in the hills of Judea. They *know* what is happening. They know that the body of God is being prepared in that very place. And in a miraculous way, the child in Elizabeth's womb also knows.

This is why the "magnificat" or "Mary's song" is such an honored thing and is regarded by many as holy. *It is Mary's awareness bursting forth in a great poem of praise.* All generations will bless her because she has prepared a body for God to be sacrificed. She knows that it is through her that God's promises will finally be fulfilled, and she speaks this truth from a heart overwhelmed with the magnificence of it. Change is coming and it will be through her.

We are told how Mary pondered these things after she had given birth to the child Jesus. It must have been with very mixed feelings that she finally saw the fruition of all the prophecies and promises. But I wonder if she knew how amazing this change to a new order was, even at that moment. Before Mary, only a male could enter directly into the presence of God and then only with a special anointing. All sacrifices were prepared and presented by these priests on behalf of the people. We mentioned two weeks ago how Elizabeth had started to break this mold when she stood before the altar insisting on special recognition for her son during his naming. But here, Mary *becomes* the priest. She is the one preparing the sacrifice on behalf of the people – *all* people, not just a select few. It is a profound change that will affect the course of the world for all generations to come. And she knows it.

This is Advent, when we await the coming. A new era is about to dawn. Watch for it. Follow the star. Find the baby, the body of God, prepared as the final sacrifice by Mary, the mother of God, on our behalf. And when you have found it, rejoice in it. Everything has changed including the relationship between human beings and the God who made them; the relationship between men and women; and the way in which we use the altar and the curtain in the temple. It is a wonderful telling and gives us hope for the peace that is the promise of this season.

A Gift Waiting to Be Received

(Meditation for a Christmas Eve candlelight service at Jasper Park Lodge)

He was in the world, and though the world was made through him, the world did not recognize him. . . .Yet to all who received him . . . he gave the right to become children of God (John 1: 10,11).

Many of us remember the Christmas cartoon feature *Rudolph, the Red-Nosed Reindeer*. Rudolph was portrayed as something of a misfit in the reindeer kingdom, laughed at by his friends and rejected, for a while at least, by his elders.

As Rudolph sought to escape the humiliation of it all, he happened to land upon the island of misfit toys. These were toys that had been rejected for some flaw or imperfection and that had been exiled so that they might not cause embarrassment to those responsible for distributing toys to good little girls and boys.

Rudolph, of course, experienced a sense of companionship and support among these creatures that were like him in so many ways. He also discovered his own unique talents and skills of leadership as he worked with these misfits to find a way out of their predicament and realize the purpose and potential for which they had all been created.

Now I hope this isn't making too much of Rudolph here on this night of Christmas expectation as we wait for the promise of Christmas Day and the coming of the child born in a manger. I have friends who have never gotten used to the idea of Rudolph being part of our Christmas culture. They think that he is a silly caricature of a secular Christmas fantasy and that he really doesn't have much to do with the true spirit of Christmas. He is, after all, a misfit.

I am, apparently, a disgrace to my profession because, as I reflected on possible meditations for the Christmas season, my thoughts drifted to Rudolph. Well, not to Rudolph so much but to the community of misfits of which he eventually became a part. As we know, he was able to save Santa's Christmas journey from disaster and the misfit toys proved that they were brave and good hearted. They would bring considerable joy to some lucky children. Rudolph and the misfit toys were created as gifts to assist in time of need or to bring happiness in a world of trouble. But for a time they were misunderstood and they were set aside as though they had no importance. They were gifts waiting to be received.

What a nice theme for Christmas! *Gifts waiting to be received.* No matter how we look at it, Christmas is all about gifts waiting to be received. It's true that we usually think about it another way. On the flip side, so to speak. We say that the gifts are waiting to be given. But tonight, just for a moment, let's look at it from the point-of-view of the gift. From that perspective, and I think also from the perspective of the giver, nothing is fulfilled until the gift is received. Until that happens, the gift is an object waiting – in a closet, hidden in wrapping under the tree, cloaked in the darkness of a hanging stocking – *or wrapped in swaddling cloths, lying in a manger.*

The story of Christmas, we all know, is the story of a gift waiting to be received – no matter how we tell it. Tonight, we have been telling it with scripture and song. It is a story so old that its phrases are a matter of memory to most of us and the songs are so familiar that we don't need the music to sing them.

Yet every year we hear this story as though for the first time. Christmas, we hear, is when God came to be with us. He was born under unusual and extraordinary circumstances. He was a gift that would bring salvation to the world – light in the darkness.

But, alas, he came to be regarded as a misfit. And like the misfits of our Rudolph story, he became for many a gift waiting to be received. We just read in our last scripture (John 1:1-14) how some received him and some didn't – but those who did became children of God – the gift that was intended all along.

So on this night before Christmas let us consider the gift waiting to be received – the child born in a manger bringing hope to the world. When we rise in the morning and consider the gifts all around us, let us not forget the one that really matters: the gift that teaches us how to be children of God, how to love, how to know the truth, and how to be at peace in this world.

The Light Shines in the Darkness

What has come into being in him was life, and the life was the light of all people. The light shines in the darkness and the darkness did not overcome it (John 1:4,5).

It is almost imperative to include our Gospel for today (John 1:1-18) somewhere in the regular Christmas celebrations of the church. I have now read this passage three times during this year's worship celebrations here in Jasper. It is included in almost all the religious devotion booklets for Christmas and is even found in some of the secular readings for the season.

While most of the readings for Christmas are related to the actual event of Christ's birth, this one has more to do with the meaning of Christ's birth. This is the Christmas reading that presents the *theology* of Christmas.

Last year, we focussed on the first line of this reading where Christ is identified as the Word that existed with God and was God from the very beginning of things. This text presents us with a difficult theology that speaks of God as being separate persons but one being (the doctrine of the Trinity). We also hear in this reading that the separate persons of God express themselves with different purpose or power. The person of Christ was the Word from the very beginning, we are told, and it was through the power of the Word that everything came to be. *In other words, it was through the Word (Christ) that God became known in the physical things of creation.* This was his purpose *and* his power. (In the Greek, "word" is "logos" which refers to reason, meaning and order.) The miracle of Christmas is that this Word became flesh and dwelt among us so that God could be fully known to men. Christ (the Word) not only made all things and gave order to them, he provided human beings with the reason and intellect to observe and appreciate his creation. All this is contained in the idea of Christ as the Word.

An Arcadian Vision

But today we want to talk about the *light*. The reference to light in this reading is largely what makes it a special part of so many Christmas celebrations. In our Christmas candlelight service, it is this passage that is read while the candles are lit. What are we to learn from this? What is the theology of the light?

It's interesting to think about the meaning of the word "light". I searched the dictionary and found that the meanings for that word filled an entire page. One possible definition of light is the scientific one where we talk about color, reflection, refraction, particles and waves.

But for our purposes today, I just want to mention four general ways that we think about light and how that relates to the theology of light that we find in our gospel reading. We think of light as physical, psychological, intellectual and spiritual.

It is hard to imagine a preoccupation of human beings more pervasive than the quest for light. Or, put another way, the effort to overcome darkness. Both light and darkness are physical phenomena that govern our existence and affect almost everything we do. No invention of human beings has been more transcendent or powerful than the creation of artificial light, whether as a by-product of fire or through the harnessing of electrical impulses. On a physical plane, we are literally able to beat back darkness reflecting a desire born within us at the very beginning of our existence. Our attraction to candle flame and electric lights of all kinds emerges out of our fear of darkness and our longing to see. The beauty of a candle or a well-constructed neon sculpture is like a healing balm. We become physically energized. We equate light with good feeling and romance.

This is the psychology of light – it makes us feel better and stimulates hope. The depressive effect of dark winters and enclosed spaces is well known to those who treat mental and emotional disorders. Light is often prescribed as a remedy or treatment for a variety of conditions. Light, it seems, is essential to our emotional well being.

Light often takes the form of enlightenment. When we make a discovery or experience an insight, we say that the "light dawns". But a mind can go dark. We know this from our own experience trying to write a sentence, remember the lines from a poem, make a speech or write an exam. We often say, when someone comes up with a great idea, that they are "brilliant". We attribute light to intellect.

Light is life. Light is truth. This is its spiritual meaning. Throughout scripture, light is the medium through which God comes to us and shows us the truth. This is not the same as light as intellect. Spiritual light comes to us as a matter of faith. We may not understand it or be able to explain it, but we can know it. This light is connected to the Word. That is why the Word and the light are side by side in our text. The Word, that is Jesus, is the light that heals our souls and makes us one again with our God.

These are meanings attributed to the word "light" and, interestingly, they are all accounted for in today's text. The Greek words for light used in our text can refer to any of those meanings. It is the context that helps us understand what is meant here.

The context, of course, is that it is the Word that is the light. The Word is Jesus, so Jesus is the light. This light is life because it overcomes the darkness of our sin. It replaces the light that went out of our souls when we separated ourselves from the Word, the source of our life.

In order to fix this, the Word became flesh and dwelt among us. We are told in our text that when this happened, we were able to "see his glory". The word for glory here is another word for light, the same word that is used to mean "insight" or "discovery". Through Jesus, we can finally see God and know the meaning of things. We have insight, enlightenment, knowledge, truth, happiness, contentment, well being and peace. All these things are included in or related to the definition of light.

We are about to complete the season of Christmas and begin the explorations of a New Year. Our Christmas season here in Jasper has been a season of light. Over and over again we have lit the candles of Christmas worship to signify the meaning of the Christmas story and the enlightenment that comes with it. We do this at the darkest time of the year in defiance of the power of darkness over us.

Yes, as human beings we have made great strides in beating back the darkness of our existence – *physically, psychologically and intellectually*. We *do* sometimes use the abilities that God has given us to our benefit.

But the real enlightenment and the essence of the message of Christmas is found in the presence of God in the world, born in a manger, waited on by shepherds and kings. This is the light that supercedes all other forms of light. It is the true light – the light of the world. It is *spiritual* light.

As we enter a New Year of life together here in the mountains, let us resolve to carry the light with us as faithfully as we can. Let us pray that we may keep the light burning with the fuel of God's Word and let us resolve to pass the flame – to share the light – with any who are seeking to overcome the darkness of their spirit.

An Arcadian Vision

With Wonder at the Birth of God

(Christmas Day)

But when the time was fully come, God sent his Son, born of a woman, born under the law . . . (Galatians 4:4).

We have come here today to see the birth of a child, the one that we have been waiting for during the period of preparation that we call Advent. The next time I see you, we will have begun the new calendar year as well as a new season in our church year that we call Epiphany.

Advent and Epiphany are long enough to give us time to reflect. Advent was the time of preparation for Christ's coming. Epiphany is a time to learn the meaning of Christ's coming, the time when he becomes manifest or known to us.

We have been trying to prepare for his coming during the days immediately leading up to this day. And, like the Three Kings or Magi who set out to find the Christ child with gifts of welcome, we will also follow the star that has signaled his coming and learn to know him in the days ahead.

But today is a day separate. We put the books of prophecy from the past and questions for the future aside. Today we live only in the present, in the moment. We concentrate on the happening that is the coming of God to live in the world as a human being. We come to see the child born in Bethlehem.

Today the language of our worship seems to change from being instructive and requiring study to being descriptive and requiring expression. The readings for today assist us in finding the words to express both what we find and what we feel as we come upon the babe wrapped in swaddling cloths, lying in a manger.

Our reading from the book of Isaiah (61:10 – 62:3) describes the effect on the world of the coming of the Messiah. It is poetry written in praise. It uses imagery that encourages the most positive feelings and the most hopeful outcomes. It is a language, often used in the Old Testament, to describe the indescribable. How, after all, does one talk about God being a child and yet leave people with any real sense of who this child is and how He touches us?

The Psalm (148) for today is a hymn of praise using somewhat different language to express what this child means. These are words that we sing. In these hymns we are reminded that nothing is left unaffected by this miracle of God's love. We affirm in our song that angels, sea creatures, animals, snakes, and birds are all somehow changed by the coming of

God to be a man. Even fire, hail, snow, fog and wind give evidence that something extraordinary has happened here. The natural world raises its voice to acknowledge the presence of God within it. This is what Luther meant when he asked us to remember that we can know God through the natural world.

In the Gospel for today (Luke 2:22-48), we are told about the first time the baby Jesus was presented to the world. He was presented to the world the way many of us are, through a rite of dedication. In these rites, a child is offered back to God as a gift for His service and receives the blessing of the people who witness the child's coming. Jesus' parents did this through a rite of purification according to the tradition of the time. This is also accomplished through the rite of baptism.

The Gospel reminds us that some of the witnesses at the dedication of Jesus could see that this was no ordinary child. He is like us but not like us. And what a difference he will make!

But the scripture that really guides us through this meditation is the one we have taken from Galatians 4. It is the scripture that seems to connect what we have been waiting for to what has actually appeared before us.

We are first presented with the condition for Christ's birth. It occurred when "the time was fully come" or, in the King James Version, "in the fullness of time". The baby was not born until the time was right. This is a great mystery to us. Time is not a limitation of God. It is a limitation imposed on God's creation. So the "right time" must be with reference to our needs, not God's. Jesus was not born until the world and its people were ready for it. We do not know why the time of Christ's birth was the right time. It is one of those mysteries the truth of which is kept from us while we live within the confines of time and space. However we recognize the truth of it by celebrating Christ's birth each year after a period of time "getting ready".

That he was "born of a woman and born under the law" is an even greater wonder. These words signify that God as man was confined within the limitations of time and space as we all are. He had to live according to all the rules that apply to any human being and, as a person, he would be subject to death. He was born of a woman so that a body could be prepared within which God could dwell.

We often struggle with the idea that a woman could conceive God's child, and we sometimes become fixated on the problem of a virgin birth. But the mystery is much more profound than that. The mystery is that

God became a human being in every conceivable way. Christ did not have superhuman strength. He got hungry. He got sick. He was tempted. All the foibles and flaws of normal human beings were experienced by him and he needed guidance as a child like everyone else.

But as God he was able to transcend his own human frailties and assist others to do so as well. He was able to heal the sick and bring the dead back to life. He could act as God but he had to live as a man. And, in the end, he could not save himself from the consequences of his own mortality. He had to die. The fact that, as a man, he had to die is not the mystery. The fact that as God he was born a man *is* the mystery.

The reading from Galatians (4:5) not only reports this mystery as fact but also gives us the reason for it. *"To redeem those under the law so that we might receive full rights as sons."* This means that God became a man (under the law) so that all men could break free of the shackles of the law and become God. He became us so that we could become Him.

This is the Christmas story. It is huge. The story is adorned with innocence, stars, light and beauty. It is a great day for us. We know that we have received a great gift and we come to this day with some gifts of our own to offer each other. But more than anything else, we come to dedicate ourselves anew to the God who created us and who, through Christ, broke the shackles of time and made us part of Him for all eternity.

4. The Festival of Epiphany (Learning to Know the Child)

Epiphany is January 6, the last day in the twelve days of Christmas. The season of Epiphany extends to Ash Wednesday. Ash Wednesday begins the season of Lent that leads to Easter. The season of Epiphany may include from four to nine Sundays depending on when Easter occurs. During Epiphany we remember how Christ and his ministry was manifested to all people, especially those (Gentiles, or non-Jews) who had not shared the history of knowing about and waiting for the coming (Advent) of a Messiah or Savior. The best known symbol of Epiphany is found in the Biblical record of the coming of the Wise Men (Gentiles) to celebrate the birth of Christ. Other remembrances during Epiphany include Jesus' baptism and his transfiguration.

On Preaching

Give me also this ability so that everyone on whom I lay my hands may receive the Holy Spirit (Acts 8:19).

I often wonder what the purpose of preaching is. Is it to *inspire, exhort* or *energize* the listener to some action or behavior? Is it to *instruct* or *teach* so that people may be informed and knowledgeable? Is it to *entertain* so that the listener is made to feel better? Is it to *impress* others so that the speaker receives notice and is revered?

People who preach struggle to answer these questions all the time. I was fascinated to read one of the definitions of preaching in the Oxford English Dictionary: "give moral advice in an obtrusive way". I must say

An Arcadian Vision

that preaching has the potential to be very obtrusive. (By the way, the word "obtrusive" means "unduly noticeable".)

How do we preach so that it is the Word of God that is highlighted, not the person speaking it (one of the reasons some preachers wear robes)? How are preachers ever to understand how the Word works through them as they struggle to put something together that is at least sensible or understandable in the language being used?

This may seem to be a strange thing to be talking about on the First Sunday of Epiphany, or the Sunday where we remember the Baptism of Our Lord. Yet it may be perfectly fitting. Epiphany is the season of our church year when we concentrate on the revelation or manifestation of Christ and his ministry. We begin this season by remembering how Christ was revealed to the Magi or Kings (Jan. 6). However, on the first Sunday after that we remember the baptism of Jesus as an adult, when he received the Holy Spirit and his formal ministry started. So today seems a perfectly appropriate day to talk about what ministry is and preaching as a part of that ministry.

With that in mind, I have decided to take our meditation from the Bible chapter that gives us our Second Reading for today (Acts 8:14-17). However, for that reading to really make sense, it is important to read the entirety of Acts chapter 8.

When we read Acts 8 in the New International Version, we see that the verses from 9 to 25 are headed "Simon the Sorcerer". Sorcery, I guess, is a form of preaching. I know of some preachers who might better be described as sorcerers.

You will also notice that this entire chapter is about preaching. It is about Simon doing his form of preaching. It is about Philip preaching and it is about Peter and John preaching.

We can learn many things from this passage in Acts, including the difference between false preaching and true preaching. We are also given some guidance about the theology of baptism and what it means to receive the Holy Spirit.

I suppose that the difference between false preaching and true preaching is pretty evident in this passage. Or is it? Simon would be seen as the false preacher, but why? Is it because he claimed to perform miracles and didn't? Was he a liar and a fraud? Is that what made him a false preacher?

I don't think so. I think that he actually could do magic and sway crowds with his rhetoric. He had "the gift of gab", as we sometimes say, coupled with knowledge about natural phenomena and some well-honed skills in manipulation. He was a *real* sorcerer and the people followed him.

He was a false preacher because he promoted only *himself* – for all his skill and uniqueness. He did not offer anything permanent or lasting and that could be used in the lives of others. In his case, the purpose of preaching was to *entertain* and *impress*. While this can be fun for awhile, it soon gets old because it is, in the end, empty and meaningless. We have preachers like that today. We have politicians like that today. And then there are all the people that we call celebrities.

Now I think that it's interesting that even Simon could recognize a true preacher when he saw one. When Philip arrived in Samaria to preach, Simon was immediately drawn to him and was even willing to be baptized by him.

(By the way, there is special meaning to the fact that all of this was happening in Samaria. Philip, Peter and John were from Judea and the Samaritans were notably resistant to anything coming from there. The Samaritans had always been considered inferior by the people of Judah and Israel because the Samaritans were a mixed race. They had Assyrian and Babylonian blood. So there was a history of bad feeling between the Samaritans and others, like many of the Judeans, who felt that they were better Jews. For the Samaritans to begin listening seriously to these men from Judea could only be considered a minor miracle. The distinction between false and true preaching is illustrated here since only true preaching was likely to overcome the suspicions of the Samaritans.)

While Simon was impressed with Philip's preaching, he apparently failed to notice that the reason it was so effective was that it was done in the name of Jesus Christ. Unlike Simon, Philip was not putting *himself* forward as someone to be observed and emulated, he was pointing to Christ.

Simon was even more amazed when Peter and John showed up. The ministry of Peter and John emphasized that all people could receive the Holy Spirit into their lives just as Christ had received the Holy Spirit at his baptism. In order to be effective in this ministry, they also had to be filled with the power of the Holy Spirit. In preparation for this ministry they worked to develop the knowledge and skill necessary to know when other people were ready to accept the Holy Spirit into their lives. This is part of being a good minister and true preacher.

A word should be said here about the distinction between being baptized and receiving the Holy Spirit. All through our readings today,

An Arcadian Vision

these things are treated as separate occurrences. This was true for Christ at his baptism and true for the Samaritans that had been baptized but who had not received the Holy Spirit. John points out in our Gospel (Luke 3: 15-17, 21-22) that while he baptizes with water, it is only with the coming of Christ that people can receive the baptism of the Holy Spirit.

Simply put, baptism is one of the means by which we receive and express faith. It is our declaration that we believe in Jesus Christ as our Lord and Savior. This prepares us to move on in the faith and enables us to receive the Holy Spirit. But even having been baptized, a person may not have received the Holy Spirit. This is why we are so careful to continue the instruction of children who have been baptized as infants. And this is why persons who have been baptized need to be exposed to true preachers who themselves are filled with the Holy Spirit and are able to pass this blessing on to those to whom they minister. Even Christ was baptized with water first and then the Holy Spirit descended upon Him.

It is clear that Simon, although he had been baptized, was not yet ready to receive the Holy Spirit. When he saw what Peter and John could do, he tried to buy their skill so he could practice it too. He thought that he was seeing another technique or manipulation in action – albeit a very impressive one. He did not understand that these powers did not belong to Philip or Peter or John. They could not package them or sell them. This was the power of God at work through some men whose hearts were right and who gave all praise to God rather than to themselves. Simon wanted another trick to perform but he wasn't going to get one from Peter. All he got was a very thorough rebuke.

We don't know if Simon got the point or not. From this scripture, it appears that he didn't. After receiving a very threatening reaction from Peter assuring him of God's wrath, Simon asked Peter to pray for him "so that nothing you have said will happen to me". I think he still thought that Peter was the one who had the power to do these things – that he was just a greater sorcerer than Simon was.

False preaching is people promoting themselves. True preaching is people sharing the power of the Holy Spirit in their lives with others and giving back all glory to God. Sometimes false preaching and true preaching look the same, and it is important to know whether or not your preacher is Simon the Sorcerer, or Peter, the Apostle.

These are some things to think about on this day of Christ's baptism, when the truest preacher of all began his ministry in this world. At Christ's baptism, the Holy Spirit descended to earth, and God's presence (Father,

Son and Holy Spirit) became complete in this world. When we receive the Holy Spirit, we have the fullness of God in us too. No wonder Simon was so desperate to have this blessing, because he could see what a great thing it was.

As we move through the days of Epiphany, we will once again hear the words of Christ's preaching and receive the power of the Holy Spirit that comes from that. May we prepare ourselves with open hearts to hear his word and dedicate ourselves to follow his teachings.

Of One Spirit

For just as the body is one and has many members, and all the members of the body, though many, are one body, so it is with Christ. For in the one Spirit we were all baptized into one body – Jews or Greeks, slaves or free – and we were all made to drink of one spirit (I Corinthians 12: 12-13).

Our meditation this morning continues the thought or the lesson of our meditations for the last two weeks. We are in the season of Epiphany and so our thoughts turn to the meaning of the ministry of Christ. What did he come to do and how are we to understand it? One very important element of the Epiphany theme is the revelation that Christ's ministry opened the way to God for everyone or, as our text says, to "Jews or Greeks, slaves or free".

It is important to note how strange an idea this was to the people of Christ's time and place. First of all, monotheism – or the doctrine that there is only one God – was not a common belief at that time, particularly within the dominant cultures of Greece and Rome. This is why there are so many warnings in the Christian scriptures about false gods and the danger of worshiping idols. Pantheism – the idea that everything may be worshipped as god – was a very prevalent belief system during the time of Christ and the Apostles.

Secondly, even in those societies that were monotheistic, such as the Hebrews, God was not understood as belonging to or being available to all people. The God the Hebrews believed in was called "the God of the Hebrews", and they had always understood that they were the chosen people and that God would stand for them against all others.

The message of Christ's ministry, as proclaimed by Christ himself and explained by the apostles, was that all this had changed. Through Christ, God was no longer exclusive to anyone. As our text says, all are now of "one spirit".

This is *the* message of the Epiphany. It is absolutely essential for all

An Arcadian Vision

Christians to understand this message. But it seems to be no easier for us to understand now than it was when the Apostle Paul was writing this letter to the Corinthians. All we have to do is look around us and we can see that many people still believe that God is somehow exclusive to them – just as the Jews did in Christ's time.

In the scripture that includes our meditation for today, Paul is trying to explain to the Corinthians what the church is and how its members should behave. There had been a lot of trouble in the young church at Corinth, partially because it was such a difficult place in which to live. Corinth had evolved under the influence of the Greek and Macedonian cultures. However the Romans were now the dominant culture and the cities of old Greece had become quite violent. There was a lot of criminal activity and a number of occult religions were trying to keep alive the pantheism of Greece's classical or golden age. Corinth was part of a great civilization in decline. It seems to be the case that when civilizations decline or societies fall into disarray the people turn on each other and corruption becomes the order of the day.

It was against this backdrop that Paul was trying to help the Corinthian church get used to the idea of being part of an inclusive religion. The Corinthian church was made up of new Christians, some Jews, living in a Greek town under the rule of a Roman authority. And Paul was telling them that no matter what their history was or how they had been taught to think about others, they had to get used to the idea that they were all equally important as members of the church. In fact he was telling them that the church could not even exist without the involvement and contribution of every member, regardless of background and culture.

The people of the church at Corinth had apparently been spending time debating which of them was the most important. They were caught in the trap that seems so common when people get together to build a community or a new institution. They wanted to know who was in charge or which skills or talents were the most important. They wanted a hierarchy of authority to be established so everyone could know their place. They were still living with the old idea that God was for some people but not for others, and that anyone who was not of God was the enemy. They could not grasp the idea that everyone was equally important regardless of talent, education or position. They had lived too long in a world of *haves* and *have nots* where power existed with some and not others and where family and the place of birth truly mattered.

The message of Christ that you are no better than anyone else, no matter who your family is, what citizenship you have, or how good or talented you are, is very difficult to hear. And worse, Paul was saying to the Corinthians that they were to actively honor and care for people that they had always considered inferior or even dangerous. Everyone that has been baptized into the faith and who has become a member of the church is equal regardless of background. Paul even seemed to be saying that anyone considered inferior or "less respectable" needed to be given *greater* respect (I Corinthians 12: 23) so that, in the end, all members would show the same care for each other. Is this our first example of the thing we now call "reverse discrimination" or "affirmative action"?

These are hard lessons but they need to be learned. The Corinthians needed to learn this lesson so they could come together as a strong, cohesive community and deal with the trouble and corruption in the world around them. They could not survive as a church if they were squabbling with each other and discriminating against each other. And, even worse, they could not maintain their faith if they were always acting contrary to it. It's not just a matter of survival as a community and a culture, it's a matter of learning how to continue and grow in the faith. If we do not grow in the faith, our faith shrivels and dies. Faith cannot just sit there waiting to be applied. We have to act on it.

Many of the parables and lessons of the New Testament are about people being "lifted up" or made equal through faith in Christ and the power of the Holy Spirit. The message that salvation is not just for the powerful or the elite is a key message of Christianity. It is sometimes a message that escapes those of us privileged to live in North America, because in a real sense we are among the powerful and the elite. We tend to think of poverty and disadvantage as belonging to others. In the time of Christ, the visible poor and oppressed were in an obvious majority. The message that everyone should be treated equally just didn't make sense either to those that had been born with wealth and status or the majority that had not. It was important then, as people believe it is important now, to strive for status and wealth and to hang on to them if you get them. It was also considered important to have the protection that wealth and status provided. Part of the reason that the Hebrew people wanted to maintain their special status as God's people was because it was the only thing that made them feel safe in a world full of oppressors. It was very difficult to understand how everyone could be equal. Obviously some had to be inferior to others.

Our Gospel for today helps us to understand that Christ's ministry

An Arcadian Vision

was about bringing all people into equal status with each other through the good news of salvation and freedom. He was the one prophesied who would "release the captives, give sight to the blind, and let the oppressed go free". All who believe in Him will be made equal in God's sight. What Paul wanted to tell the Corinthians was that this is a done deal. Get used to it. In God's house or in Christ's church you cannot discriminate. So don't waste time trying to figure out who is better or who deserves more.

Last week a day was set aside in the United States to remember the legacy of Martin Luther King. His image has been reproduced on the face of our bulletin for today.

I suppose Martin Luther King has been featured today because he represents one modern expression of an attempt to bring freedom and equality to the poor and oppressed. It might seem fitting to think of Martin Luther King on this day when we remember that one of the central messages of Christ's ministry was that he came to bring good news to the poor. The legacy of Martin Luther King reminds us that there are people in our time and place who may also be considered inferior or less respectable even by people who consider themselves religious or Christian. We are reminded today that this is not a Christian way to think or behave, whether you are a Corinthian or a Canadian. Just as Paul did with the Corinthians, Martin Luther King tried to apply the idea of reverse discrimination, described in our text today, to overcome the extreme disadvantage and prejudice so many were facing in his time and place.

It is hard not to express bigotry and prejudice. We grow up with so many biases. But we cannot allow these attitudes and opinions to control us and, especially, to influence our lives as members of the body of Christ. I worry about our church when I read about the bitter disputes that drain its energy and divert it from its purpose. One need only pick up a copy of our own national church magazine to see some of this going on. We apparently aren't that different from the church at Corinth.

Yes, we should be as clear as we can be about our teachings and those things that are essential to our faith. But we should never discriminate against anyone who comes among us with questions unanswered or a background that is different. The only way any of us can stay true to our faith is through humble attention to the lessons of God's word and the message of Christ's ministry. We are all equal in that.

The last sentence in our second reading for today says "strive for the greater gifts". We all want to know more and become more excellent in our faith and we should encourage each other to strive for excellence as well.

But, as the very next chapter in I Corinthians points out, *the greatest gift is love* and if we cannot love one another in the face of our differences then there is no hope at all, for us or for the church.

It is through Christ's sacrifice and his ministry to us that we can learn to love each other and continue to proclaim Christ's message as members of his church. May God grant us the power to do this in a world that continues to experience so much trouble and where it is so easy to become dissatisfied and discouraged with the behavior of those around us. Maybe we do need to practice a little more reverse discrimination so that those considered less respectable are treated with greater respect and the church is made better for it.

Made for a Purpose

Now there are varieties of gifts, but the same Spirit; and there are varieties of services, but the same Lord; and there are varieties of activities, but it is the same God who activates all of them in everyone. To each is given the manifestation of the Spirit for the common good (I Corinthians 12:4-7).

We are just concluding a rather lengthy season in both the secular and church years where the emphasis has been on gifts. For much of this time, our attention has been directed to the Festival of Christmas. Of course, Christmas is all about gifts no matter what perspective you take on it. We can worry about what Christmas really is as a holiday and whether or not the true spirit of Christmas gets lost in the commercial fury of buying and selling. But in the end the one thing we know is that this has been a time for thinking about gifts and what they mean in both superficial and profound ways.

On Christmas Eve we talked about gifts from the perspective of the *gift*. In order to do this we really did mix up the sacred and the secular by considering the meaning of gifts in one of the stories featuring Rudolph the Red-Nosed Reindeer. Rudolph encounters a community of misfit toys that had been rejected because they weren't quite up to snuff. We described these toys as "gifts waiting to be received" and considered how they must have felt being rejected as gifts when that was their whole reason for being. They had been made to be gifts and they became convinced that, because of their flaws, no one would be willing to receive them. For a child especially, this story can help us think about Jesus, who was born in a manger as a gift to all of humanity; and yet it seemed that so few were willing to receive him. He, too, was a gift waiting to be received and, like the toys, that was his whole reason for being.

An Arcadian Vision

We have come out the other end of Christmas now and you might think that we would be moving on to other things. But here we are, talking about gifts again.

We have reminded ourselves about the idea of gifts as *objects, talents or people waiting to be received* because our lesson for today builds on that theme. If we accept the idea from the Rudolph story that a toy's only reason for existence is to be received and valued by someone else, then we can begin to grasp some of the meaning found in our Second Reading for today. In this scripture we, too, are presented with the idea that we are gifts or, more accurately, that we have gifts within us that are there for the purpose of giving value to someone else. It is helpful to consider how we also are gifts waiting to be received. But in order for us to be received and used by others, we need to understand what kind of gift we are and how we can best make ourselves available for use. As our text says, "there are varieties of gifts . . . varieties of services . . . varieties of activities" and no one of us is, or can perform, all of them. No mortal human being can be all things to all people. We each have a gift. We each have a purpose. And in order for our lives to have meaning, both to ourselves and to others, we need to find out what that gift is and learn to know its purpose.

Wise parents try to instill this idea into their children. "Find out what you like. Discover what you are good at. Don't try to do everything. Identify that one thing that fulfills you and become good at it." Parents can do a lot of harm if they try to mold a child into an object that they cannot become. Helping children find their essence or who they truly are has always been at the heart of parenting.

But this is more than just a parenting goal. This is a life goal and, as our reading encourages us, it is at the center of understanding about how to live a Christian life. Think of what our lesson for today says:

First, all Christians have the same Spirit. They have the same source of power for living their lives.

Second, all persons are different and express this Spirit according to abilities that are unique to them.

Third, Christians know that their abilities are gifts of the Holy Spirit, given to them for the purpose of making Jesus known in the world. By our gifts we make Jesus manifest to others and this is how our gifts contribute to the common good, by helping to bring salvation to the world.

Last week we said that Epiphany is the time during the church year when we celebrate the manifestation of Jesus. It is the time when we remember how people began to recognize Jesus for who he was and how he imparted his word to them – especially to his disciples. Part of Christ's word was to charge his followers with the mission of continuing his ministry in the world after he was gone. We are charged with continuing the Epiphany of our Lord by helping to make him known in the modern world.

Our reading for today reminds us that we do this through the gifts that are unique to each of us and that come to us through the power of the Holy Spirit. We use these gifts in the service of our Lord because we are not confused about our purpose as we might have been before we accepted Jesus as Lord (Read I Corinthians 12:1-3).

So the message here is that *we* are gifts of God waiting to be received by others. That is how we make God known in the world. We are part of this Epiphany that we celebrate every year.

Once we understand what our gifts are, we simply offer them. In other words, we just live in the world as the person God has made us to be, filled with the Holy Spirit, and living as witness to the life and ministry of Jesus our Lord.

No gift is so small or so homely as to be unworthy of this great ministry. Not all persons can be preachers or teachers. Not everyone can understand complicated things. We aren't all good examples of a faithful life nor do all Christians set a high spiritual standard.

Some of us are good companions. Some are notable for their regular attendance at church. Others are famous for their charity and compassion. Some give the gift of music. There are some whose gift is faithfulness in the face of doubt and who are known for their questions and constant searching. Some are parents whose gift is an idea of family and who sacrifice endlessly for those they have brought into the world.

The gospel (John 2:1-11) for today is an example of a small gift made great. Jesus did this more than once in his ministry (water into wine, fish and loaves to feed thousands) and it is an example to us that the humblest gift can become great in God's hands. Through the power of the Holy Spirit we, too, can accomplish great things in Jesus name.

Like the toys in the Christmas story, we have been made for a purpose. We are to bring the Spirit of God into the world and by that contribute to the common good. How we do that is determined by who we are and the gifts we have been given. Our responsibility is to get to know who we are, discover our gifts, and develop those gifts to share with anyone willing to receive them.

Sometimes we can be disappointed when we offer our gifts and they are not received. I have talked to a number of persons who have seemingly been discarded by others when all they wanted was to be a friend, or a partner, or a parent, or a lover. It is heartbreaking to talk to people who have suffered rejection in this way. They offered their gift, it wasn't received, and they don't know why. It seems to happen to every child as they go through their school years. Friends are fickle and it is sometimes hard to figure out what to do to be accepted or received.

Jesus certainly experienced this. Even his own disciples let him down on occasion. His people, the Jews, rejected him and the whole world has participated in denying him.

So we must be prepared as Jesus was to be rejected from time to time. But it isn't all about rejection. As with Christ, our gifts are often received by those who see them for what they are. We are also comforted in knowing that these gifts really are gifts of the Holy Spirit, and so the power in them is very great. We must simply continue to put our gifts out there and let the Holy Spirit do what he will with them. It is God's will that must be done – not ours.

So let us use our gifts to carry on the work of the Epiphany – making Jesus manifest in the world. Like the water that was changed into wine and the few fish and loaves that fed thousands, God will make them great in His service.

Images on a Flannel Board

Who shall I send, and who will go for us? (Isaiah 6:8)

I think that this sentence from the Book of Isaiah may be the first Bible verse that I ever learned (although I am sure John 3:16 was at least a close second). I remember attending a church before I started public school where the tradition was that children should start memorizing Bible verses almost as soon as they could speak coherently. In Sunday school we were assigned a Bible verse that we would speak from memory the next Sunday in the regular church service. If I ever had any fear of public speaking, I soon lost it in the repetition of public utterances that particular church required of all of us.

One of the things that I remember about learning this verse is that it was accompanied by a very memorable Sunday school lesson. This verse is God's call to Isaiah, and I still think that the context in which it occurs is one of the most dynamic in all of scripture. As a result, this story lends itself to some fairly spectacular art and theatrics. In those days we used something in churches and schools that was called a "flannel board". You would hang a sheet of flannel on an easel or on the wall and cover it with figures also cut out of flannel cloth of various colors. The flannel pieces would stick to each other and you could form a picture or a scene (unless you tried to put too many together and then the whole thing would fall apart). This was a common method used to illustrate Bible stories or just to make a decoration for use in the church.

I especially remember the flannel board presentation of the call of God to Isaiah. This call and the incidents surrounding it happened "in the year that King Uzziah died". As a child, I remember wondering why they had to tell us that. I did not understand then that the Hebrew people spoke their history chronologically by marking the time of death of important persons. While I didn't understand the reason for that information, it did give the story a tone of solemnity and even mystery that it might not otherwise have had.

Not that this story needs more mystery. The angels with six wings *("with two they covered their faces, with two they covered their feet, with two they flew")*, the temple shaking and filling with smoke, and the angel touching Isaiah's mouth with a live coal provokes plenty of mystery or mysticism. I remember that all of us kids sat around in a circle with our mouths hanging open at the wonder of it and, of course, there was the child who just had to try and see if someone could really stand putting a live coal on the mouth.

This is a great story, of course, and it is often told in worship services or at other gatherings of the church where the purpose is to discuss the ministry or mission of the church. This story focuses not so much on the ministry itself but on how the ministry or mission of the church gets accomplished.

The book of Isaiah begins by recounting the fall into disrepute of the tribes or "houses" of Israel and Judah. King Uzziah was a king of Judah and during his reign the people of the house of Judah had turned rebellious and degenerate in their relationship with God and in their dealings with each other. Many had abandoned their faith and taken on the practices of the Philistines, Assyrians and Babylonians, worshipping idols and engaging in all sorts of heathen practices. It had become so bad that God finally rose up to threaten the very existence of the houses of Israel and Judah.

But there in the midst of it all were Isaiah and a few others, who were known as Isaiah's disciples. They were trying desperately to keep the faith and warn the offending tribes and nations of the degree to which they were endangering themselves by denying God and associating with unbelievers.

But it looked grim. There seemed little likelihood that the people could be called back from their arrogance and degeneracy.

Then King Uzziah died and God called a meeting in the temple with one of the few remaining persons willing to meet Him there. It's pretty evident that God wanted no mistake about who was waiting in the temple that day. This was not a false god of the kind so many were worshiping during that time. This was "the Lord sitting on a throne, high and lofty, and the hem of his robe filled the temple". The word that He spoke out of the smoke and trembling of this glorious presentation still sounds in the midst of the troubles and misbehaviors of the world. *"Is anyone out there that I can send to speak for me?"* (And the little children sat in a circle around the flannel board with their mouths open in wonder.)

All the readings today are about God calling people, and they all have the ring of the spectacular about them. The call of God is apparently a pretty awesome thing no matter how it occurs.

And it's always the case, isn't it, that when someone answers the call and says "here am I, send me", hope and possible salvation arise even in the midst of the smoke of God's wrath. It is interesting that God tells Isaiah that he must speak damnation to the people. He must tell them that they have gone too far and that, in their sin, they are going to be utterly destroyed. *"Until cities lie waste without inhabitant, and houses without people, and the land is utterly desolate . . .."*

But the one who hears the call of God and faithfully speaks God's word is a person who not only speaks for God but also for the people. He becomes a mediator and, while he does not withhold the sword of God's wrath, he begs on behalf of the people for the blessing of God's mercy and grace. And so three chapters after Isaiah receives his call and accepts it, one of the most beautiful passages of promise to all humanity is spoken by him (Isaiah 9). *"The people who walked in darkness have seen a great light – those who lived in a land of deep darkness – on them light has shined."* We read this every Christmas to remind us that the child born in Bethlehem is the salvation of all people, including those people from Israel and Judah who lived in Isaiah's time.

The call to mission always seems to be especially strong in times of trouble or when people most need to be reminded of God's presence among them and His promise for them. And often the call to serve God has to come in a way that will be noticed. It is often accompanied by a vision or a miracle (Moses and the burning bush is another example).

We have three commentaries on the call to mission in our readings for today. In every case, the ones called are made afraid by their call, believing that their own humanity and sinfulness somehow makes them ineligible to serve God in this way. Isaiah says, "woe is me! I am lost, for I am a man of unclean lips, and I live among a people of unclean lips." Paul, in our second reading (1 Corinthians 15) says, "for I am the least of the apostles, unfit to be called an apostle". And Peter, in our Gospel (Luke 5) says, "Go away from me Lord, for I am a sinful man!"

Of course, no one is good enough to speak for God or to speak to God on behalf of others. And it seems that God has to use images on a flannel board to show these men that *it is not their goodness that matters to their call, it is God's power and grace that makes it possible.* So, for Isaiah's benefit and in order to demonstrate His power, God fills the temple with fantastic images of heavenly beings. Similarly, He confronts Saul on the way to Damascus in the person of His Son, Jesus Christ, and Saul is blinded by the glory of it. (Saul, of course, becomes Paul and goes on to become one of God's great spokespersons.) In our Gospel, God provides the miracle of the fishes, again through the person of His Son, to take the minds of Peter, James and John away from their petty struggles and point them in the direction of becoming fishers of men.

We are now beginning to wind down our Epiphany meditations. Next Sunday we celebrate the Transfiguration of Christ. That Sunday is also considered to be our last Sunday in Epiphany. After next Sunday we will be following the way of the cross where Christ finishes his work for us here on earth.

So today is a good time to think some more about the work of the church in continuing Christ's ministry in the world. And to think about the call to mission and especially those who have agreed to speak for God in this world.

We have been reminding ourselves these past few weeks that we all have gifts to contribute to the mission of Christ in this world. No gift is more honorable than another gift, but we all have a tendency to feel that our gifts are not sufficient and that we are certainly unworthy of anything as great as the call to speak *for* God in this world or *to* God on behalf of other people. As we have already noted, even Isaiah, Paul, Peter, James and John felt that way.

Isaiah learned from the touch of the hot coal that he could withstand the word of God and speak it without injury. Paul apparently found peace with his calling by letting go and giving in to it. I like the way he describes this. "By the grace of God I am what I am, and his grace toward me has not been in vain." All the called of God finally realize this. *I may not consider myself worthy but that doesn't matter. It is the grace of God that makes me what I am.*

Paul was sure that God's grace toward him had not been in vain because, as he says, "I worked harder than any of them". Paul took pride in the fact that through God's grace he could do good work even in the face of his own limitations and disabilities. Like a great athlete, he learned to strive more than others, and as a result, the message and ministry of Christ spread throughout the world. Let us hope that we too can have the confidence that God did not waste His grace on us and that when He called we were there to answer "here am I, send me".

Love is an Adult Thing

Love is patient; love is kind; love is not envious or boastful or arrogant or rude. It does not insist on its own way; it is not irritable or resentful; it does not rejoice in wrongdoing, but rejoices in the truth (I Corinthians 13:4,6).

When I was a child, I spoke like a child, I thought like a child, I reasoned like a child; when I became an adult, I put an end to childish ways (I Corinthians 13:11).

During this Epiphany season, we have been working our way through lessons about the meaning of Christ's coming. We have talked about the purpose of his ministry. We have discussed how all humanity has benefited from the ministry of our Lord, both through his words and his actions.

For much of this time, beginning with the Christmas celebrations, we have talked about Christ's life and ministry as gifts that we receive through faith and that we learn to use in his service. We have said that the gift of salvation or eternal life is universal and equally available to everyone. We have also learned that each individual receives specific gifts and that together we combine those gifts to do the work of the church while we live here on earth. The work of the church, of course, is to continue to proclaim the ministry of Christ until he comes again.

Last week we talked a little bit about the different kinds of gifts people might have and the importance of recognizing the equal value of all gifts whether great or small. However, at the end of that discussion we learned that no matter what our gifts are, we are always to strive for greater things and develop ourselves to the full extent of our potential – to the glory of God. We also said that the greatest thing to strive for, the greatest gift to both give and receive, is love.

Today's meditation, taken from the Second Reading for today (I Corinthians 13), is about the gift of love.

Have you ever wondered when in life a person is able to love? We like to think that children can love, even as newborn babies. It is a comforting thought to believe that our children actually can and do love us. And when two people reach the stage in their lives where they decide to commit themselves to each other and enter the estate of Holy Matrimony, we like to think they are doing it for the love of one another. Very often, the 13th chapter of Corinthians is read to couples as part of their marriage ceremony to remind them that their commitment to each other is about love. Marriage counseling may be offered or requested to assist people with the practicalities of a loving relationship.

But if we accept that I Corinthians 13 is an accurate presentation of the meaning of love, then we know that it is not a childish thing and that even many adults are not ready for it. It is probably fair to say that most people who enter into marriage have only a vague idea about what love is, if they have any at all. This does not mean that they lack affection for each other or that they don't share other strong feelings such as appreciation, respect, physical attraction or desire, fondness, admiration or even need. But for most of us, love, if it comes at all, comes as an expression of our growth and maturity as human beings. It is the fine gold remaining after the fires of daily living have burned away the dross arising out of our confusion about what is important in life. It's what is left after we give up trying to feed our own ego and truly give ourselves over to another person.

In order to love, you have to be able to give yourself up while still remaining confident and self-assured. It takes a long time and a serious effort to learn how to be that way, and for some it never seems to happen. It's pretty clear that true love is not possible for people who are narcissistic or self-centered. This is why children, while they can be extremely loveable, probably do not have the maturity to actually love. If they are lucky, they have parents who do know how to love and who, as a result, are able to raise their children to maturity also knowing how to love.

Listen to what the attributes of love are. These are the things that need to be evident in a life for anyone to know that love exists there. Love can be described both positively and negatively – what it is and what it is not. Love *is* patience, kindness, a passion for the truth, a willingness to carry the burdens of life, an undying faith, hope in the face of uncertainty and disappointment, and endurance beyond strength. Love is *not* boastfulness, arrogance, or rudeness. It doesn't cope by expressing irritability or resentment about the conditions of life or the things that are happening in the world. And love simply does not accept that two wrongs make a right or that sometimes it is okay to get back at someone.

These are the qualities or characteristics of a mature and loving life. Of course, we have to acknowledge that even the best of us fail at love from time to time. The kind of maturity and wisdom required to love truly and consistently is just not possible for human beings since the fall into sin. This is why Paul takes a little bit off the edge of his demands about love by pointing out that we all struggle to acquire the kind of knowledge and wisdom that can reflect itself in consistent love. It is in the context of a lesson about true love that Paul points out how imperfect our knowledge is and how difficult these lessons can be. ("For now we see through a mirror dimly . . . now I know only in part" v. 12.)

We are usually patient with people who don't yet know how to love or who have experienced life with someone who doesn't know how to love. We see this often with children, but we also see it with adults who struggle with their marriages or who become involved with the wrong crowd and begin to do harm to themselves or to other people. We know how hard it is to deal with life sometimes and what difficulty we all have in trying to learn how to love successfully.

This is why the ministry of Christ is so important to us. *Jesus came to teach us how to love.* He did this with both words and actions. He was the ultimate example of a mature life. He knew how to love selflessly and completely. He gave himself up for others while retaining perfect assurance about who he was and what he believed. Sure, he sometimes struggled too. As a man living in the world, he experienced the doubts and temptations that we all feel. But he knew where to go when the load became too heavy. He went to his father. He prayed. He asked for help.

This is part of the secret of a mature, loving life – *knowing how and when to ask for help.* People who are boastful or arrogant do not know how to ask for help. People who insist on their own way often cannot ask for help. They suffer from the sin of pride and it requires humility to seek assistance on the way of life. Only mature people can ask for help. Only they know where to find it. This is why it is important for mature people to assist immature people and why parents must help their children. It's only when we know how to love that we know where to go to keep that love going.

Love comes from God. God is love. When we know God, we know how to love and where to go to keep that love alive. We help other people learn to love by pointing them to God. Sometimes we do that by teaching them about God. Often we point people to God by being godlike ourselves – by reflecting God's love in the way we behave and in the things we say.

It's interesting that Paul lifts three qualities up as the chief gifts of a human life – faith, hope and love. The reason he says that love is the greatest of these is because it is through love that we achieve the other qualities. Faith comes by love, especially the love of Christ. Hope exists because of love. And if faith becomes weak and hope fades we can be confident that love still continues. As a matter of fact, *love is at its best when trouble comes, when we are filled with doubt, and when hope has been buried in the rubble of disaster.*

So what does it mean to be a Christian? It means knowing how to love. How do we learn to love? From the ministry of Christ: from his teachings, from his life, from his death and resurrection. He gave himself for us so that we may know how to give ourselves for others. Love is a work in progress but at least we have been given the power, through Christ, to begin loving and to grow in love throughout our lives.

At the Heart of the Matter

And being found in fashion as a man, He humbled himself . . . wherefore God has highly exalted Him . . . then make my joy complete by being like minded, having the same love, being one in spirit and purpose (Philippians 2: 8-9, 2).

The transfiguration of Christ can be a difficult topic for a preacher, especially one who follows the patterns of the church year with the various remembrances or observances that are built into the flow of it. This is one of those times when the church year and the secular year collide. We have, of course, encountered that problem before and have commented on it in various ways.

During this season, on the secular side we have Valentines Day and the more recent local observance of Family Day. These observances provide us with an opportunity for some good-hearted fun and even, possibly, an extra day of leisure. As we learned last year, Valentines Day has its roots in a more serious remembrance of the life and death of a priest named Valentine or Valentinus who lived in Rome in the third century. He was martyred because he tried to preserve the sanctity of love and marriage in a time when those things had been seriously devalued.

But Valentines Day for us is not a remembrance of an ancient priest. It

An Arcadian Vision

has evolved, as most of these observances do, into a celebration of *us* and of *our* love relationships.

In the church year, we are about to observe Transfiguration Sunday, which is the last Sunday before we begin the celebration of Lent. The transfiguration is a mysterious singular event in the life of Christ and in the presentation of his ministry. This event seems somewhat difficult to understand from a theological perspective. Ministers sometimes just ride over the top of it and talk about other things. And, of course, Lent is a time of dark remembrance where the focus is on the way of the cross and the conclusion of Christ's ministry on earth.

These things don't seem to go well together: the giddy celebration of a secular love festival and the mystery of the transfiguration leading toward a walk of death. So it may be no wonder that choosing a topic for a time like this can be difficult. And, as I have already said, we sometimes resolve this difficulty by simply not commenting on one or the other of these apparently incompatible observances.

I'm not sure that we have to give up on trying to bring these things together in some way. For example, it is possible to view the Transfiguration of Christ as evidence of love at work in the world. And we get an idea of what love is by understanding and acting on our own love relationships. So maybe we can observe the Transfiguration, Valentine's Day and Family Day in a way that helps us grasp what love really is – as the love of God for us and as the love we have for each other.

What was the Transfiguration anyway? It was an event intended to demonstrate to the world that the man who admonished people to love each other and who was about to offer himself up as a love sacrifice for the salvation of the world was actually who he said he was. It was an event intended to prove that he *was* God and that he had come *from* God as the promised Messiah. It was, if you will, an opportunity to demonstrate that he was not a false lover and that he could and would accomplish what he had promised.

The readings for today (from Exodus 34, Psalm 99, 2 Corinthians 3 and Luke 9) are about the problem of seeing God and knowing Him for who He is. Moses is mentioned in the Psalm and the First and Second Readings as someone who had seen God but because of that had to cover his face with a veil so the glory of God's spirit and light wouldn't blind or confuse other people. The veil became a symbol of the sin that separates people from God. If we try to look on God in a state of sinfulness or hard heartedness we are blinded by His glory and, as a result, cannot see Him at all.

The message of the gospel is that because of Christ the veil has been lifted and we can see God and share in His glory. This is what Paul is talking about in the Second Reading.

The Transfiguration is the event where a transition is made from the idea of God *hidden* behind the veil to the idea of God *revealed* in the person of His son, Jesus Christ. In the Old Testament, Moses and Elijah were two people that had been chosen before Christ to enter into God's presence and bring back God's Word to the people. They were able to step behind the veil and see God during a time when God was hidden or inaccessible to most people.

However, with Christ all people can see God. The veil is now lifted. The sign of this is that Jesus the man is revealed as God in the Transfiguration. This revelation is in the form used in the Old Testament where God presents Himself as the spirit of light. The difference is that once this light was too bright for men to see, but now the light of God is in the person of Jesus Christ so everyone can see it. Moses and Elijah appear as witnesses to this presentation because they have already seen God and can testify that it is really God who is present at this event. Some of Jesus' disciples are also present as witnesses of this transformation or transfiguration. Moses and Elijah are witnesses from the past. Peter, John and James are witnesses from the present. They are all there to fulfill the requirement in Hebrew law that a statement can only be accepted as fact when it is confirmed by three witnesses. *The fact here is that Jesus the man is also God the Son, the promised Messiah.* This fact is further confirmed at the Transfiguration by the voice of God the Father saying, "this is my Son, listen to him".

During these days when many of us are thinking about love and family, the confirmation of Jesus as the author of true love in the world is comforting. It means that we have a source from which to draw to sustain our love for each other.

Love between persons is often a difficult thing. We don't always know how to practice love, and even small differences or disagreements can seem to ruin love relationships and even render them irreparable. And families are sometimes cauldrons of turmoil rather than places of solace or comfort. What is usually missing when love relationships go wrong is knowledge of love itself. God is love and the source of love. When we know God, we know love. But to know God, we must know who God is, and how to get to Him. That is what the Transfiguration is all about: *knowing who God is and understanding that we all now have access to Him* through the life and death of a man who was God walking among us in this world.

Religion and theology sometimes seem to be about things that have no practical use in the world. We may ridicule the study of these things by relating them to debates on questions like "how many angels can stand on the head of a pin?"

It *is* hard to take time for the deeper things. Our lives can become relegated to the mundane details of living, and the energy required for that can be overwhelming. But this is why we set time aside to think about things that may not, on the surface, seem to have any practical use – like deciding who, this year, will be our Valentine. Or what, this year, we can learn from the record of the transfiguration of Jesus. Or is it worthwhile, this year, to try and do something special as a family?

All these things are about love. Love is one of the deeper things whether or not we relate it to religion and theology. But at least when we look to God's word to find some instruction about what love is and how God has expressed it, we get closer to the source of love and we can become better at practicing love.

In our Gospel for today (Luke 9:28-43a) Jesus is confronted by a man who wants a favor on behalf of his son. Jesus appears to become angry with the man but performs the act of healing for the man's son anyway. Why would Jesus become angry at this request for help? It is because he has perceived that the people, including this man, don't yet know who he is or what his message is even though they acknowledge his ability to teach and to heal. Jesus knows that very often after he has spoken to the people or performed a miracle of healing they go away and live exactly as they did before. They still do not know God. The veil is still before their eyes. (This is what Paul is talking about in our Second Reading – 1 Corinthians 3:12ff). The people will accept acts of love from him but they do not learn how to offer love themselves.

But loving someone and helping someone in need cannot depend on a right attitude or understanding on the part of the ones asking for help. So Jesus cannot turn away from the child in need even though he regrets that the child's father does not see him for who he is. As we have learned from our study of First Corinthians 13, love is blind that way. Anyone who has true love will give it whether it is appreciated or not. But if you have love yourself and know the source of love, you don't have to always be dependent on the love of others to solve your problems for you. The power of love is within you.

John W. Ekstedt

This was the frustration of Jesus. "How long", he says, "will you refuse to understand that the power is in you too and that you can love as I do?"

So as we think about love today, let us also remember that because of Christ we, too, can be transfigured by the love of God into people who know how to love all the time – not just on these days of special remembrance.

5. The High Festival of Easter

While Christmas may be the most popular of the high festivals, most agree that Easter is the central feast of the Christian liturgical year. Its date is not fixed and instead is determined by a formula established at the First Council of Nicea in 325AD. This Council established the time for Easter as the first Sunday after the full moon following the vernal (spring) equinox in the Northern Hemisphere. The method of determining the date for Easter is very interesting and tells us much about the connection between Jewish and Christian ritual as well as historical methods for telling time, determining seasons and organizing remembrances. The council of Nicea was the first attempt to develop a consensus throughout Christendom about statements of belief and some matters of church organization and worship.

Lessons of the Passion (Lent)

Lent is the forty days before Easter. It is used to prepare for the celebration of the death of Christ (the Passion) and his resurrection from the dead. It is normally a time of contemplation and penitence. There are several specific festivals within this period including Ash Wednesday, Maundy Thursday and Good Friday. As advent prepares us for Christmas, so Lent prepares us for Easter.

Celebration or Sacrifice: a Petition for Lent

If anyone would come after me, he must deny himself and take up his cross daily and follow me (Luke 9:23).

As we begin the season of Lent we are reminded that this is the time when Christ began the walk of death. Every year we enter this season sensing the darkness of it. This is symbolized in our adornments and acknowledged in our readings.

It is a practice in many parts of the world to precede this season with a party or elaborate celebration. In some places this is known as carnival or Mardi Gras and the streets are filled with symbols of temptation and excess.

The idea that a remembrance of suffering and death is preceded by such lavish celebrations may seem strange – especially when we are looking ahead to the path of suffering that we refer to as the passion of Christ. But we can use the time just preceding Lent to remember Christ's temptation by Satan. By doing this, we may understand more about the magnitude of Christ's decision to go the way of the cross. We might have a better feel for the meaning of Christ's temptation by taking a last deliberate taste of earthly pleasure and excess before entering into a time of self-imposed sacrifice and self-denial. In this way, we might be better prepared to follow Christ on his journey to death.

Lent is intended as a very dark and reflective time. Christ is on his way to die. He is beginning his descent into hell. During this time, he experiences all the changes human beings experience when they know that they are going to die. Even though he has just been revealed as God in the Transfiguration, he humbles himself and walks as a man to that end that we all must face. He will overcome death of course, though he does experience it; and because of that we will overcome death, though we will also experience it.

Lent is about learning what it means to follow Christ. Christ came to earth to die for us and it is important for us to learn the meaning of this. But while we follow him along the way to the place of death, we don't follow him to learn how to die. We follow him to learn how to live. This is the mystery of Lent and why it is such a remarkable time in the life of the church.

All the readings for today are about living. But they are not about having a good time. Or about being happy. Or about being content. Or about being satisfied or successful. These *are* some of the positive moments or outcomes that we experience in life but some of us may think that life *is* those things. We may feel that if we are not happy or successful or satisfied then life is cheating us.

Our culture doesn't deal well with tragedy or death. Some argue that we have had so much of what life has to offer and our expectations about

An Arcadian Vision

self-satisfaction are so high that when tragedy comes or death happens, we can be overwhelmed. We may blame others for our misfortunes even when the tragedy that befalls us is of our own doing or simply part of the problem of living. And, of course, the occurrence of tragedy or death in our lives is the perfect time to deny God or blame *Him* for the troubles we are experiencing.

In recent years, scientists have researched the way in which people deal with tragedy. Their findings seem to confirm that many people, especially in North American culture, are simply not prepared for the occurrence of tragedy or the event of death. In simple terms, many of us may actually feel that we don't deserve to experience these things.

In many places, the practice of preparing for Lent with a great party or carnival has become part of the culture. The idea that we cannot walk in the shoes of our Lord unless we, like him, have faced and overcome the temptation of earthly pleasure is a well understood "theology of the street". Some people are quite used to the idea of using the carnival to taste of the temptation that Christ experienced at the hands of Satan during those forty days before he entered his passion. Caricatures of Satan often dominate at these celebrations, especially during the opening and closing ceremonies. The party or the carnival symbolically tempts the people with the idea that life is really a quest for personal pleasure and happiness. The party offers them various ways to achieve this. Can they resist this temptation and, instead, take up the cross to follow their Lord? This is the question of carnival as well as the question of Lent.

But, as with so many things in life, people can become enamored of the party and turned off by the self-denial. Today, for many, the party is the thing. We do not see the party, or all the grand promises of Satan, as something to be rejected or overcome. We see these temptations as desirable, as things to be sought after, even as the purpose of our work. It is interesting that even those who have little money or minimal prospects of success can often find a way to party much of the time. We see evidence of this in our little town. In the midst of the affluence, there is real poverty here, but for some of us even poverty can afford us just enough to waste our lives seeking pleasure. And, in the end, we obtain nothing from it but regret.

The original idea of carnival as a time of preparation for Lent was based on a different reality from ours. When these celebrations originated, almost everyone struggled with the basics of life. And among those basics were the constant specters of tragedy and death. A grand party was a rare thing for most people. Any kind of party at all was a rare thing. These days people may prepare for Lent with a party or a parade, or eat to excess (Mardi Gras means Fat Tuesday), because it is the *last* time they will do that before participating in their self-imposed period of denial. But for those who rarely had a chance to experience mindless personal pleasure or the bright lights and fancy costumes of a grand celebration, the party of Lent became a real and present temptation. They were not used to such excess. It signaled for them how hard it must have been for Christ to be offered so much from Satan (see our Gospel for today, Luke 4:1-13) at a time when he was about to face the greatest suffering of his life.

Historically, it was relatively easy for people to get into the intended spirit of the rituals of the church both before and during Lent. Much of life was about the struggle to survive, enduring the conditions of poverty and fighting the temptation to give up morality for even the briefest taste of pleasure or the smallest amount of material gain. For most people, the rituals of organized religion provided the means for dealing with these most basic of life's concerns. Carnival could be a time of real temptation to see if they could withstand even a short time of promised pleasure and excess. In this sense, carnival actually could prepare them for the remembrance of Christ's temptation and his participation in the struggles of life on our behalf.

Sometimes carnival is called "anti-Lent" because the costumes often feature the devil or people wearing masks to hide their identity as they follow the devil. It is a moment when people symbolically give in to the very thing that Christ faced in our gospel for today. The devil is featured in our gospel tempting Christ with promises of power, authority and escape from the torments of life, even death itself. When observed as a religious experience, the carnival is a remembrance of this moment of temptation. Lent, which follows, teaches us the magnitude of the sacrifice made by Christ in turning away from earthly pleasure to a life in service to God, his father.

However, we probably shouldn't make too much of the rituals of carnival or Mardi Gras as we begin the Lenten season. In most places, these retain little of their original religious intent and have become mostly secular experiences. Also, there are those who argue that these practices evolved from pagan traditions as have many other Christian rites and ceremonies. In the context of modern religious practices, especially in North America, we might find it difficult to get in touch with the intended spirit of it.

An Arcadian Vision

Lent *is* a celebration – even though it is about temptation, suffering and death. And some prepare for it in extravagant ways. We know that Christ could have given in to the temptation of the devil and avoided the way of the cross. He could have chosen to "party on", but he did not. As a result, we are all able to endure suffering and face death knowing that it cannot defeat us – that we are saved from the consequences of our sin through the sacrifice of God's son.

Lent prepares us for life, even though Lent commemorates a journey to death. And that, after all, is what life on earth is, isn't it – a journey to death. We often say that death is part of life and that we understand death better if we see it that way. But there is a greater meaning to this sentiment. The death we remember at Lent, including the time of temptation that precedes it, is a guarantee of life. Our Lord refuses to be swayed by the temptations of the devil and he gives in to his suffering knowing that he will die. In his dying he shows that he is a man, but in his resurrection he shows that he is God. Because he suffered this way, our suffering on earth can be made bearable, even satisfying. And our death is not a loss but a victory, as his death was not a loss but a victory. This is the meaning of Lent.

It is so important to remember that Lent prepares us for life *before* death as much as it helps us to understand the meaning of life for us *after* death. What do we need to know about this life here on earth? Well, we see part of the meaning of our earthly life illustrated in the readings for today.

According to the First Reading (Deuteronomy 26:1-11), life is trouble, harshness and affliction but with a promise that God is able to bring us out of these things victorious.

According to the Psalm (91), life is the promise that there is help in times of trouble and that we need never be alone in this world.

According to the Gospel (Luke 4:1-13), life is full of temptations, but they can be overcome.

According to the Second Reading (Romans 10:8b-13), life is salvation and it is available to everyone.

Life is trouble but life is also hope. Life is temptation, but life is also strength. Life is danger, but life is protection and support. Life is dying, but life is salvation from the consequences of death.

We have talked before about what prayer is as an activity of life. One of its aspects is as *petition*. Prayer is our opportunity to come before God with appeals, pleas or requests. We can petition on behalf of ourselves or on behalf of others.

Lent is a good time for prayer. We observe Christ doing it throughout the journey to the cross. And it is especially a good time for prayer as petition.

What might our petition be as we enter Lent? Some, who may have partied excessively to get ready for Lent, may want to petition for a promise of a better life. For a life that is more satisfying all the time, not just at carnival.

Some, who take their religion seriously, may petition for the grace and the strength to actually engage in some form of meaningful self-denial so that they can live a better life and be more understanding of the life of Christ.

But most of us have not partied to get ready for Lent and most of us will not make any particular effort to engage in acts of self-denial. So for us, what might our petitions be?

Each of us may have different petitions. One petition might be to follow the promise of the Psalm and ask God for the protection of an angel. In the spirit of the First Reading, we might ask for a better life. We might ask for escape from the things that oppress us and be "brought to a better place". In the spirit of the Gospel, we might ask for the ability to overcome temptation. Or we might follow Paul's encouragement from our Second Reading and petition God for our salvation. These are all good and proper Lenten petitions.

But I have a suggestion. Lent is a great time to give special attention to the greatest petition of all. The one taught to us by Christ himself – the Lord's Prayer. As a Lenten meditation, maybe in preparation for each church service during Lent, it might be a very satisfying practice to open a Bible to one of the two places (Matthew 6:9-13 and Luke 11:1-4) where the Lord's prayer occurs and read that prayer in its context.

We speak the Lord's prayer every Sunday, but maybe during Lent we can say it as our Lenten petition. This prayer gives honor to God, asks that our basic needs be met, seeks forgiveness, offers the promise that we will forgive others, asks for help in the face of our daily temptations and pleads for protection from evil. It is the perfect Lenten petition and will remind us to keep the spirit of Lent faithfully as we follow Christ along the way of sorrows.

An Arcadian Vision

To Die in Jerusalem

Jerusalem, Jerusalem, the city that kills the prophets and stones those who are sent to it! How often have I desired to gather your children . . . (Luke 13:34a).

It might be useful this Lenten season to keep track of where we are going on this journey that we have called the walk of death or the way of dying. We started with the Transfiguration, the time when Christ was revealed as the Son of God. We then proceeded into the desert where we were witnesses to the temptation of Christ, and now we find ourselves in Jerusalem where it is becoming obvious that Christ is in mortal danger. As we have noted before, it is a dark time, this period leading up to the crucifixion, and it is important to try to grasp the meaning of it, if we can.

Of course, many things transpire along the way between these events. For example, Christ performs much of his recorded ministry as he and his followers journey between the desert where he is tempted by evil, the place of his Transfiguration where he is revealed as God, and the city of Jerusalem where death is waiting. He performs miracles, speaks parables, teaches lessons on life and living, explains the relationship between God and human beings, and talks about the meaning of death – including his own. He confronts evil (or the devil) on several occasions, engages in personal counseling sessions, instructs people on how to understand the scriptures and teaches them how to pray. From his teaching on prayer, we get the Lord's Prayer that we have chosen this year as our "petition for Lent".

I read a newspaper article this week in which the author was concerned about the growing lack of familiarity with the Bible (William Ingram, "Even atheists need to read the Bible", National Post, Feb. 22, 2010). He wrote, "our antipathy toward reading the Bible is creating a situation of increasing cultural and intellectual illiteracy". He was concerned that "a lack of understanding of the Bible undermines the ability to fully appreciate the greatest works of art, philosophy, music and literature". He argued that the importance of the Bible was not dependent on approaching it from a perspective of faith. "Biblical literacy", he said, "is a prerequisite for cultural understanding".

It's true, isn't it, that our culture is loaded with Biblical metaphors and allusions. Moses' vision of the Promised Land at the completion of the Israelites' wilderness journey is the basis for one of Martin Luther King's most famous quotes: "I've seen the Promised Land. I may not get there with you. But I want you to know tonight, that we, as a people, will get to the Promised Land". Our article writer rightly points out that if we don't know the story of Moses and the suffering of the people of Israel in their quest for the Promised Land, the true meaning of Martin Luther King's remarks will elude us.

Some people avoid organized religion or don't read the Bible because they are turned off by the positions of extremists and militant fundamentalists. And yes, Christianity has extremists, some violent and dangerous, just as other religions do. Some avoid the Bible because they think that many people who read it are anti-intellectual or literal in their interpretation of it. These people, it is imagined, are narrow minded in their views about things like human sexuality, the role of women in society and facts concerning the existence of the world and how it came to be.

But the truth is that the Bible has to be grossly misinterpreted to be used in support of bigoted views and superstitious assumptions. The worst use of the Bible happens when people are ignorant of it. This is true whether a person uses the Bible to promote bigotry and violence or condemns the Bible as a work of superstition.

It is not my intention here to discuss or defend the Bible – as either the Word of God or a great work of literature. We have often talked about what the Bible is as the Word of God and have even marveled at some of the difficulties involved in interpreting the Bible because of problems of translation and historical context.

I raise this issue of Biblical literacy, which *has* worsened in recent years, because it helps to illustrate the frustration Christ was experiencing in our Gospel for today (Luke 13:31-35).

Jesus was on his way to Jerusalem to die. This was his destiny. For all the reasons that we have discussed many times, he had to die in Jerusalem – and he knew it. But the problem was that the people of Jerusalem should have known it too. Jerusalem was the great and holy city of the people of Judah. The people of Judah were one of the major tribes of God's chosen people and had been taught from birth about the coming of the Messiah. It was ingrained in their culture and bound up in their traditions. All of their great works of art, literature and music were remembrances of their lives of captivity and oppression as well as reflections on the promise of their salvation. Everyone in Jerusalem should have known that the events that would save them from all the oppression and misery of their lives would happen in *their* land and that the Messiah would rise up from among *their* people. The promised Savior would be born in Bethlehem of Judea

(Judah), and he would come announced by the angels of God and many signs of prophecy would precede him. If they had read their scriptures, if they had been Biblically literate, they would have known this. The signs would have been clear to them and they would have recognized the Son of God when he appeared.

But they were not Biblically literate. They did not know their own history. They did not understand their own destiny. And from their ignorance they committed grievous crimes, including killing the prophets and teachers who over the millennia had been sent to instruct them on the signs that would announce the coming of the Messiah. And they were about to participate in the killing of a prophet again, without knowing who he was or understanding his reason for coming. Or that he was the promised Messiah himself.

We have talked before about the frustrations experienced by Christ along his way of sorrows. Remember how the gospel for Transfiguration Sunday told us of his frustration at the attitude of the people as he came down from the mountain after he had been fully revealed as God in the form of a man. Frustration is, of course, a human emotion. It was part of Christ's expression of his humanity as he took this hard road to his death. As we pointed out on Transfiguration Sunday, he didn't let that hinder his work. He didn't stop loving people or caring for them just because they frustrated him. (Good lesson for parents, I would think.) He didn't try to avoid his time of dying just because the people he was dying for didn't appreciate it or understand it. But still, there were times when we get the feeling that it must have seemed a bit too much to endure, even for the Son of God.

So here Christ was, inside the gates of Jerusalem – the great holy city – knowing his time of death was close and the path of his dying would begin to get rough and mean. And along comes a Pharisee, one of the elite scholars and teachers of the law.

Last week, we talked about the Torah which is the Pentateuch, the first five books of the Bible, or the five books of Moses. We talked about how scholars have dissected the Torah, added footnotes and study notes to it and debated its nuances and perspectives. These efforts have inspired profound intellectual and spiritual debates that have themselves emerged as important books for study.

In Christ's time such deep study of the Torah was the work of the Pharisees. They were supposed to know the scriptures backward and forward including every reference, no matter how oblique, to the coming of a Messiah from the House of Judah who would be condemned to die in God's holy city of Jerusalem.

It was one of those very Pharisees who confronted Jesus inside the gates of Jerusalem. He warned Christ, "hey, you'd better get out of here. Herod wants to kill you". As some of our children like to say these days, "well duh"!

Once again Jesus shows his humanity by responding somewhat sarcastically. "Well, you just tell that sly fox that I'm going to remain here for a few days to attend to some of the spiritual and physical needs of the people. Then I'll leave Jerusalem for a while. After all, no one gets assassinated outside of Jerusalem. If you are a prophet you have to come to Jerusalem to die. But I will be back and then you will see me for who I am."

Jesus is saying that he has a little more work to do in Jerusalem before he leaves town to prepare for his return to die. He knows that it is dangerous in Jerusalem and his sarcasm fairly drips as he taunts the Pharisee. He is saying to the Pharisee that there is considerable irony in the fact that the holy city of Jerusalem is a dangerous place to be, especially for holy people. And it is even more ironical that part of the reason for this is that the religious leaders and scholars of Jerusalem are so illiterate in their own scriptures.

Biblical illiteracy is a problem on many levels. It is a problem for people who refuse to read the Bible and it is a problem for people who claim that they are experts in the Bible. People who refuse to read the Bible because of false perceptions about it deny themselves the possibility of developing their own opinions about it. They may spend their lives dependent on the advice or opinions of others for what they know or believe about Biblical matters. People who read or study the Bible in order to be experts and gain glory for themselves as great teachers deny themselves the possibility of seeing beyond their own intellectual vanity. It can be said that they may be in danger of blinding themselves with their own brilliance.

I agree with the author of the article on Biblical illiteracy, William Ingram, that not knowing the Bible removes us from an understanding of our own history and culture. Such illiteracy lessens our ability to understand the things around us, reduces our imagination, and separates us from really understanding some of the greatest things our culture has produced.

But the journey to the cross helps us understand that it is about more than that. Biblical illiteracy may mean that when God comes to us we won't know it. When the truth is in front of us, we won't see it. And the problem with that is that we may make bad decisions about how we live our lives and deal with others. Or worse, we may make no decisions at all and just drift with the mob. Every one of us has experienced or heard about the psychology of the mob. In the midst of mob frenzy people will destroy property and endanger lives when they would otherwise have no inclination to behave that way. People become part of a mob when they have no opinions of their own, no faith, no conviction and no confidence.

So the lesson for today is to seek Biblical literacy as we follow Jesus on his way to the cross. To study God's word in order to know what the way of the cross means for us and to recognize the person who is making this journey on our behalf. We should encourage each other to be Biblically literate so that our lives can be better on all levels: the level of knowledge, the level of culture and, above all, the level of faith where the face of God can actually be seen.

It Just Isn't Fair!

(All) these years I have been working like a slave for you, and I have never disobeyed your command; yet you have never given me even a young goat so that I might celebrate with my friends (Luke 15:29).

Today's gospel (Luke 15:1-3,11b-32) is the parable of the prodigal son. We all know this parable. We usually interpret it positively, and its message is comforting to us, because in it we are reminded of the love of a father for his son, no matter how rebellious or wayward that son may be. We see this parable as an allegory for the love that God the Father has extended to us, no matter how rebellious or wayward we have been.

In our discussion today, we might want to look at this parable a different way, from the perspective of the good son rather than the bad son. We are going to assume that the good son actually was good. There is no reason for us to believe otherwise. He was one of those who consistently performed good works. He was faithful, he attended to his duties, he was respectful of others and he was willing to sacrifice for the good of his family and his community. By all appearances, he was one of those people we admire wonderingly. They just seem to be so focussed. They appear to be unaffected by the siren call of self-pleasure. They are happy in their work. Men like this, we think, probably make good husbands.

However, in this parable, the good son appears to be selfish and petulant in his response to the return of his brother. He appears to become jealous about the way his father responds to the wayward son. And the good brother's reaction seems to indicate that he has been hiding these feelings, or similar ones, for a long time. His father's response to the return of his brother is simply the last straw.

We often look at this parable and talk about what is right about it – about the return of a wayward child and the unconditional love of a father. But at least from the point-of-view of the elder brother, there is a lot going wrong here.

I remember a comment often heard from social workers and correctional officers: "fifteen percent of the people on your caseload take up eighty percent of your time". It was easy to tell that those fifteen percent had been taking up eighty percent of the time of the people around them for their entire lives. Finally they did something that couldn't be fixed by all that attention and they ended up on the caseload of some social worker or as a prisoner in a secure institution.

This same sentiment applies in all situations where people live and work together. Schoolteachers, coaches, program directors, psychologists, physicians, nurses and parents with more than one child, all give testimony to the reality in their lives that some people require more energy or demand more attention from them than others do.

The prodigal son is a type. The word "prodigal" has come to mean reckless, wasteful or irresponsible. Our association of this word with the parable in our gospel (Luke 15:11-32) has made us think that it means "lost person" or "returned wanderer" and you can even find these definitions in some dictionaries. But, as usual, the language and sense of the original script for this text give us more subtlety than that. Yes, the son in this parable is reckless and wasteful and lost. But he is not lost in the physical sense. The use of the word "lost" here does not mean that he cannot be found. *It means that he has not come back from the place he has gone in his mind, body and spirit.* And the use of the word "found" in this parable does not mean that anyone went out to search for him. It means that he has returned from his place of excess and loneliness and confusion to the home that he always knew was there for him. Instead of using the English word "found", we might be better to use the word "returned".

It is also interesting that the word "prodigal" is from the same root as "prodigious" and "prodigy". These last two words are usually understood positively. To be prodigious is to be extremely or unusually productive. Two of its synonyms are the words "marvelous" and "amazing". To be a prodigy is to be a marvelous person or a wonderful example. It means to

An Arcadian Vision

have unusual abilities, as with the child who can play Beethoven at the age of four.

It isn't a mistake that the word prodigal comes from the same root as prodigy. All the potential of productivity and unusual ability is in the prodigal. But people are called prodigals when they have wasted their potential on excess and self-pleasure. Or when they have become lost in their minds and cannot use their talents in a positive way. They become needy and self-serving and begin to take up a lot of other people's time. I have met some of these people in prison but I also see them on the street every day. These are the prodigals of *our* time and many of them never return from the place to which they have gone.

We could preach at length about the meaning of the prodigal and the lessons that emerge from this parable of the prodigal son. It is a good and interesting topic. From a discussion of the true meaning of being a prodigal, we can understand the nature of much of the trouble in the world. It is also a good Lenten topic since the prodigal obviously has problems with the concept of self-denial. (By the way, if you've ever seen the movie *A River Runs Through It,* you will have seen a good modern parable about the problem of the prodigal son.)

But there is another type of trouble to think about today. This is the trouble facing those who must put up with the prodigal. This is the problem of the elder son in our parable – the good son. The one who stayed home and did his duty. The one who never returned, because he never went away. The one who was willing to stay focussed on the details of everyday life. The one who attended to his father's business.

It is quite likely that none of the derivatives from the Latin words, *prodigus* or *prodigium* applied to the elder son. He was neither amazing, in the sense of the prodigy, nor wayward, in the sense of the prodigal. He was, as most of us are, a plodder. He was a regular guy doing what needed to be done and, no doubt, his world was a better place for it.

So why is it that the prodigal son, the irresponsible son, gets all the attention? Why does the father become ecstatic when this wasteful human being shows his face again? For those who stay in the trenches and do the dirty work, it's enough to drive a person crazy! *It just isn't fair!*

And, indeed, the eldest son finally rebelled. He became jealous, angry and vindictive. He criticized his own father. He threw a tantrum. He acted totally out of character. He became a lot more like his brother and, in the moment, it was probably good for him. He needed to let it out.

You will notice that the father didn't berate the eldest son for his outburst. He responded in a loving way, reminding his eldest son that he was aware of his constant presence and all that he had done and that, as a result, everything that the father owned belonged to him. But then he said something to this effect, "come on, think about it, I thought that I had lost your brother to his craziness. I thought that I had failed in the worst possible way with him and it scared me to death. Given his excesses, it's a miracle that he has returned. So give me this moment of happiness and share it with me. He may not deserve such a party, but I do. Give this to me because he is my son and he was lost but now is found."

Fairness is a concept with which human beings seem to have a lot of trouble. The reality of our existence is that nothing we do can assure that we will be treated fairly or that we will be compensated in proportion to the attitudes we have or the efforts that we make. We get most confused about the issue of fairness when we observe the conditions of others in this world and we see how the rich get richer and the poor get poorer – and disproportionate trouble seems to happen to those who deserve it the least.

And, of course, we sometimes think that, if there is a God, that Being should have made sure that things work out evenly for everyone and that no trouble happens to anybody – especially to those who don't deserve it.

In the sense that we are talking, life is *not* fair, or at least there certainly are times when unfair things happen. This, as we know, is because there is sin in the world. The world is disordered and exists as a shadow of its created self. There is much that is in ruin, including the way human beings treat each other.

But if there is not fairness, at least there can be justice and mercy. In the case of the parable of the prodigal son, *justice* is that the eldest son loses nothing from the waywardness of his brother. He may not gain some of the things he would have liked, like a lavish party he could share with his friends, but nothing is taken from him including the trust and admiration of his father.

There is *mercy* here in that, regardless of the younger son's waywardness, he is welcomed back home with sincere joy and unconditional love. But *justice* applies to him, too. He has received his inheritance and wasted it. He cannot get that back. He has been shown to be irresponsible and, as a result, his father must watch him now. There is a problem of trust here.

In a way, it isn't fair, or it doesn't seem fair, that there should be so much attention given to this wayward son. But many things trump fairness, the main one being love. The eldest son has an opportunity to really be the bigger man if he can remember to love his brother in this moment when things aren't fair.

What do the parables of Christ do for us? They teach us about our relationship with God and how we are to live in this world in service to God. They also remind us of the conditions in which we live and how hard it is sometimes to live with joy, in service to Christ, when so many things don't seem right or fair.

The *love* of the father overcomes the lack of fairness that the eldest son experiences and brings both justice and mercy to the wasted life of the younger son. This is the promise of God to us. Life may not always be fair but, from the Father's love, justice and mercy are extended to us. And besides, in our sin we all deserve condemnation of one kind or another. As has been pointed out, over and over, we all deserve death and instead have been promised life. How fair is that?

The Work of the Church

You always have the poor with you, but you do not always have me (John 12:8).

Today our meditation addresses the dilemma of the church as a worldly institution. What is its duty and to whom? How are we to behave as Christians in a world of trouble and need? And when we come together to form a fellowship, a community of like-minded and like-spirited people called a church, what is it for?

Recently, I was in a meeting discussing the problems of the modern church – especially the concerns that we all have about declining memberships. Someone, with reference to Jasper said, "yes, but at least in Jasper the whole town knows how to do church".

The conversation stopped as people considered this statement. What did that mean? How does a town "do church"?

What the speaker no doubt meant was that Jasper has a reputation for extending services to people in somewhat unique or unusual ways. The town organizes itself to provide community dinners for seniors and transient workers. (The Jasper ministerial association helped to sponsor one of those dinners just last week and members of our church were actively involved.) There is a very good community outreach program here that I have used several times as a local pastor to provide food and other support for people in immediate need. It wouldn't be difficult to provide other examples of the way in which the town of Jasper organizes itself to serve its resident population as well as its many and diverse visitors.

I don't know if Jasper is more notable for its community services than other communities might be. But it is a somewhat unusual place, and quite a large percentage of its population at any given time can be living on the edge and in need of some form of assistance or another. I have certainly noticed this in my own ministry.

But it was something of a startling proposition to have this work described as "doing church" and I found myself reflecting on the meaning of such a statement and what it might say about our perceptions of what a church is and what its members do.

This is not the first time that I have been faced with this question. It was at the forefront of my awareness over forty-five years ago when I began my graduate thesis at seminary. Completing that thesis was to be my last formal academic activity before the Board of Regents would decide whether or not I had successfully completed the requirements for graduation. But, more importantly, they would be deciding whether or not I was qualified for the office of the ministry.

The year was 1964. This was a time of extreme upheaval in the United States. President Kennedy had been assassinated just a few months earlier. President Johnson, who replaced him, was initiating a "War on Poverty" and the most significant piece of civil rights legislation ever passed in the United States was about to be drafted (Voting Rights Act). The country was being torn apart by racial strife. Poverty as an aspect of American life was being profiled as never before. Not even during the depression had poverty been described as such a wicked and debilitating aspect of American culture and politics.

One of the problems for the church during this time was that the inner cities were breaking up or disintegrating. It was in these places that the church had committed most of its energy during the first two thirds of the twentieth century. In every major American city, very large "mother churches" of the various denominations filled the skyline and set the tone for much of the city's cultural experience.

These churches were the fortresses of European immigrants who had used them to preserve their culture and protect their community during the difficult transition to a new land. The families that occupied these churches produced the political and community leaders who controlled the wealth that, in turn, supported the great cathedrals of North American Christendom. As crime and racial strife escalated, these white, middle class Americans began fleeing the inner city and abandoning the churches that they had built to preserve their way of life.

Within the course of a decade, the foundation of language and culture on which these churches had been established became irrelevant as a community force. The churches had trouble relating to the growing poverty of the inner cities as well as to their changing color and language. It was an uncertain and difficult time and, in one form or another, this problem still exists. For the Lutheran church, the cultural and linguistic base was German or Scandinavian. Now it found itself surrounded by African and Asian ethnic groups, many of which had themselves been corrupted by almost two centuries of discrimination and mistreatment enforced by the very community and political leaders whose families had sustained the old European enclaves.

Within the churches and seminaries of Christendom, a number of attempts were made to study the conditions that were affecting how the church was performing in these changing city environments. Much was made of the need to redefine the ministry of the church in the new inner city as well as within the changing rural and suburban landscape.

One movement that emerged was based on a concept called "social gospel". The idea here was that the gospel could be made relevant in places like the new inner city through programs of the church directed first to the needs of the disadvantaged people who lived there. This was partially based on the idea that people suffering from hunger or needing medical attention have trouble receiving the message of spiritual salvation until their physical needs are met. This approach was also based on the theological assumption that a primary purpose of the Christian community is to serve Christ by helping others without qualification and especially without regard to their spiritual commitment or affiliation with any particular church.

In a short period of time, churches in the inner cities began to evolve as social service agencies and treatment centers. Money began to be diverted from church coffers to the development of housing and food service programs. People started coming back to church, not for the word and sacraments, but for food stamps, education vouchers and housing assistance. The changes were extreme because the times were perceived to be extreme. The church at every level from its youth to its Bishops was caught in the confusion created by a changing constituency and an uncertain mission.

I proposed to my graduate program advisors that I be given permission to study this problem as research for my thesis. I received permission and a year later published a thesis titled *The Christian Ministry in the Poverty of the Inner City*.

I did a lot of research for that thesis. This included visiting several large inner city churches and studying their programs. Reviews were completed on the start-up of most of the programs funded through the War on Poverty legislation initiated under the administration of President Lyndon Johnson. I participated in civil rights marches and interviewed inner city politicians as well as church leaders. I attended youth conferences to get the view of people from my own generation and younger. But the most important advice and guidance that I received during my research came from the scripture that provides the gospel lesson for today and that has formed the basis for this meditation (John 12:1-8).

There is much to consider in the gospel for today. We will not nearly get to all of it. This story is loaded with images for discussion. Christ is having a meal with a man that he had raised from the dead. Mary, Martha and Judas Iscariot, some of the most significant people in Christ's human life, are present. Judas is portrayed as a man known to be of weak character even before he betrayed Jesus (we heard in an earlier sermon that he was the only one of Christ's disciples who was not a Galilean). Mary uses expensive perfume to perform the ritual of foot washing on the feet of Christ. All of these aspects of the story give us something to talk about. I have often thought that the story of this supper meeting presents a perfect allegory for what the institution of the church is meant to be.

But today we want to highlight the portion of the gospel where Christ rebukes Judas for his criticism of Mary and speaks that relatively famous line "you always have the poor with you, but you do not always have me".

People are sometimes startled and confused by the apparent callousness of Christ's response to Judas in this passage. But it would be the height of foolishness to assume that Christ had no regard for the poor or for others with various needs. The point here is that there are some things of greater moment or greater importance than attending to the physical needs of fellow human beings. Sometimes it is more important for the soul, *and to our ability to help others*, that we first attend to the things of God. First things must come first; otherwise we become like Judas, who is a fake. Judas pretends to care for others but he is a thief. He steals from the poor while professing to be an advocate for them. His soul is shriveled because he has not fed it and he can be of no help to anyone.

I met many people like this, especially during the time of my study, when the church was struggling to find its place in a world consumed by the specters of poverty, need and discrimination. The poor were crying out "feed us, teach us, heal us, give us a chance to make a life in this harsh and violent world. Sell your churches, tear down your altars, donate the land to us, convert the space for us." *And some in the church said, "wouldn't it be better to sell these things and give the money to the poor?"*

I wish that I could share all of the things I experienced while struggling with this issue in those days of my own uncertainty. But for now I can only say that I concluded what Christ's words in the gospel have already informed us. We must clearly see what the priorities are. We do not, of course, give up on the poor *but we must know who we are as a church and what we have to offer, otherwise we are of no earthly use to anyone.*

As I have already noted, the images in the gospel for today are, for me, images of the church. These are people coming together to be with their Lord. They did this by attending to the ritual needs that they all had. They came to serve each other, remember their history together and listen to the Word of God. And attend to the traitor in the midst of them.

This is what the church is and it keeps itself alive by directing its energies to the preservation of itself as a gathering of believers, by attending to its houses, by confirming and giving meaning to its rituals. And by inviting everyone, including the poor and disadvantaged, to join with them in the receiving of God's Word and the sharing of resources to meet each other's needs.

Allow me to read a couple of excerpts from *The Christian Ministry in the Poverty of the Inner City*:

Whenever the church enters new territory, it must re-ask itself two basic questions: What is our purpose? and, How do we accomplish that purpose in this situation?... The church is the body of Christ. As the body of Christ it can have only one purpose: to do the will of Christ. The will of Christ is learned from the Word of Christ which is the Word of God ... What does this mean in the poverty situation of the inner city?

It means that the church is in the poverty situation of the inner city to proclaim salvation from sin and its consequences (and) the church proclaims that Christ, not affluence, is their salvation. The church is there not to make the poor middle-class, but to bring the poor to Christ. The church brings the message that sin, not poverty, is the cause of death.

It means that the church in the poverty of the inner city owes its first allegiance to Christ and His Gospel, not to the poor and their poverty. It means that the church is, first of all, Christian, not, first of all, humanitarian. Whatever is done is done in the name of Christ for His glory, not in the name of the poor so they may escape their poverty (pp. 35-36).

When I read this again after all these years, I am struck with the sound of it. Like Christ's words in our gospel for today, these words seem harsh and maybe even uncaring.

But, in fact, this is the most important help we have to offer anyone who is in trouble – that regardless of their condition, they are children of God and have been offered God's blessing and salvation just like everyone else.

If the church has a warm place to stay or food to offer or education to provide, it offers that as well – not *as* gospel but *because of* the gospel. This is why the church's first duty is to preserve the gospel and point the way to salvation. This is why the widow gave her mite to the church rather than buying food for herself. This is why Mary scrimped and saved to present a special gift to Christ at a special dinner prepared especially for him. She knew that recognizing and giving honor to her Lord was the only way she could be of use to anyone else. This is why we have our churches, this is why we preserve them, and this is why we offer our gifts within them.

We have many exhortations in scripture about how we are to be with the poor and the needy. We are to feed them, give them drink, and visit them in prison – among other things. But our giving is special because of the person we are representing when we do it. That person is the God who made us. Our gifts to other people have power because we first offered ourselves as gifts to God for His service. When we give ourselves to others in Christ's name, they can be truly helped.

It Is My Passion!

(A meditation for Palm or Passion Sunday)

Blessed is the King who comes (Luke 19:38) . . . *every knee should bend* (Phil. 2:10).

This is a Sunday of the church year with an interesting history that might leave some of us a little confused. As a child, and well into my years as a pastor, this Sunday was Palm Sunday, and Passion Sunday was the Sunday before this one or the Sunday that we now refer to as the 5th Sunday in Lent. Passion Sunday was the first day of a two-week period called Passiontide, the second week of Passiontide being Holy Week. So in the relatively recent past Passion Sunday and Palm Sunday were two different Sundays and we celebrated them in a particular way in the sequence of our remembrances about the journey of Christ to the cross.

Some of you might remember when actual palm branches were distributed in churches on Palm Sunday. I remember that happening in several of the churches that I attended as a child. Even though we were in the Passiontide and about to enter Holy Week with its harsh remembrances marked by dark colors, Palm Sunday always seemed to set a tone for Holy Week that was more like Easter than Good Friday. Setting Palm Sunday aside as its own specific day to concentrate on Christ's triumphal entry into Jerusalem made the commemoration of Christ's suffering and death seem brighter and more worthy of celebration than sorrow. It helped me, as a child, take a different perspective on the meaning of death as seen through the eyes of faith. Death was not something that was defeating but something that could be faced courageously and overcome. It was not a tragedy – it was a victory. Christ's impending death was being announced by cheering crowds and with Palms laid like a carpet or waived like flags. Palm Sunday was a happy day.

Maybe someday a liturgist will explain to me why we have changed these elements of our Lutheran tradition. I am aware of the changes that were made during the 1960s within the calendar of the Roman Catholic Church and how the great ecumenical movement of that time encouraged a review of all church traditions to make church life more relevant to a changing society. Many churches attempted to reform their liturgical practices in keeping with other doctrinal reforms that were taking place. You may remember hearing about the Second Vatican Council, or Vatican II, that began in 1962 and ended in 1965. This great modern reform council of Roman Catholicism, also called the Ecumenical Council, set in motion a number of sweeping reforms in church practice. Anglicans and Lutherans followed suit by reforming some of their liturgies and entering into a growing ecumenical dialogue on church dogma and practice.

One result of all this has been an attempt to standardize certain elements of church practice across all the liturgical churches of Christendom.

It probably isn't that important how we choose to arrange our church year or emphasize events within it. But it is important that we devise a way to assist each other in our effort to worship God faithfully and search intelligently for the meaning of His message to us as it is received through scripture and the doctrines of the church. What the church year does with its sequences of readings, its symbols and its colors, is to give us a way to direct our worship and think on the Word that He has spoken to us. And, clearly, our liturgical practices should reflect our beliefs. They should not be for any other purpose.

In the case of these Sundays that precede the commemoration of the death and resurrection of our Lord, we seem to have moved to a more somber expression of the Passion. Some of these changes have been very recent. Within the last five years we have moved from labeling this Sunday as both Passion and Palm Sunday to removing the Palm part altogether. You will note that the passage from Luke chosen for today's gospel does not even mention the palms or branches laid along the path of Christ's entry into Jerusalem. All the other gospels put their emphasis on this common method used by the Jews to announce the coming of royalty.

Again, I want to emphasize that this is not an issue of great importance. It is, in fact, part of those church matters that we refer to as "adiaphora". Adiaphora is a Greek word that means "indifferent things". We use this word to refer to anything we do in the church or in our private lives that is not essential to our faith. These are things that are neither required nor forbidden. Anything that is a matter of choice or opinion is adiaphora and we often warn each other not to create dissension among ourselves about such matters. The Palm Sunday issue is one of those things.

Nevertheless, such matters are worth talking about because our choices or opinions are important even if we are talking about something where we can end up disagreeing without harm.

In the case of the Palm Sunday/Passion Sunday issue, I think that we should at least talk about how these observances help us understand God's message to us. Regardless of what we call our days of observance, we should not lose the meaning of them, or at least we should try to get as much meaning out of them as possible.

You might be able to tell by now that I would rather start Holy Week with Palm Sunday. I am quite ready to admit that this is because of my tradition. Someone else's tradition can be just as effective and powerful in their lives. However, I think it is unfortunate that we seem to have removed or at least de-emphasized the parade of ecstatic people who entered Jerusalem with Jesus. These people were announcing Christ's coming to those along the way as they would any king or other important ruler. Of course, this was a procession with a difference. This king was embarking on a journey that would change the world. Christ's entry into Jerusalem was an act of courage for a man and a humbling act of mercy for a god. He was there not to end his life by being killed, but to confirm life by conquering death. His dying would bring life and salvation to all people.

It was exactly one month ago that we talked about the Pharisee who confronted Jesus on his first trip to Jerusalem. You will remember that the Pharisee told Jesus, "you'd better get out of here because Herod wants to kill you". Jesus told the Pharisee that he would leave when he had finished

An Arcadian Vision

the work he wanted to do but he would be back. And in saying that, he knew he would be back to die. Even if Jesus had not been God, he would have known his return to Jerusalem would result in his death. He had plenty of warning. He knew, the Pharisees knew, Herod knew and, deep in their hearts, the disciples knew. Maybe they didn't yet understand why Jesus would die, but they knew he would.

But in spite of this, Jesus returned to Jerusalem triumphantly. And he was aiming for Easter, not Good Friday.

It's true that the parade and the demonstration would fall apart in disarray, as so many do. The participants would experience trouble, confusion and significant heartache as some in their number would fall away, some would deny their affiliation with Christ, and some would even conspire in his capture. The sun would drop behind a cloud, the palms would be kicked aside and the cheering would stop. But for just a moment the true meaning of Christ's coming to die filled the spirits of the people. So much so that when the Pharisees tried to stop the revelry, they were told that all of creation had caught the spirit and if the people didn't shout for his coming, then the stones would.

If this isn't passion, then what is? We often interpret the word passion in this context to mean the passion of Christ as seen in his suffering and death. And, yes, we can understand it that way. But what about the passion of the people who prepared the way for him on this day and who could see that he was the Lord of life? What about the passion that comes with the realization that God is moving through these dark paths of human existence so that we, too, can face suffering and death in the knowledge that they have been defeated on our behalf by God himself? This is our passion too.

As usual, all the readings for today reflect a common theme. In this case, the theme is the passion found in the relationship between human beings and their God. David's lament in our Psalm (31) refrain for today was so powerful that Christ repeated it on the cross. The courage and bravado of Isaiah (50:4-9a) is seen in the challenge to his enemies to do their best because "it is the Lord God who helps me". These are statements of passion that have moved and motivated the church through the ages.

In the second reading (Philippians 2:5-11) Paul says, "yes, Jesus obeyed the call to die even though he was God. He humbled himself in a way that we cannot fully understand. But look, it was an act of triumph! He was exalted above all others and because of him everyone can know who God is". This is an act worthy of a royal procession and we should bring our palms to spread before him. This is something to be truly passionate about.

So I guess this really is "passion" Sunday and we are right to remember it that way. But the palms help us understand the nature of that passion and we should remember that too.

Self-denial and Repentance

Do you think that because (these) suffered in this way they were worse sinners . . .? No, I tell you; but unless you repent, you will all perish just as they did (Luke 13:2,3).

Many people believe that Lent is a time to give up something. Some are quite faithful in using this time to try to get in touch with the whole idea of self-denial or self-sacrifice. Today our scriptures give us some insight into these concepts and the related idea of repentance.

Briefly, the connection between these things goes like this: self-denial is a form of penitence and penitence is an act of repentance. In self-denial, we give up something that we truly want or desire. When we do this for spiritual reasons, it is in recognition that the thing we have desired somehow has the power to interfere with our spiritual progress. It may be endangering our relationship with God as well as with other people. Many things may inhibit our spiritual progress. There are attitudes like greed, pride, conceit or other forms of self-love. There are behaviors like gluttony, excessive drinking, brutality, fraud and other forms of deception. We can all make our own list or think of the things from our own lives which have threatened our spiritual welfare.

When we give up something or engage in an activity that is meant to repair a broken relationship, especially with God, or when we wish to show true remorse for a sin we have committed, we are said to be engaging in an act of penitence.

To give up something as an act of penitence is to show that we are truly sorry and want to heal any relationships that have been broken or any other damage that might have been done. This is repentance. When I repent, I not only stop doing the hurtful thing, I engage in some positive activity to fix the damage done by it.

So, again, spiritual *self-denial* happens when a person realizes that something needs to be denied because it is hurtful to the soul and, when the soul is damaged, a person can become hurtful to others. When self-denial is done with this understanding, it is an act of *penitence* that shows we are truly sorry, that we *repent* and are ready to make right any wrongs we have done.

Admittedly, the things we usually give up at Lent are mostly symbolic of greater spiritual needs. We may give up a certain kind of food or engage in some kind of fast. We may stop smoking or drinking. We may reduce or temporarily eliminate television viewing or movie watching. We may even delay or postpone sexual intimacy. All of these things and many others we can each think of represent important moments of self-denial, forcing us to concentrate on other behaviors and needs. Such self-sacrifice reminds us that some things are more necessary and more satisfying to our spirit than feeding or entertaining our bodies.

Now we need to ask why any of this matters. Well, these things matter because they have to do with the quest for a meaningful life. They may even have to do with the preservation of life itself. The readings for today (Isaiah 55:1-9; Psalm 63:1-8; I Corinthians 10:1-13; Luke 13:1-9) warn us that there are certain things we should deny ourselves. If we do not deny ourselves these things, we need to repent. If we don't repent, we may perish.

It is also worth remembering here that these things that hinder us, that get in the way of our relationship with God and with others and that, in the end, can threaten our very lives, are the *temptations* that we face daily and that Christ faced on our behalf. Because of Christ, we can have victory over these things and maintain a right relationship with God. But we have to be proactive about it. We need to stop doing the things that can hurt us before they actually *do* hurt us – perhaps beyond redemption. This is the message of the Gospel lesson for today.

The context for our Gospel lesson is interesting. We read that Jesus had been informed that some Galileans had been killed. As an insult to them, Pilate, the Roman governor, had mixed their blood with some of the sacrifices that these same Galileans had prepared in the temple.

It is quite likely that the reason Jesus was told this was because he, too, was a Galilean. There was a strong feeling in the Jewish community that if a terrible thing had happened to some Galileans, they probably deserved it. In order to understand much of the New Testament and especially the ministry of Jesus, we have to understand a little bit about the Galileans and why people felt so negatively about them.

The Galileans, first of all, were a relatively new addition to the Jewish community. They had originally been part of the Assyrian nation but had been conquered by Israel approximately a century before Christ's birth. It is said that the Galileans are the only Jewish people ever forcibly converted to the Jewish faith. Galileans were regarded as troublemakers by the Roman authorities and as deviant Jews by the Jewish authorities. This was because they either failed to practice the rites and rituals of Judaism or because they practiced these rites in extreme ways, as zealots. By the time Christ was born, the Galileans had become ghettoized and were generally despised as either ignorant newcomers or outlaws within the Jewish community.

It is also important to remember that Jesus and all his disciples but one were Galileans. The one that was not a Galilean was Judas Iscariot, Christ's eventual betrayer. From the very beginning of Christ's ministry, his movement was considered a Galilean aberration, just another rebellion by these intruders who were not quite Jews. It is possible that the High Priests of Jerusalem approached Judas Iscariot as a potential informer about the Christ movement because he was considered more loyal to the Jewish cause than the other followers of Christ.

Rome identified the Christ movement so much as a Galilean thing that the emperor Julian even forbade the followers of Christ from being called Christian. He decreed that they had to be called Galilean.

So it was in this context that someone said to Christ, "look what happened to these Galileans! Their rashness and persistent deviance finally got them killed". Among other things, this taunting or baiting of Christ, the Galilean, was a test of his loyalties to both the Roman and Jewish authorities.

It is common for people to discriminate against groups that have something different about them or behave in some different way. This may be especially true of those groups that do not quite fit, that aren't quite like us. When something goes wrong that involves these groups, people might say "see, they're getting what they deserve". And, of course, we sometimes focus on the trouble of others in order to make ourselves feel better or even superior.

But Christ would have none of that. "Do you think", he says, "that people have trouble in this world because they are worse than you are? You'd better not think that because, if you do, you will fail to see your own sin, you will not give up the evil that you do and you, too, will perish."

In order to make his case, Jesus points out that just a few days earlier the tower of Siloam (in south Jerusalem) had collapsed and killed eighteen people. "Do you think", he says, "that they were killed because they were worse sinners than you? If you do think that, you will fail to see your own sin and you will not repent and you will perish."

An Arcadian Vision

The character flaws that must be denied by Christ's questioners are pride and prejudice. Pride in the belief that there is no need for self-examination in their own lives and prejudice in thinking themselves better than others.

Jesus is saying that they must exercise self-denial and give up these attitudes, re-examine their own lives as an act of penitence and repent so that they can receive forgiveness and be saved from the consequence of their sin, which is death.

Jesus, as part of the Galilean minority, was saying, "when something happens to us, it is not because we are worse than you. If you believe that, you are in danger yourselves".

Christ tells a parable in today's gospel (Luke 13:1-9) that illustrates the seriousness of his warning while offering a reprieve or a ray of hope. What he is saying is that if your life is like a tree that is diseased and, as a result, is barren or not bearing fruit, there is still hope, but you'd better attend to it.

The sacrificial activities of Lent (self-denial, penitence and repentance) are all illustrated by this parable. Self-denial is the pruning necessary to give the tree a chance to breathe again. Penitence is the fertilizer that offers sustenance to a barren life. And repentance is the dedicated commitment to the continuing care of the tree. With these things, life can be restored and the tree will be saved to contribute faithfully within the vineyard.

The Second Reading for today (1 Corinthians 10:1-13) is a good companion to the gospel. In it we are reminded that the problem of self-denial and the requirement for repentance has been with us from the beginning of man's relationship with God. In this reading we are given examples of the kinds of things that we must let go. But also we are reminded again that everyone is subject to the same tests and that no one is better or worse than anyone else.

The word that we will end with today is the last sentence of the second reading. It reinforces the promise of the gospel parable that with a little care the tree can be saved. "God is faithful, and He will not let you be tested beyond your strength, but with the testing he will provide the way out so that you may be able to endure it."

Christ endured many temptations and much suffering for us on the way to the cross. As a man, he was, after all, a Galilean. When we find ourselves facing temptations or suffering along the way of life, it is important to remember that Christ has also walked this way, that he has shouldered the same burdens and overcome the same temptations. He does not remove temptation or suffering from us but gives us a way to deal with these things, to face down our troubles, to live with certainty in the present and with hope for the future. The way of life is sometimes hard and we have to learn to deny those attitudes and behaviors that can separate us from God.

These days of Lent are filled with the dark mood of a man dying. But this man was God suffering and dying for us in the form of a man. Through this sacrifice we receive the promise that we can endure our own suffering and through faith overcome death to receive life eternal. Through even minor efforts at self-denial and self-discipline during this season, we participate a little bit in Christ's suffering and learn a little more about the meaning of sacrifice. This can only be good for our souls.

Stay Together! Stay Awake!

(Maundy Thursday mediation)
My time is near; I will keep the Passover at your house with my disciples . . . you will all become deserters because of me this night . . . could you not stay awake with me one hour? (Matt. 26:18b, 31a, 40b)

We come here tonight to continue our commemoration of Christ's passion. We have chosen to enter this time as Christ did, by having a supper with our earthly companions.

In the Hebrew tradition, the supper Christ had with his followers was the Passover feast, an occasion to remember the escape of the Hebrews from slavery in Egypt. More particularly, this supper commemorates the instruction of God to the Hebrews to sprinkle the blood of a lamb on the frame of their doors so the angel of death would pass over them.

Much has been made of this Last Supper of Christ. We are familiar with the image of it – at least the imagined image of it. There are many paintings of it, some famous, and every year passion plays feature this gathering of people around a table adorned with candles and the ritual food of the Passover – and, of course, the chalice. The chalice used by Christ when the Last Supper became the Lord's Supper has become the stuff of legend. More importantly, it is remembered in an on-going ritual of the church – an object of Sacrament that carries forward the message and meaning of Christ's sacrifice for us so that two thousand years later we, too, can "gather 'round the table".

We could talk at length about what the mood must have been like on that night. Jesus had announced his impending doom and the traitor he spoke of sat among them. They were all uncertain and afraid and some were already wondering how they were going to get along without Jesus.

Nevertheless, the passion of our Lord that we remember this week is all about promise. It is full of moments of transition between Old Testament promises and New Testament fulfillment. This supper is one of them. This is where the Old Testament blood promise made to the children of Israel would become the New Testament blood promise made to every person of every tribe and nation on earth. The salvation of God's chosen people at the time of their captivity in Egypt becomes the salvation of the entire world for all time and in all places.

Those of us who regularly attend to God's word and sacraments are familiar with these things. Like the disciples who knew how to do the Passover and understood its meaning, we know the Lord's Supper and understand its meaning.

And so we have come here tonight to share the Lord's Supper and remember the passion of our Lord. His agony and suffering were endured for us. We know that. But like the disciples, the world encompasses us and the weight of worldly things sometimes overwhelms us. Like the disciples, we may sometimes want to deny our Lord before the world so that the world will leave us alone and give us some peace. This is a great temptation. And, in this sense, Christ's passion becomes our passion. We, like the disciples, want to follow him on this road and we swear we will. But it is a hard road and, like the disciples, we don't know what lies ahead for us.

So it is not enough for us to promise that we will be true to our Lord. We must take action to protect ourselves from the temptation to fall away. Like the Hebrews in Egypt, we must heed the Word of our Lord and follow His command so that the angel of death will pass over us.

What is it that we can do?

Generally, what we can do is what we are doing tonight: we can *stay together* and we can *stay awake*.

We stay together by doing what the Hebrew people have done for thousands of years and what we do week after week. We gather to remember the promises made to us and to share the Word of God as it comes to us.

But we must also stay awake. Over and over in scripture we are reminded to be vigilant, to watch and to pray. It is not enough to hear the instruction to cover the door's frame with the blood of a spring lamb. It must actually be done. The church does not exercise true discipleship if it is asleep while the world is seeking to destroy the church or discredit it. We must all be ready and alert when God calls us to stay with Him a little while. This is why we are here tonight. Let us use this time to pray with him and remember the promise.

John W. Ekstedt

A New Day Coming

Then he entered the temple area and began driving out those who were selling. "It is written," he said to them, "My house will be a house of prayer, but you have made it a den of robbers" (Luke 19:45-46).

After several weeks of dark moments and dire predictions, a glimmer of light (lightness) has appeared. I have been interested to observe how proceedings in the secular world have mimicked some of the themes of our forty-day journey during Lent. As we note the dramatic effect on our world from the excesses of those who seek fame and fortune for themselves (the economic crisis, the failure of the banks, etc. 2008-2009), we are reminded of the moneychangers in the temple and of Christ's outrage at their behavior. It seems that the journey along the Way of the Cross includes for us, as well as for Christ, a series of encounters with people who become stark examples of why the cross is necessary. The way of men, or the way of the world, seems to be about striving, selfishness, greed, exploitation, and, perhaps worst of all, ignorance. (I have often thought that the best line in Charles Dickens *A Christmas Carol* was when the ghost of Christmas present introduced two children under his protection and told Scrooge to be afraid of them. One of the children was called "want" and the other was called "ignorance". The ghost points to the child called ignorance and tells Scrooge, "but most of all fear this child".)

Many find it simply outrageous, in this current climate of economic loss and political uncertainty, that those whose self-interest and greed have contributed to the current difficulties that we are all experiencing now claim that they may be the only ones smart enough to fix it. They argue that they should continue to be rewarded handsomely for their involvement in the money changing business. What they have done, of course, is to create a self-fulfilling prophecy. They have built the shady and secretive system that has rewarded them. They know how it works better than anyone else does. They now insist that it is only their knowledge that can make all of this go away. In one of our lessons last Sunday, the apostle Paul spoke about "the wisdom of the wise" and how those who count themselves wise in the world often seem to miss the point. To people for whom earthly wisdom means power and success, the message of the cross is foolishness. Those who believe only in themselves devise a wisdom that can only be hurtful to others. They do not get the point of self-denial or service to others. They cannot imagine that there is anything to be learned by following the path of someone who lived to give up everything, even life, for the sake of others.

An Arcadian Vision

So it was as Christ walked his way of sorrow. He confronted the entrepreneurs and moneychangers of his time about the manner in which they did their work or pursued their professions. There is no reason for us to believe that Christ was in any way opposed to commercial enterprise such as selling goods for a profit or running a money exchange. What he opposed was the wickedness of using God's house as a retail store or public market and of engaging in business practices that were usurious (unfair to the consumer). These practices resulted in a high level of personal gain to the seller while raising the cost of living for consumers beyond the point where they could sustain it, resulting in serious harm to the general economy. And it was happening under the cover of religion. Sound familiar?

I guess that it is always a bit discouraging to realize that the lessons of the Bible remain relevant because nothing has changed about human behavior since Biblical times. It is actually quite astounding how much parallel there is in the lives of the people Christ confronted on his way to death and our lives as we meet together to remember this epic journey.

The Lenten theme is continued in our readings for today but, if we pay attention, we will note that something seems to be changing.

All of the readings today emphasize the foolish and self-serving tendencies of people, so amply demonstrated by the commercial activities Christ confronted in the temple. In the Psalm (107:17) we read "some were fools and took rebellious paths". The Old Testament reading suggests that even in ancient times people had a habit of confessing their sins (when caught) and then begging for a way out as though they were victims. We read, "the people came to Moses and said, 'we have sinned by speaking against the Lord and against you; pray to the Lord to take away the serpents from us" (Numbers 21:7).

We hear about the spirit of worldliness that causes people to concentrate on what pleases them and how, in their selfishness, they become children of wrath who cheat others and damage the well being of whole communities. The Epistle (Ephesians 2:1-3) says: "You were dead through trespasses and sins in which you once lived, following the course of this world, following the ruler of the power of the air, the spirit that is now at work among those who are disobedient. All of us once lived among them in the passions of our flesh . . . and we were by nature children of wrath". (This passage is worth an extra comment. When the things of life seem to be going especially well or unusually badly, have you ever thought or said "there is something in the air"? What we usually mean by this is that sometimes there seems to be a spirit at work affecting all of us and driving us in a certain direction. In this reading, the phrase "the power of the air" refers to Satan's influence or the power of evil working within and among us. There are times when you can just "feel it in the air". This certainly must have been true during Christ's journey to the cross.)

However, in spite of all this, the readings for today move from the despair of human tragedy and mistakes to the promise of salvation and escape. It would appear that indeed there is a new day coming. The Psalm, for example, recovers from the lament about human foolishness and rebellion and becomes a hymn of thankfulness in the memory of past blessings. "Then in their trouble they cried to the Lord and you delivered them from their distress" (107:19).

The first reading (Numbers 21) moves from a plea for escape from God's punishment to a recording of the miracle that saved them. "So Moses made a serpent of bronze, and put it upon a pole; and whenever a serpent bit someone, that person would look at the serpent of bronze and live" (v 9). This is a precursor of the salvation that would be rendered by Christ's death on the cross, the event for which these scriptures ready us.

Then our readings take us to two of the great promises of scripture. The first is the promise of salvation for all people that so occupied Luther and that became central to his theology. "For by grace you have been saved through faith, and this is not your own doing; it is the gift of God – not the result of works . . . for we are what he has made us, created in Christ Jesus for good works . . ." (Ephesians 1:8-10). It's interesting that Luther had his own problem with moneychangers. But in his case they were not just working in the church, they were the officials of the church. Luther protested the use of indulgences to take money from the poor thereby giving them false hope that they could buy forgiveness or salvation. Through indulgences, it was said, a person could buy remission for sins that somehow had not managed to be forgiven through the regular offerings of absolution by the church (e.g. Holy Communion). Through this scripture, Luther was able to confront the church on that practice and clarify his own beliefs on the nature of salvation.

The Gospel for today contains the sweetest promise of them all – recited by children, sung by choirs, posted on walls and in corridors and carried in wallets or purses. "For God so loved the world that he gave his only Son, so that everyone who believes in him may not perish but may have eternal life" (John 3:16).

So, what has happened here? We are, after all, still on the way of the cross and we have not yet arrived at that awful moment when the Son is lost in darkness, crying after his Father, "why have you forsaken me?" It is as though a decision has been made to deliberately stop the painful procession so that we can reflect on why this is happening and find some hope in the purpose of it.

On the journey of the cross, Christ needed to be helped by a man named Simon and have his face wiped by a woman bystander. He needed moments along the way to be refreshed so that he could pick up the cross and walk again.

So it is with us. This is a long and difficult journey – forty days and forty nights. We need to be helped, to stop for a moment and be refreshed.

These passages do refresh us by reminding us of the purpose of it all. We are promised that, no matter what the trouble, the people will be delivered. We learn from the story of the serpent that God can, through his mercy, heal the wounds of our own making that have resulted in such catastrophe. We learn that, even though we suffer the consequences of our sin in this life, we will be delivered to a new life through the sacrifice of Jesus Christ. There is a new day coming.

We are saved by faith and not by works. This is not of our own doing. We cannot boast about it. It is a gift of God.

We need to be refreshed in this way right now. We need to know in the midst of Christ's passion that "God did not send His Son into the world to condemn the world, but in order that the world might be saved . . ." (John 3:17). It is a great relief to stop and have the weight lifted from our shoulders and the blood wiped from our brows. Now we can pick up the cross again and move on in the knowledge of where we are going and the reason for going there. God is merciful and will not give us a load greater than we can carry. We thank God for these mercies.

From Death to New Life (the Easter message)

Is This What We've Been Waiting For?

(Readings: Acts 10:34-43, I Corinthians 15:19-26, Psalm 118:1-2, 14-24, John 20: 1-18).

They put him to death by hanging him on a tree; but God raised him on the third day and allowed him to appear . . . . He commanded us to preach to the people . . . that God shows no partiality, but in every nation anyone who fears him and does what is right is acceptable to him (Acts 10:39a-40; 42a; 34a-35).

As we move from week to week in the church year, we seem to always be reminding ourselves that something is coming. We look forward a lot and we spend a lot of time waiting.

This is, of course, because the church year takes us through an organized sequence of events each of which involves prophecies or promises (Old Testament) and fulfillment (New Testament). These events are intended to evoke memories, instill comfort or encourage action. The moments when we recall God's promises and look forward to their fulfillment are essential to the life of the church – not just the church as an institution or an organization, but the church as the body of Christ. The church organizes its rituals and worship activities so that God's Word can be shared among the people clearly and with attention to those things that strengthen our faith and teach us how to serve God.

God's Word teaches us who we are, why we are here, what we have done and what we need to do. It also teaches us about who God is and what He has done. The central theme of God's Word is about the relationship between God and the people of the world. It is a great and continuing saga that feeds the church, gives it energy, and which governs what the church does and the way its members behave with each other.

Think about who we are here and what our business is. Our work is to bring God to the people and the people to God. We know the secrets of God's intentions as He has revealed them. We know mysteries that transcend the struggles and worries of our everyday existence and that allow us to transcend them too. We know about eternal life. We not only know about it, we have it.

It is not fashionable to say these things. To the ear that has not heard the sound of God's voice, this is considered strange talk that should best be kept private. But then we learn from scripture that it has never been fashionable to say these things. That's why they killed Jesus. Two days ago we celebrated his death at an event in the church year we usually call Good Friday. We even organized the physical space of our church differently this last week so that we could remember events in the period of time we normally call Holy Week. We remembered Christ's Last Supper with his disciples and meditated on the words spoken there. We recalled the encounters of Christ along the way to the cross and pondered the meaning of them.

We do these things to help us remember. We do these things to keep us strong. We do these things because we are waiting for a time when we will do them no more.

Right now we are creatures of time and space. We are temporal which means that we are "in time". Everything is boxed and contained for us. Everything we know and experience is defined for us by its limits – how high, how far, how long? The church as it exists in the world is also temporal and so we are required to contain great truths in small spaces and short ceremonies. We believe that we go to church to meet with God, but we are often told that God cannot be contained in our little places. Yet still He comes to meet us in them and we wonder at the mystery of it.

We praise God with song but our songs are limited to the range of our voices and instruments – and the imagination of our minds. We are limited by age. Our singing fades, our thinking weakens and we chafe at it. It seems unfair that we have so little time in our lives to realize our potential and that, when we do, our potential seems so terribly limited.

So we wait for something better. We wait, as we are instructed in scripture, on our salvation. Scripture tells us that this need to learn how to wait has been the condition of human beings since the fall into sin. Many of the accounts of scripture are about the promise of a recovery from the loss of immortality that came with the fall. We learn in scripture about heroic human beings who have lived their entire lives trusting in that promise, about a whole people who followed God based solely on his promise of relief from oppression, forgiveness for their sins, and a home where they could serve God and worship Him.

Scripture says that final and complete relief will come from among these people. These are the people talked about in our first reading for today (Acts 10:34-43): the people of Judea, from Galilee, of Nazareth, in Jerusalem – the chosen people of God. The relief that will arise from among these people is not just relief from the oppressive circumstances of everyday existence but from existence itself, as we know it. We are promised a transition from temporal life to eternal life, from sorrow to joy, from confusion to certainty, from lack of knowledge to full knowledge. Promises, promises, waiting, waiting.

Today we celebrate another event in the church year. It is among the highest of our festivals. At this festival, called Easter, we celebrate a moment in time when the limitations of temporal existence were broken, when death was defeated. When God, who had taken on the limits of temporal existence in the body of Jesus Christ, solved the problem about how human beings could overcome death, He did it in such a way that everyone who believes could participate in this miracle.

So is this what we have been waiting for? Have we finally reached a place where we can stop waiting? Is it, in the words of our Lord on the cross, "finished"?

Well, yes, in a sense it is finished. The central promise of God to us has been kept. From among God's people has risen a Messiah who, as a sacrificial lamb, has been offered up before God so that our sins may be forgiven. He is the last of these sacrifices. From his death to the present, our task as a church has not been to provide an altar for blood sacrifices but to provide a venue of thanksgiving for the fulfillment of God's promise in the blood sacrifice of His Son.

We have passed through the dark days of remembrance concerning the sacrifice of God's only son. We have seen the drama of it and what an amazing thing it was for the people who stood and witnessed it. The savior of the world did arise from the oppressed people of Galilee who were among God's chosen people – those who had kept the promises alive for so long.

But now the bond of temporal existence has been broken, the veil separating people from God has been torn, and the work of the chosen people has been accomplished. Our readings today remind us that now God favors no one, that all are chosen, that there is no partiality, and that every nation is acceptable to Him.

When we come to this holy day we can remember it in any number of ways. People the world over practice the ceremonies of Holy Week and they do it with particular attention to their own histories and cultures. But however Holy Week and Easter are celebrated, there are two aspects of it that are common everywhere.

The first is the *fact* of it, that Christ who was killed is alive again. This resurrection is the event that we remember in the rituals of Easter. It is the evidence that Jesus was not only a man but that he was also God. He died as a man, as we all must, and he rose again because he was God who is life itself. As with his birth, this coming together of God and man is the mystery that is the greatest pillar of our faith.

The second aspect is the *message* of it. Easter is not just about life again for Jesus. It is about life again for everyone.

You will note the use of the word "fear" in the first reading and the portion of it that I have taken for our meditation (" . . . anyone who *fears* him . . . is acceptable."). It is probably worth being reminded again that most of the time in scripture, especially in the New Testament, the word "fear" does not mean "to be afraid", it means "to hold in the highest regard".

The message of Easter is that the promise of God is now available to *anyone* who gives God the highest regard, not just the people who were originally chosen and who had kept the promise for so long. We are all, Jews and Gentiles, children of God and keepers of the promise of salvation. And the promise of salvation is eternal life. Death is conquered for us too.

It's an old message now because the death of the man Jesus happened a long time ago. But we have kept the promise and we continue to share it. This may be the real miracle of Easter.

They Have Taken Away My Lord

They have taken away my Lord, and I do not know where they have laid him (John 20:13b).

What happens to you when you lose someone? And what do you do when that someone has made your life worthwhile, has given your life meaning when nothing else could? And how can you cope when the circumstances of your loss are unexplainable? When you literally don't know why this has happened. When you don't know who is to blame and, even if you could find out, what could you do?

The circumstances surrounding Christ's death were something like that. At least it was so for Mary Magdalene. She was one of the women whose faith seemed to consistently outshine that of the men around Jesus. The men who followed Jesus were rational and analytical in their response to Jesus. How many times did their reaction to Jesus include questions like "Lord, how can this be?" or statements such as "Lord, certainly this must not be". They felt the need to understand with their minds before they could accept with their hearts. The men in Christ's life often brought their own agendas to his ministry. These expectations, often unspoken, sometimes hindered the men in their search for the truth. It was the men, his chosen disciples, who so often disappointed Christ along the way of sorrows. More often than not, it was the women who cloaked him in love and compassionate support. The women seemed to see what Christ's coming meant for a world in conflict and for children not yet born. The women seemed to take Christ into their heart without the need for elaborate explanation.

I suppose that it's important not to leave the impression here that the men were less worthy than the women, or that the women were less sinful than the men. Nor should we judge the men in such a way as to assume that they had no defense for their actions. The men, and especially the disciples, had experienced severe disruption in their lives. Some had left everything behind, including their families, livelihoods and possessions, to follow Jesus. All had been exposed to constant danger by being identified with Jesus. Some of them were rejected by their own communities and seen as traitors to the cause of the Jews in an occupied territory. And they were all struggling with their status as students, sitting at the feet of Jesus, trying desperately to understand the meaning of his words and what it was he actually expected of them.

Nevertheless, it has to be said that the women often painted quite a different picture of what it meant to be a follower of Jesus. The story of Mary Magdalene, especially, has intrigued Christians since the earliest days of the church. Her faith comes to us as being simple and straight from the heart. Her faith is not complicated by the need to be right in her opinions or to prove others wrong in theirs. Her faith did not depend on knowing the right words or slogans to defend her faith before others. She did not have the need to explain why she followed Jesus. She probably could *not* have explained why she followed Jesus. And when they killed Jesus, she did not think that he had failed her or had, somehow, been a false prophet. She just followed him, even in death, going to the tomb to pray for him.

It's important to remember that Mary did not hope for Jesus' resurrection. She had not been part of those discussions. She could not have imagined that she would again see him alive when she had seen him die. She did not understand the prophecies about his death and resurrection. Even the men, who had been personally mentored by Jesus, did not hope for a resurrection – for all their discussions with Jesus and questioning of him. *Mary didn't go to Jesus' grave with hope. She went with faith. And there is a difference.* Mary was prepared to accept this tragedy. She came to grieve for herself and pray for him. She didn't believe in him any less because he had died. She knew that he had come to bring God's word to people and he had done that faithfully and well. She had been uplifted by his words and astonished by his life. She had learned faith from him and it had settled her down and given her life real meaning. So she brought that faith with her to the tomb where she thought that he must surely be dead. *And because of her faith, she would find hope when there was no reason at all to expect it.* She would be honored for her faith and her faithfulness. Angels would speak with her and she would be the first person to see Jesus alive.

But when Mary approached the tomb she knew none of this and she was unprepared for what she found. She was shocked to find the tomb empty, not because she thought that he had risen from the dead, but because she thought that another indignity had been perpetrated on her Lord. She had been brave and strong up to that point, but this was too much. She thought that, after everything else, they wouldn't even let him rest in peace.

So Mary appears to have become frantic and hysterical. She ran to some of the men for help. Surely with their superior learning and analytical powers they could help her figure out what had gone wrong. But they could not. They came to the tomb, for Mary's sake, and checked things out. They agreed with her that the tomb was empty and that the body was gone. They could not explain this nor did they seem curious to follow up in any way. It is quite likely that they just wanted to be done with all of this. After all, it was their loss, too. They went home and Mary remained at the tomb, weeping.

It is interesting that it is only in our gospel for today (John 20) that Mary, or any woman, is identified as a witness to Christ's resurrection. In our other readings on this subject, she is not mentioned. Elsewhere, when the witnesses to Christ's resurrection are identified, it is in the context of verifying the resurrection as a fulfillment of Old Testament prophecy or as the foundation on which the church proclaims the promise of salvation from sin and death. The accounts have more of a tone of theological importance or of validating the authority of the church.

Are we to take any meaning from this? Mary was the first to see Jesus and it was she who informed the men of this miracle. Yet, except in this one instance, she doesn't appear to receive the same stature as the others in accounts seeking to verify the fact of the resurrection.

I'm sure that there is much we could say about this. We could talk about the paternalistic culture of the time or the traditional place of women in the religious community from which Christianity sprang. No doubt these things played a part in how the story of this miraculous event was told.

But I think that the important lesson here may be of a different kind. The kind of faith that sustains the effort required to preach the gospel and teach the word of God to a hostile and unrepentant world is not the same as the kind of faith that can find Jesus in impossible or improbable places. Mary wasn't a teacher or leader of any kind and she did not aspire to become one. She did not walk the countries of the Middle East bringing the good news of Christ's resurrection to warring tribes or Roman occupiers. She did not try to explain the meaning of Christ's words while he was present in the world. Hers was not the kind of faith that could *explain* Jesus. Hers was the kind of faith that could *find* him when everyone thought that he was lost forever.

This is an important message. The faith of Mary Magdalene is the type of faith that we should all seek. Some of us, like Peter, John and Paul, also witnesses to Christ's resurrection, are called to wrestle with the finer points involved in understanding the word of God. Organizing the message of the Law and Gospel for the purposes of teaching and preaching is a difficult task requiring an exercise of faith that can accommodate doubt, confusion and uncertainty. We remember how Luther wrote that he felt attacked at every turn and confused in his thinking by none other than Satan as he tried to develop a theology for the people of his time. He was a man of faith but his faith was constantly assailed by his own need to defend that faith and explain it to people who had rarely heard any of it in their own language.

Mary Magdalene didn't have to explain anything nor did she want to. She just loved Jesus and lived for him, dead or alive. When he went missing, she looked for him. She didn't try to explain how he could have disappeared and then appeared again. When she found him, she just announced it. "I have seen the Lord and he has spoken to me".

Sometimes we Lutherans work really hard to explain things. We act as though our mission on earth will be accomplished if we can work out a theology that is consistent and explainable. One that allows people to know where we stand on things like the existence of God, human nature, the concept of sin, the definition of God, the virgin birth, the death of God as a man and the resurrection. These are important things. God has given us the ability to reason and understand. We should use our reason to know God better. And if we have the talent, we should serve God by teaching his message and preaching his word. Peter, Paul, John, Matthew, Mark, Luke and all the others, men and women, who have followed them as church leaders, teachers and evangelists are people of faith whose work it is to bring the message of faith to others.

But the example of faith is Mary Magdalene. Hers was a faith devoid of the politics of the time and of the religious debates that swirled all around her. She did not try to figure out why some people believe and some deny or why some people suffer and some prosper. She did not question things for which she had no answers. The truth of it is that she had very little hope for the things of this world. There had just been too many disappointments and too many things left unexplained. The only thing she had was faith.

But she was the one who found Jesus when it appeared to others that all was lost.

For me, this is the story of Easter. The message of Easter is not explainable in *anyone's* theology. Like the men who followed Mary to the tomb to comfort her, they just end up looking foolish. Maybe those who seek to explain it all should take a lesson from Peter and John – have a look at the empty tomb and then just go home.

It is not through knowledge or analysis that the resurrection becomes real for us. We know the resurrection through the kind of faith that shines from a life of innocence and love – the kind of faith that can see the angels and find Jesus in a garden.

Mary brought only her faith and love to the tomb. There was not much hope in her life. But what she found because of her faith did give her hope. Hope did not give her faith – it was the other way around.

And so here we are, this Easter morning. We have come with our faith and we will leave full of the hope that the resurrection brings. Because he has defeated death, death is defeated for us as well. Because he has ascended to the Father, we will ascend to the father as well and live with Him forever in eternity.

What a day! Let us rejoice in it for we have seen the Lord and he has spoken to us!

Unless I See . . . I Will Not Believe

Put your finger here and see my hands. Reach out your hand and put it in my side. Do not doubt but believe (John 20:27).

Don't you think it is interesting that one Sunday after we celebrate the resurrection, we are confronted with a test of faith? The first question of Easter seems to be "do we believe it or not?"

What is this thing called faith? Some say it is the capacity to believe something exists without seeing it, to accept a proposition as true without any way to prove it. Some say it is a way of dealing with things you can't control, such as death – or a way of having hope when everything seems hopeless. Whatever it is, people of faith seem to suffer a lot of ridicule for having it. As I look back on my own life, I have to admit that the problem of faith has been among the most difficult of my struggles.

Part of the reason for my struggle with faith may be that my life and work have taken me to places where reason is the highest priority and faith is considered an enemy. Many of my close friends and colleagues, while respecting my attachment to things of faith, have been severely critical of faith as a concept and of people of faith as deluded and probably unintelligent. My best friend in high school, who eventually went on to become a very successful theoretical physicist, could never understand why I wasted my time on the idea of faith. Still, we reveled in our competition with each other to achieve the highest grades in our science classes (which I usually lost). Many years later, when I was teaching law and policy courses at secular universities, I found myself in the same discussions with other members of faculty that I had shared with my high school friend so long before.

I wonder if anything has changed in these encounters or disagreements about faith since the time of Thomas' engagement with the risen Christ in our gospel for today (John 20:19-31). We remember also how Adam and Eve were asked by God to accept *on faith* the proposition that eating of the tree of the knowledge of good and evil would kill them, and how Abraham accepted *in faith* that sacrificing his own son would be a good thing. Do we understand the character of faith, or its demands, any better now? (If you want to see a long list of faith encounters, read Hebrews 11.)

Something that has changed human perception, and that is fairly unique in recent times, is the advent of applied science. The ability of human beings to manipulate the things of the natural world through the exercise of their intellect seems to have added weight to the side of reason in arguments about the value of faith, and how it is defined.

However, there is another matter concerning the idea of faith that seems somewhat unique to our modern age. Those who say that they are people of faith now very often make claims for faith that cannot possibly be true, and they may use faith as an excuse for denying the value of human intellect (or even of common sense). As a result of this, there are people of faith who are "anti-science" and may even view science as a form of atheism set up specifically for the purpose of denying the existence of God. People like this may take pride in how little they know. They are happy enough just to have faith and they would never want to be identified as intellectual. Worse, as we all know, faith can be an excuse for the commission of all kinds of sins in the name of God – and you don't have to be a scientist or an intellectual to see the foolishness of that.

So what do we do with this thing called faith? And especially now when, as a church *and* as people of faith, we are celebrating the resurrection of a man from the dead, the same man who is said to have been born of a virgin. And what are we to make of the Thomas of our gospel who has become a symbol of the antithesis of faith? For instance, it is interesting that, in his memory, we may call a person who refuses to believe *any* proposition a "doubting Thomas".

Like so many characters from antiquity that have been made symbols of the worst attributes of human beings, I think Thomas has been given a bum rap. Thomas was being a perfectly reasonable man (notice the word "reason") in this narrative. The other disciples who told him about the miracle of Christ's resurrection *had* seen Christ. *They* had believed because they *saw* Christ. Why should Thomas be expected to accept their story without having the same opportunity?

We need to reemphasize something that we mentioned on Easter Sunday when we were considering the event of Christ's resurrection. We are temporal creatures. That means that we are creatures "in time and space" and because of that we are limited in the way we think and act. We cannot understand the concept of eternity because eternity is something that is outside of time and space and, consequently, alien to our experience. Similarly, we cannot understand immortality because, since the fall, we are creatures who must die. We not only exist in time, but our time is limited. We have a measured existence.

So everything about our lives is subject to definition and measurement. If we cannot know the dimensions of something, then we are likely to doubt its existence. We have to see it for what it is. We have to handle it. We have to manipulate it. This need encompasses things that we cannot see like atoms or microbes. We don't accept their existence on faith. We have to see them at work or build an instrument that can expose them. Without that, we can only say – at best – that they exist in theory, not in fact. This is the demand of science and it is perfectly legitimate.

This is also the dilemma of being human. Because of our limitations we struggle with concepts like faith, eternity or immortality. We cannot prove them or measure them or describe them. And this may put in doubt the very existence of God. So people may feel that they have no choice but to doubt the existence of God and any concepts that seem associated with the idea of God (atheists) or at least to claim that people can't possibly know one way or the other (agnostics). And then, given our other weaknesses, some of us choose to ridicule anyone who insists that the things of faith do exist. This was the dilemma faced by Thomas. *How can I believe what I am being told when I have not seen the proof of it?*

This brings us to another problem of faith. Faith is about accepting things that are beyond our understanding and that will probably *always* be beyond our understanding as long as we are limited by time and space.

By faith, we are asked to believe in things that transcend time and space. Sometimes we are required to act on something *too fantastic to be believed*. An example of this was when Noah was asked to build a giant boat on dry land, in a desert, with no water in sight. Or when we are given *an unbelievable promise*. An example of that is when Abraham was told to sacrifice his son while at the same time being promised that this very son would be the father of Abraham's progeny for all generations to come. Or when we are asked to accept an *outrageous proposition*. Thomas is one example of that. Moses parting the Red Sea is another.

But perhaps one of the hardest things about faith is that it applies to things we normally think we cannot have but wish that we could have, like eternal life. It is about things that *are* fantastic, unbelievable or outrageous to us but which we truly desire. In Hebrews 11:1, we are told that, among other things, "faith is being sure of what we hope for".

So here we have Thomas, a simple man, being asked to believe that his companions have seen Jesus alive when he knows for sure that Jesus was killed. Still, even in his doubting, it's certain that, in his heart, he hoped that it was true.

But give Thomas credit. He didn't ridicule his friends. He just said that he had to have some evidence from a credible authority. In this case, the only authority for him would be Jesus himself.

Faith is not about things that can be proven – at least in the scientific sense. But it *is* about evidence. It is about knowledge and authority. Faith is *not* blind. Blind faith is stupid and it *is* worthy of ridicule. Faith is based on something. And our task, as it was for Thomas, is to know what authority we have for the leaps of faith that we take.

For Thomas, in the end, his faith was informed by the physical presence of Christ just as it had been for the other disciples who had told him the story of Christ's appearance. And it is true that Jesus gave Thomas a reprimand for not accepting his fellow disciples' witness as the authority on which he would base his faith. Thomas, after all, had the opportunity to be the first person after Christ's resurrection to believe in the resurrection on the word of the other followers of Jesus – the apostles. This is the word through which the Holy Spirit has brought people to faith ever since – the word of God as given to us through the apostles. So Jesus said to Thomas, "you are lucky. You have seen me in the flesh. But many will believe who will not have that opportunity. Their evidence will be the word of the apostles – the very word that you could not accept".

Faith is based on evidence. It is not blind – *it is informed*. Just as the faith of Thomas was informed by the wounds in Christ's hands and side. *Our* faith is informed by the testimony of the apostles and, as they promised, the Holy Spirit has worked faith in us through those words so that we might believe. As Christ told Thomas, we are especially blessed for that.

But again, let us not be hard on Thomas. As we will discuss in the weeks to come, a great deal happened after his encounter with the disciples, and then with Christ, that paved the way for people to come to faith and for the church to be formed *and informed* about the reality of Christ's resurrection. Thomas didn't have the advantage of that. He was on the leading edge of a new thing and it's not surprising that he didn't know how to act.

But Thomas did teach us that it is not unreasonable to expect evidence for the things that give us hope. It is just a question of what that evidence is. We are to follow our Lord intelligently, not stupidly or unaware. Scripture constantly warns us about being sloppy or unthinking in our faith. We may understand that the only way we can accept the miracle of Easter is through faith, that there is no way to reason it out. But we also understand the authority we have for that miracle. The message of Easter and the story of Thomas confirm that our authority comes from God – either directly, as with Thomas, or indirectly through God's Word and the witness of his apostles.

We know that faith is not unintelligent or uninformed and is worthy of respect. As Christians, we understand how we came to faith and what the basis is for our beliefs. For this, Thomas is a positive example, not a negative one.

Who Are You, Lord?

Now none of the disciples dared to ask him, "Who are you?" because they knew it was the Lord (John 21:19).

Saul, Saul, why do you persecute me? He asked, "Who are you, Lord?" The reply came, I am Jesus, whom you are persecuting (Acts 9:4b, 5).

We are in that period of the church year when we remember Christ's ministry after his resurrection from the dead. It seems that from the time of his resurrection to his ascension, Christ was concerned with two things. The first was to "prove" or give evidence to his resurrection by appearing before his followers and making sure that they knew who he was – that he was the same one that had been laid in the tomb. He wanted to give his followers as much *evidence* for his resurrection as possible. (Remember that last week we talked about knowing the evidence for our faith and how faith is based on knowledge. It is not blind or groundless.)

His second concern was that his followers would understand the *meaning* of his resurrection so that they could build his church with confidence. The time between his resurrection and his ascension would be used to confirm his power over death and teach the message of hope that this power offers to all human beings. It was this message that his followers would be charged with spreading throughout the world. In the scriptures, it is the gospels that present Christ and his teachings while he is *in* the world. The books following the gospels, beginning with the book of Acts, are about the work of the disciples presenting Christ and his teachings *to* the world.

This is the part of the church year when we discuss things that happened in the transition between Christ's ministry *in* the world and the church's ministry *to* the world.

Today, we are going to discuss the question that is heard throughout our readings for today, "Who are you, Lord?" We will begin discussion with the first of the two purposes for Christ's appearances after the resurrection: *that his followers should be certain of his identity* and be able to answer the question, who are you?

Now it's interesting that the question "who are you" is asked in two different settings after the resurrection. The first setting is early after Christ's resurrection when he appears to some of his disciples by the sea and the second is after Christ's ascension when he appears to Saul while Saul is traveling along the road to Damascus.

It seems a simple question: "who are you, Lord?" Yet it is not. It actually is quite a difficult and awkward question. Think about how you might respond to being asked, "who are you?" – especially if the question is followed by your name. If someone already knows your name and yet still wants to know who you are, then the question is an attempt to get at the essence of your being. It is as though the questioner is asking you to define yourself and justify your existence. In our readings for today, it is also a question concerning authority. Who are you that I should listen to you or bother with you or waste my time on you? Justify yourself so that I will know whether to trust you or believe you or follow you.

So it is a substantial question, "Who are you?' And it is one not to be taken lightly.

We have noted that this question appears twice in our readings. But it is asked only once. On the occasion when it is not asked, it hangs in the air

An Arcadian Vision

like a lead weight. The matter of knowing God's essence troubles everyone who encounters Him regardless of the context or the circumstances. Once we know God is there, we must know who He is.

In the gospel for today (John 21:1-19) some of the disciples are gathered by the Sea of Tiberius. Thomas, our hero of last week, is there with Peter and several others. They are getting on with their lives after Christ's death and resurrection. They are going fishing again.

This was a rough time for them. They were faced with a problem that we all experience from time to time. They had just finished having what some might call a "peak experience". This is one of those times in a person's life when the mundane is transcended and enlightenment or great insight is experienced. Certainly the disciples had just been through a very powerful religious or supernatural experience. Their time with Jesus while he performed his ministry, including his encounters with the high church officials and government leaders of the day, must have left them euphoric. His death was crushing but his resurrection had lifted them up again. They had gone from having hope dashed to seeing their world open up with possibilities again. Jesus was alive! Death had been conquered!

But the realization soon hit them that they were still living in the world. They still had to eat and care for their families. Their enemies were still at large. The Romans were still in control. The leaders of Judaism were still bent on crushing their movement.

It had all been so crazy during those days when Christ was with them and they were somehow free from the cares of daily life. They had been able to stay together as a group and enjoy each other's company. People gave them food and, when that wasn't possible, Christ made miracles that turned small meals into large banquets and water into fine wine. It had been, as they say, a heady time – a halcyon time. At one point, it looked like it had all been destroyed, but Jesus had come back.

Yet things seemed different now. They had to get back to work.

I think we have to realize that in this instance, by the Sea of Tiberius, the disciples were in the process of letting Jesus go after a roller coaster of a ride with him. They had been left with hope because of his resurrection and were pleased that he seemed to have accomplished what he came to do. They knew that their lives were forever changed. But their kids were hungry. Their taxes were due. Their businesses needed attention.

And then Jesus appears again. They receive him into their presence with mixed emotions. What will happen now? Is it all going to start again?

But Jesus seems to accept that things have changed and that his disciples have to find a way to get on with their lives. It is as though he has come to help them get started with their earthly life again. He doesn't start out preaching or making demands. He just helps them catch fish and has breakfast with them.

It's worth noting that, in the midst of this, John feels the need to tell us that none of them *dared* ask the question "Who are you?" The reason given is that they knew it was the Lord.

It was evident that the time had come for Jesus' followers to find a way to organize their affairs and establish some routine for their lives again. It was also clear that for some of them that routine would be different than it had been before their time with Christ. For example, Jesus follows the breakfast by challenging Peter to leave his fishing business and become a minister of the gospel. This call to Peter is about helping Jesus' followers find a way to get back into their lives after Christ is gone. Peter is to become their leader now and do it in a way that will assure Christ's work is carried on while most of his followers get on with their normal lives. At that moment, the office of the ministry is established. The task of continuing Christ's work on earth while people continue on with their daily lives is what the office of the ministry is all about.

I think that the reason the disciples didn't *dare* ask "who are you?" was that the answer would have been too much to bear. They weren't ready for the answer. Of course they knew this was the risen Christ, and while they were sure of that, the question of who he *really* was still lingered for them. Recent events had left them in such turmoil and they still didn't know what it all meant. I think they knew that with all the things of the world pressing in on them and with the aftermath of Christ's persecution and death still so fresh, it probably was just too difficult a question to ask.

I believe the narrative shows us that Christ understood this. They had all kinds of questions remaining about who he *really* was but at that moment it was too much to know and too dangerous to ask. So Christ chose to pull Peter aside and say to him, "look, if you love me, take care of these people – they are going to need help".

We *all* need help when dealing with the things of God in the midst of life's routines and responsibilities. As Paul has reminded us, there are some things we never fully understand this side of heaven. We "see through a glass darkly". The problems of faith always seem to plague us. Sometimes it's just too hard to ask the questions that seem unanswerable or unknowable. So we don't dare ask them. This is another reason why the institution of the church exists, so that we can take care of each other in our times of doubt and difficulty.

The second setting where the question "who are you?" occurs is found in Acts 9:1-20. This is where Saul receives his call to follow Jesus. The circumstances of the call are dramatic. Christ has ascended to heaven and is no longer physically present in the world.

But Christ's presence in the world is still a very fresh memory for Saul. He was a leading figure in Judaism and had always considered Christ and his movement a significant threat to Judaism and its leaders. He had taken it upon himself to rid the country of this rebellious sect. He knew that Jesus had been killed. Yet Jesus' disciples remained and he had vowed that their movement would not survive. He does *not* know that Christ has risen.

So the encounter with Jesus on the way to Damascus is a shock because Saul knows as soon as he sees the light that he is in the presence of the Lord. Of course, Jesus is there for the same purpose that he had when he appeared before his disciples by the sea and had his conversation with Peter – to insure that the people who would spread his message of salvation throughout the world were clear about his identity.

As it had for the disciples, the question "who are you" presses in on Saul. He knows that he is in the presence of power and authority and that this is the Lord, but he has to ask the question that the disciples did not dare to ask. Saul cannot survive this encounter without knowing who it was that struck him down. In this moment, he knows that his life is going to change and he cannot or will not go into it without knowing what he is getting into – and with whom.

The answer that Christ gives – "I am Jesus, whom you are persecuting" – is far more that simply telling Saul his name. He is telling him that he is the one that was killed while heading the movement that Saul is committed to destroying. He makes clear to Saul that the persecution of the Christians is a persecution of him, the Christ.

It is too much to take in, of course, so Saul is temporarily blinded. He must be helped and led along while in total submission, a hard thing for a proud and dedicated man. He is told that he will be taken to a place where he can get his answers. And, as we know, Saul did get his answers. He became Paul the apostle, and God's answers to him have become God's answers to us through his preaching and writing.

"Who are you, Lord?" is an *Easter* question. It is a question of faith asked by human beings who have heard the word of Christ's resurrection or been confronted by it in some way and need to know how they are to respond. Who are you, really? Why should I believe in you? Why should I change my life around just because you have appeared before me?

One way or another, we all must ask this question. Sometimes, we ask it out of frustration when life beats us down and trouble seems to be our middle name. Sometimes we ask it in a state of euphoria, when life is good and we feel especially blessed. But most of the time we need to ask it when life is routine and our worldly obligations seem to be our priority. When we must attend to our business, assure food is on the table and take care of our family. It is at these times – which is most of the time – that we need to keep our eye out for Christ's appearance and not be afraid to ask the question, "who are you, Lord?"

How Long Will You Keep Us in Suspense?

So the Jews gathered around him and said to him, "How long will you keep us in suspense?" . . . (John 10:24).

During the Sundays of Easter, we are encountering questions of faith, one after the other. We have noted this with some interest and we have realized that it makes sense that the miracle of Easter should be followed with questions or tests of faith. Easter presents us with one of the great mysteries of Christendom. Without Easter, nothing else in our theology seems to have much meaning. Without Easter, Christianity is like a philosopher's tale, a course in popular psychology, or the study of a book with pithy sayings. Christianity as a movement might still have some relevance in assisting people to live in peace and with respect for others. The Bible might still be a book worth reading for its nuggets of wisdom and its stories of times gone by. But if Easter is removed, Christianity is just another community program and the Bible is just another interesting book.

It is the mystery of Easter that gives us the need to consider the questions of faith. When we ask ourselves, or if we are asked by others, "Do you believe?" it is the event of Easter that we normally call to mind.

However, it is important to remember that faith and belief are not the same thing. A person can believe in many things without faith. Faith, at least in the Biblical sense, is a supernatural ability. Belief is perfectly natural. Faith is not even required to believe that there is or might be a god or a higher power. Faith is not required to believe that people are spiritual creatures as well as being physical, emotional or intellectual.

We are told in scripture that a person cannot have faith without

An Arcadian Vision

receiving the Holy Spirit. This is because faith is a gift of God given to us so that we can experience God and know who He is. It is the work of the Holy Spirit to instill faith in us. Because Easter is about a man doing what only God can do, we cannot believe it without faith. It is simply beyond our natural human abilities to grasp the existence of God in a human being. And it is especially difficult when we are told that the entire human existence of that person was dedicated to correcting the sin or wrongdoing of every other human being. It all seems such an unlikely and impossible story.

The questions of faith that follow Easter may all be summarized as one question, "do you believe that Jesus the man was also God and that he was killed for us and became alive again"? That is what Christians celebrate at Easter – and without faith, we just don't get it.

We have noted this Easter season that questions of faith may be asked in different ways. Sometimes a question of faith appears as a statement as with Thomas who said, "unless I see the mark of the nails and put my finger in his side, I will not believe". In saying this, Thomas was affirming that, on his own, he did not have the power to believe that Jesus had risen from the dead – that he could not know Jesus for who he was. Jesus' response to him was that he would agree to give Thomas the faith to believe by presenting himself to Thomas physically. But he also said that almost everyone else who believed would believe without seeing or touching him. The faith of those people would be a particular blessing because it would come *by the power of the Holy Spirit*. It would be *a spiritual revelation*, not a physical one.

Last week we discussed what a faith question looks and sounds like when it is asked *as a question* or when it is hidden *in a statement,* such as the one made by Thomas. The question that we found in both cases was "who *are* you?" That's what Thomas wanted to know and what the disciples wanted to know (but were afraid to ask) and what Saul *had* to know on the road to Damascus. It is a matter of curiosity – even hope – to want to know who God is and if He lived on earth in the form of a person. This is a question of belief. The question of faith wants to know if Jesus is that person.

So we come to the gospel for today and find another faith question.

I really like the context of today's question. Having just been through the time of the Passion, we are used to dark images and rough circumstances. But the context for our gospel today is a pleasant moment in the ministry of Christ's final days. His message has taken on a comforting tone as he describes his relationship with his followers as like that between a shepherd and his sheep. From this image we get some of the most pleasing art that decorates our churches and some of our books.

I also like the description of the context within which Jesus spoke his words of pastoral comfort. It is the time of the festival of the Dedication where the rededication and purification of the great temple in Jerusalem is remembered. Almost two hundred years before Christ the temple had been desecrated and committed to pagan worship by the King of Syria. Judaism was outlawed at more or less the same time. The story of the rise of Judaism and the role of the Maccabees (a Jewish rebel army) in the return of the temple to Jewish worship was remembered in Christ's time at the Festival of Dedication. Today it is remembered during Hanukkah or the Festival of Lights. (The word Hanukkah comes from the Hebrew verb "to dedicate".) From before Christ's time to the present this festival has been a very important cultural and religious remembrance of the Jewish people.

In our gospel for today, Jesus is walking in the very temple that is being honored during this important festival. He is in the portico of Solomon, the great King who originally built the temple. It seems an almost idyllic setting for our Lord to contemplate his work and the prophecies that preceded his coming. He remembers King David, his earthly ancestor, who wrote of the Lord as a shepherd in the Psalm (23) selected for this day of worship.

Jesus kept the festivals of the Jews. He honored the history and culture of his people. He was often angry with those of his own people who failed to keep their religion well and who dishonored their own culture and history. One can see him wandering the corridors and patios of this great temple remembering the work of God among his people and thinking about all the things that had transpired to bring him to this place.

It was fitting that *another question of faith* would be asked here by the very people whose ancestors had built the temple to worship and keep the scriptures. These scriptures had contained within them the promise of the Messiah, the one who would finally relieve them of their oppression and fulfill for them all of God's promises.

So the Jews gathered around Christ and asked him "How long will you keep us in suspense? Are you the Messiah or not?"

The Jews insist that they want a plain answer and many commentators have wondered why Jesus didn't give them one. His answer does not seem to be plain. It seems to be obscure. But Jesus knows that the question comes without the faith needed to accept the answer. It wouldn't matter if he had answered "I am the Messiah". After all, he had told them that before. The question was being asked to incriminate him, not to know who he really was. It was a question that required faith and they had none.

So Christ said, "you do not believe even though you have had all the evidence put before you. You are not my sheep, that is, you do not have the faith to believe. Those who believe follow me. They know who I am and I know who they are. So do what you will. You cannot take anything away from me or from anyone who believes in me".

It is a difficult thing, this faith. We cannot get it by paying for it. We cannot get it by working for it. We cannot get it by asking the right questions. Instead we need *it* to get the questions right.

What we need to do, as we are told over and over again in scripture, is to seek out the Holy Spirit so that we might receive faith and by faith believe. We do this by asking for the Holy Spirit to come into our lives through prayer. We learn how to pray by attending God's house and by listening to His word. Faith is not a difficult thing to find but we must be open to it. We must give ourselves over to God and let Him work in us. Only in this way can we see with faith and therefore believe. It is only in faith that we can accept Christ, as God made man, without having him standing in front of us and offering us his hands and his side.

The faith questions that are asked in our meditations following the Passion of our Lord and the miracle of Easter are faith questions whether or not they are asked and whether or not people are ready for the answer. We may reject the answer, but we will never even hear the answer if we don't ask the question.

In our other readings for today (Acts 9:36-43, Revelation 7:9-17) we begin to get a glimpse of what faith does once it is received in a person. We see Peter, following his conversation with Jesus by the Sea of Tiberius, finally beginning his new life in the office of the ministry. He experiences right away the power of the ministry when it is an expression of faith in the life of a person called to it.

In Revelation, we see how many and diverse the people are who have received faith and how faith brings them together in the kingdom of God as a great and wondrous assembly of believers.

So let us rejoice at this Eastertide not only in the miracle of the resurrection but in the miracle of faith that gives us the vision to believe it.

John W. Ekstedt

Everything Here Is New Again

See I am making all things new (Rev. 21:5a).

We have now reached the point in our Easter meditations when we begin to see the results of the Easter event taking form in the world. Up to this point we have remembered the Easter event as a physical happening and have meditated on the questions of faith that have followed from it. It is as though Easter is a seed planted that is fed and fertilized by our faith. We now begin to see the shape of the things that are growing from this.

We cannot begin to overstate the enormity of the Easter event and how it changed everything in our world. Our readings today (Acts 11:1-18, Rev. 21:1-6, Psalm 148 and John 13:31-35) give us an idea of the changes that would come from Christ's death and resurrection. For purposes of our discussion today, we will categorize those changes as being *theological, teleological, spiritual* and *cultural*.

In order for us to follow this thinking, we should spend a moment defining the terms that I have just used:

Theological – When we say something is theological or has theological implications we mean that it tells us something about the essence of God or the meaning of our faith. Theology is the study of God or of systems of faith (religion). The scriptures for today show us how the Easter event changed the way people understand God and the meaning of their faith.

Teleological – This is a somewhat harder word or concept to understand. Literally, it means the study of ends or final things. Some people simply define teleology as the study of the last things or the end times. But it is also the study of conditions or events that lead to or cause final things. In scripture, we usually think about the book of Daniel in the Old Testament or the book of Revelation in the New Testament as being the most concerned with teleology. These books talk about things that foretell the end of the world. Armageddon is an example of a predicted event or happening that is said to be a sign of the end times. Most people have heard of that. Again, we see today how the Easter event is teleological in that it changes our view about how things are going to end both for ourselves as people and for the entire world as we know it.

Spiritual – In a general sense, the word spiritual is taken to mean "not physical". It is common these days to equate spiritual with psychological or emotional and to describe spirit as the feeling one has about something or the mood that is created by a phenomenon like a sunset or an expression of love. But in the Biblical sense, spiritual refers to the soul and the way it is acted on by God. We talk about "feeding the soul" by attending to God's

Word. We talk about the Holy Spirit as God acting in our lives to make us spiritually whole. In the religious sense, something is spiritual when it is about how God speaks to us, or how He completes us. Soul is God in us. This is why we say that neglecting the things of God causes our soul to shrivel and darken. Today we see how the Easter event feeds our soul and changes our spiritual nature.

Cultural – This is another one of those words that we tend to use loosely. Most of the time, we mean a particular people behaving in a particular way like French culture, Amish culture, Swedish culture or Canadian culture. But what the word really means is "to improve" by specific actions or techniques. We can improve the soil for planting by tilling and fertilizing it. We can improve the production of foods or other substances by the way we raise and process animals, fish or insects (like bees). These are all cultures.

We also use this word to describe groups of people in various stages or forms of civilization. When we do this, we often say that certain people have "developed a culture", and we usually mean that they have improved themselves in some way such as through language, politics, economy or lifestyle.

We will use the word *culture* to mean *"improvements in the lives of people living together and sharing similar traits or goals"*. Today we see how the Easter event has improved the culture of all people, especially those who share the same faith in Jesus and who seek to do the will of God while living in this world.

I think all of this is summarized in the sentence from our second reading for today (Rev. 21:1-6), *"see, I am making all things new"*.

Let's look quickly at an example in each of the four areas that are defined above.

Our understanding of God (*theology*) is given new meaning because of the Easter event. Christ's resurrection proves that God lived in the body of a man and that His glory can exist in the bodies or in the lives of all people. God is not distant but close. He is actually in our lives, not separate. This was a new revelation, especially to God's chosen people. This doctrine or teaching is central to our *theology*.

Our understanding of the last things (*teleology*) is also improved because of the Easter event. It is as though the sight line between heaven and earth has been opened up. Again, in our second reading we hear the apostle John proclaiming, "I saw a new heaven and a new earth". We have often talked about how the veil between people and God was torn away by Christ's death and resurrection. We now have direct access to God's mysteries. So we can have a clearer understanding of the life that awaits us in eternity.

Our ability to nurture our souls (*spiritual*) is clearly improved by the Easter event. The main way that we grow spiritually is to learn to love. We first love God and then we love each other. Jesus' demonstration of love in his death and resurrection guides us in our own pursuit of love. In the gospel for today, Jesus gives us love as a commandment, something we do for him because he did it for us. This is *spiritual enlightenment* and it comes to us because of the Easter event.

The Easter event contributed significantly to our social awareness or the idea we have of ourselves as people (*cultural*). It's not just that love became our foundation for living together. It is that people who had been totally separate from each other and even mortal enemies are now bound together because of the Easter event. This is the message of our first reading (Acts 11:1-18) where the actions of Peter finally start to convince some of the Jewish people that their God is the God of the gentiles too. This not only had an impact on the culture of the people originally chosen of God, but it changed the culture of every other nation that became exposed to the message of the Easter event. It is possible to write the history of the modern world from the perspective of the cultural changes that have occurred since Christ's life, death and resurrection.

As usual, the Psalm for today summarizes all of this as a poem of praise. David reminds us that everything has been and will be affected by the miracle of God's love and the fulfillment of the prophecy that God would send a Savior to bring us back to God again, full and complete as we were at creation.

In the Easter event, we have seen this promise fulfilled. Some have experienced it *physically*, as did Thomas and the other apostles. Some have experienced it *spiritually*, as did David for whom it was only a promise, and as it is with all of us who rely on the testimony of the witnesses to the event that fulfilled the promise. We hear this testimony because it is recorded in God's Word and we are able to believe in this miracle through the power of the Holy Spirit. The death and resurrection of our Lord has affected every aspect of our lives: theological, teleological, spiritual and cultural. Everything is new again and we praise God for it.

Death Will Be No More

He will wipe every tear from their eyes. There will be no more death or mourning or crying or pain, for the old order of things has passed away (Revelation 21: 4).

It is said that human beings are unique in God's creation in that they can think about their own thoughts.

I don't know if you have ever considered this ability that we have. It is the power that allows us to be inventive and literate, to think ahead and learn lessons from the past, to understand our own behavior as well as the behavior of others.

Because of this ability we can create new things and propose new ideas. We are not stuck within the limits of our own experience as animals might be. We are able to break off the shackles of our experiences and transcend them. When our experience has been walking or running, we can imagine riding or flying – and make it happen. When our experience has been poverty and sickness, we can imagine health and prosperity – and make it happen.

If we have learned nothing else in these years of our lives, we have learned how amazing human beings can be. We have created wonders in the arts and sciences. Technology, an object of our creation, takes us to places and allows us to do things that seem impossible – even as we do them. Music expresses us in ways that are truly astounding. Hundreds of songs can be created from six chords of music, and they are vastly different from each other in the gifts they offer of melody and emotion. Artists transfer ideas into form and form into meaning with an energy that seems almost mystical, and we stand in the great galleries of the world wondering how human beings can have such imaginations and present them so well.

We have words. We can give expression to our thoughts. But we can go further. We can create thoughts with our words. I was reading a book about writing some years ago and the author was trying to point out that a good writer actually creates thoughts in the head of the reader. He was arguing that a good book is a creative collaboration between the writer and the reader. Because both the writer and the reader have the ability to use words, they build on each other's thoughts. The reader "reads between the lines" and adds new meaning to the story created by the writer. A good writer gives readers space to create their own meaning from the story.

We should be amazed at what we can do. We are truly children of God.

Being able to think about our own thoughts allows us to be transcendent, even magnificent.

I guess that we could keep going like this. But I hope that by now you have started to feel a little uneasy with this portrayal of the glorious things wrought by human beings. I'm sure that we can all identify with the capacity of human beings to produce wonderful works. However, it must leave us with mixed emotions to realize that for all this ability and for all this creativity, things don't seem to be going so well for human beings, and much of the time we don't feel so good about our efforts. Sometimes we imagine things and *can't* make them happen.

It appears that this ability to think about our own thoughts is not simply a blessing taking us to utopian wonders, it can also be a curse dragging us into deep despair. Sometimes I wish that I could turn off my mind because the places it takes me are so unpleasant and the problems it gives me are so irresolvable.

Those of us who are familiar with God's Word and Christ's teaching understand this phenomenon. It is a consequence of sin and disobedience. Yes, we were created in the image of God. We were given creative power and free will and we decided that with those powers we could go it alone and create a world of our own making. We separated ourselves from God, the source of our life and the reason that we have the ability to think about our own thoughts. We were created immortal but we chose mortality. We were told that if we ate of the tree of the knowledge of good and evil we would surely die. And now, in the creativity of our minds, where we think about our own thoughts, we are faced with the specter of our own death.

We still have these great abilities to create and invent, although they are noticeably diminished from the powers given us at the moment of God's creation; but it sometimes seems useless to have these powers when we cannot save ourselves from our own demise. This realization dampens our spirits, dilutes our energy and drives us into despair. And, in our despair, some of us may even turn to using our powers for evil.

Today's readings are about death. I suppose this is fitting since this is All Saint's Sunday. On this day we usually remember those who have gone before us, especially those that have died in the faith. (I was installed in this church last year on All Saints Sunday and one of the visiting pastors was quick to point out to me that you don't have to be dead to be a saint. I think that he was trying to elevate the day and remind us to rejoice in the saints who are living and who add meaning to our lives every day.)

Nevertheless, even in the midst of life we can become consumed by

An Arcadian Vision

the problem of death, our own and that of others. In the midst of all the evidence of our moments of greatness comes the reminder that we cannot continue to live in this world. That we will die. This realization can reduce our will to do great things or to do anything at all. What's the point? We're just going to die. And, as they say, "you can't take it with you".

The gospel for today (John 11: 32-44) is the story of Lazarus. We are all familiar with this story. The raising of Lazarus is difficult because it asks us to believe something that is apparently impossible in our experience. The story intends to illustrate that Jesus is God, the source of all life. In his human form, he is subject to limitations but, at the same time, he remains one with his father. Jesus makes a point in the story of having the people hear him talk to God as his father so they can know the source of his power to raise someone from the dead.

There is a great deal in this story that is worthy of study and discussion. Today we will note that this story comes to us as an affirmation that Christ can conquer death and because of that he is our hope in the despair of our everyday lives.

This hope is amplified in the first and second lessons for today (Isaiah 25:6-9 and Revelation 21:1-6a). The main message in these writings is that there is no reason to fear death while we live because God has promised to restore us to a life of immortality. This world of darkness and death will pass away and there will be a new heaven and a new earth where "death will be no more".

The removal of the fear of death from us is the most direct and most important result of our salvation. As the Psalm for today (24) points out, we receive blessing from the God of our salvation. And what is this blessing? It is freedom from the fear of death, not only for ourselves but also for those we love. We no longer need to live with an inhibiting and debilitating despair that saps our energy and removes any motivation to aspire to great works.

Because we are saved from the consequences of death, "the shroud that is cast over all peoples" is removed from us and we see the possibilities for a new heaven and a new earth. We can shake off our despair, wipe away our tears, and think about our own thoughts without the cloud of hopelessness descending upon us. We can do good works in the name of God and make contributions to the affairs of men in this world that give evidence of our salvation and theirs – just as Christ did when he raised Lazarus from the dead.

We remember the Saints who passed before us, including many of those we knew and loved, without despair, because we know of Christ's power and of his promise. It is this same promise that can make us Saints while we live. If death cannot drive us to despair then surely life becomes better and more productive of those virtues Christ commands such as faithfulness, temperance, joy, love of others, patience and excellence in the gifts and offerings we bring before God.

In the Old Testament, God asked His people to bring the most perfect offerings before Him. He wanted the best of what the people could give – the best animal, the finest fruit and vegetables, the most accomplished art and the greatest music. They could do this only if they were released from the constrictions of their own worries and limitations. So God gave them the promise of His salvation and they were able to live by it.

We have seen the salvation promised to all peoples. Our second lesson ends with the words "it is done". Christ's power over death was confirmed for us when he raised Lazarus from the dead, and we have followed the disciples to the empty tomb of Christ himself.

And so we live in joy because death cannot conquer us, and we remember those who have passed before us in the spirit of that same promise.

While we live in this world, we will sometimes remember those we love with tears, and we will even cry for ourselves in our awareness of our own mortality. But when this happens, we have the promise of God and the example of Christ that death, in the end, will be no more and that we will live with all the saints forever in God's presence.

These are thoughts worth thinking about.

Great Grace

Blessed are those who have not seen and yet have come to believe (John 20). *Now the whole group of those who believed were of one heart and soul . . . great grace was upon them all* (Acts 4).

How many of us have had those times in our lives when everything seemed just right? Such times usually present themselves when we are young and healthy, inquisitive and surrounded by people who – at least in some way – are just like us. They, too, are young and healthy and seem to be looking for the same things – even if they don't yet know what those things are. There is a shared energy and a willingness to support each other and to disregard the little quirks and foibles each of us have. Such times are usually shrouded in an atmosphere of forgiveness and acceptance. No one is interested in being judgmental or critical. Everyone is just happy to be with everyone else.

Sometimes the glue that binds people together during such times is a "cause" that is considered to be greater than any individual involved or all of the individuals taken together. The power and energy that is generated from such a situation can be enormous, and those who are involved are likely to remember it the rest of their lives.

Sometimes the cause may be something with which none of the individuals had chosen to be involved. War is an example of that or a natural disaster such as the fires now being experienced in the province of Manitoba or the earthquake and tsunami causing such destruction in L'Aquila, Italy. I have talked to veterans of great wars and survivors of terrible catastrophes who, in spite of all the suffering and death, have lived the rest of their lives in the glow of that experience.

When I was teaching at university, a graduate student was assigned to me as a research assistant. While we were working together, a major environmental conflict emerged in an isolated area of our region involving the government, private resource development companies, indigenous people and environmental activists. Because of the isolated location of this incident, anyone participating in it had to journey a great distance to reach it and, while there, live in fairly primitive circumstances.

My research assistant was a city girl who belonged to one of the politically powerful families in our area. She had never wanted for anything and could easily be judged as someone who had been "spoiled". She was writing a thesis on environmental issues and was intrigued by the reports of this event and the issues surrounding it. After some discussion, she decided that she wanted to study what was happening in this remote area, so we arranged to get her attached to one of the groups leaving the city to participate in the protests.

The experience changed her life. She spent several weeks living in rain, wind and mud. She participated in confrontations with police, company officials and forest workers. She lived in intimate circumstances with people from places she had never been and who lived lifestyles that she had never experienced. She got sick. She returned dirty, disheveled and hungry. But by her own admission she had never been happier. She was convinced that she had never met better people, nor had she ever had a more meaningful experience.

Many of us have stories like this. I have a few more of my own. People who share these kinds of moments consider themselves very lucky, even though they often come out the other end of such experiences with lasting scars and with more questions than answers. Yet somehow their lives have been challenged at a level and with an energy that they could not have previously imagined. For many, these moments quite literally happen "once in a lifetime" and no experience will ever be like that again. Sometimes, for these reasons, such experiences are life changing and the person affected takes a totally unexpected new direction in life. The apostle Paul's conversion (as Saul) on the way to Damascus is often considered an example of such an experience.

However, these experiences can be dangerous because sometimes people get stuck in them. The experience may be so stimulating and mean so much that a person might not know how to carry on and live successfully again in the mundane world of ordinary living. If you read the story of the conversion of Saul, you discover that, after his conversion on the way to Damascus, he had a very difficult time readjusting. Saul needed help as people often do who return to the "real" world from a life-changing experience.

Sometimes I wonder if people who go through such experiences have some quality that they share in common either going into the experience or coming away from it. In one of our worship services, we discussed the difference between faith and hope. We remembered Mary Magdalene and speculated about what it must have been like for her during her time with Jesus. It would have been the highlight of her life and, if asked, she would likely say that she could never again expect to experience anything like it. She would live in the memory of it for the rest of her natural life.

We remember Mary Magdalene as a woman of great faith. Surely, it was her faith that made her time with Jesus what it was. And it was clearly her faith that sustained her in his death.

Is it faith that is the common theme in all these types of experiences? Maybe not faith in Jesus, as we saw in Mary, but faith nevertheless? People who have these great singular moments in life likely have them because they believe in what they are doing, the possibilities that are present and the people they are with. Like my research assistant, they give themselves over to something without any way of knowing the outcome. Is it faith that brought them there, whether or not they know it?

We talk about faith all the time. We say it is central to everything we do as Christians. Yet if someone asks us what faith is we may become tongue-tied, unable to find the words to express it. Yet people of faith always seem to be sure of its existence and comforted by its promise.

Faith may be described or experienced in many ways but they all seem to include the idea of a promise. To be a person of faith is to be faithful and to live in the promise of faithfulness. Listen to those who have had unusual or spectacular experiences. If other people were involved, they talk about the people. The people of the experience are almost always described as loyal, constant, conscientious and trustworthy. They were comrades in arms. With them and because of them almost anything seemed possible. Life is worth living with people like that. You can have faith in them and that's what makes the experience so great.

It is faith at the highest level that makes our life as Christians so worthwhile. We have received the ultimate promise from the most loving and faithful being anyone could ever know. Mary Magdalene knew this. It gave her hope that, even in death, the promises of Jesus would be kept. Hope is a powerful thing. But without faith, hope is only a dream or a mirage.

Faith is what makes it happen. Faith is what gives an experience its power. It is the common factor that all those great moments of life share.

We are still basking in the glow of Easter. All our readings for today are about the happiness and joy flowing from the resurrection of Jesus and his appearance among his disciples. The resurrection was an event like no other. In our Second Reading for today we see the witness of John to this event. His witness allows others to share in the knowledge of it and through faith to accept its certainty. From John, Peter, James and the other witnesses to Christ's resurrection there emerged a church that was a community of people living with faith and sharing a common experience of life together. The church in the world has become a unique and exciting community where faith is learned and expressed in moments of great grace and joyful praise. But what the church also provides is a way to live in the transition from the experiences of faith to life in a difficult and sometimes hurtful world. Like Mary Magdalene, we have to learn to come back from the amazing encounters with Jesus to give witness of his resurrection to people who may be troubled and confused by the cares of this world.

In the gospel for today, we are reminded again of Thomas. He was not with the other disciples who saw Jesus after his resurrection. He was left confused and troubled by the events surrounding Jesus' death and the stories of his resurrection. We have talked about Thomas before and have tried not to judge him too harshly. He was, after all, like we are. He demanded proof. He did not yet know how to exercise faith. It was so important at that moment for the other disciples to remain faithful and continue their witness to Thomas. And when Thomas finally saw Jesus again, Jesus demonstrated great grace in giving Thomas the proof that he asked for, while using the opportunity to teach Thomas faith so that he could continue with his life and witness after the experience of touching Jesus' hands.

We read in the book of Acts how the church grew in the promise of Christ's resurrection. The people shared everything. They were supportive and caring. They lived in the promises that had been made to them and that they had shared with each other. They worked hard to strengthen their faith and make it more perfect.

However, as is often the case with those who come back from great experiences, members of the early church sometimes found it difficult to carry on in the world of everyday things. The church has struggled ever since to "keep the faith". The church in Jasper, like so many others, has struggled for many years to keep itself alive in the spirit of the resurrection.

Sometimes it is helpful for us to return to the moment when the first churches basked in the glow of Christ's resurrection and were able to be sustained by the word of the witnesses who had seen and touched him. Returning to that place in faith and prayer can give us hope for ourselves and for our ministry to others.

Having remembered the moment of great grace that was visited on the disciples of Jesus and, especially, Thomas, we need to come back to our world and remember how blessed we are that we have believed without having seen him. We have the gift of the Holy Spirit which Christ breathed on his disciples and which is now given to all of us. Through the Holy Spirit we have the faith to hear the words of the disciples with understanding. Through faith we, too, share in the experience of great grace given in a dramatic way to some and in the routine of regular life to others. However we have received it, we know it as a sure thing that gives our lives meaning and allows us to also become witnesses of Christ's life, death and resurrection.

Sometimes we are not sure how to express our faith or whether we are effective witnesses. But it is not up to us to make our witness meaningful to others. This is the work of the Holy Spirit. We can only live out our faith as honestly and openly as possible. God will work through us to accomplish His will. We can only declare what we know and be who we are.

We are together in this, a community of faith living in a sometimes harsh and troubled world. Each of us has returned to the world of daily living from our own experience of faith. We bring with us a message of peace and love and it is great grace for all that receive it.

6. The Festival of Pentecost

Pentecost means "the fiftieth" and is celebrated fifty days after Easter Sunday. It commemorates the coming of God in the form of the Holy Spirit to be the presence of God among human beings after the ascension (return to heaven) of Christ. It is usually thought of as signaling the birth of the church and the beginning of the commission to all people to take responsibility for their faith and communicate that faith to others.

Becoming What We Were Meant to Be

(A meditation for Pentecost)

If you love me, you will keep my commandments. And I will ask the Father, and he will give you another Advocate, to be with you forever. This is the Spirit of truth, whom the world cannot receive, because it neither sees him nor knows him. You know him, because he abides with you, and he will be in you (John 14:15-17).

Today is the day of Pentecost. Pentecost was a festival of the church long before the time of Christ. When Peter and the rest of the disciples were in Jerusalem to attend the day of Pentecost celebration, it was being observed as a festival of harvest according to instructions found in Leviticus 23:15-17. This celebration took place on the fiftieth day after the second day of Passover. In more recent times, within Judaism, it is celebrated in remembrance of the giving of the Law on Mount Sinai.

For Christians, the day of Pentecost has been given new meaning by the events described in our first reading for today (Acts 2:1-21). We now use this day to celebrate the coming of the Holy Spirit as promised in our Gospel for today (John 14:8-17 and 25-27). Within Christendom, Pentecost normally falls on the seventh Sunday after Easter and is sometimes called Whit Sunday or White Sunday, referring to the white robes of those baptized at Pentecost.

I mention these historical connections because continuity is important. The history of God's relationship with His creation and with His people is of one thing. Christ did not come to destroy everything that had come before him but to build on those things. He did not declare that the teachings of those who preceded him were wrong or should be ignored. He came to fulfil those teachings and help people understand them.

For weeks we have been talking about the changes that were brought about by Christ's death and resurrection. You will remember that we categorized these changes as *theological* (how we understand God), *teleological* (how we understand the future), *spiritual* (how we understand our personal relationship to God and His creation) and *cultural* (how we understand our relationship to other human beings). It is important for us to know what these changes are and how they affect us, but *we also need to understand God's work to assist us in coping with these changes.*

Our readings during the Easter season have helped us focus on the meaning of these changes in their various categories. Now, as we enter Pentecost, the Word of God is instructing us about how God works to assist us in living with these changes, especially after Jesus left this earth and returned to his Father.

In a sense, the change that was transforming the world reached its apex when Christ ascended back into heaven after completing his ministry here on earth. Christ's disciples were among those most immediately affected. The era of change and renewal had begun when God came to earth as the Christ child in Bethlehem. During his earthly ministry, Christ's physical presence provided comfort and security to those who followed him. He was able to instruct them and answer their questions. He was able to demonstrate the power of God in tangible ways through events that his followers and others often regarded as miraculous.

But toward the end of his earthly ministry he began preparing his disciples for his leaving. He did this by presenting his message in two parts. One was to begin instructing them on *his expectations* of them after he was gone. The other was to promise or assure them that they would have *the ability to meet his expectations* and carry on his work.

These were hard lessons, and the disciples tried to think of questions that would help clarify things for them. They began asking these questions of Christ and placing other demands on him as it became more apparent

John W. Ekstedt

that his physical presence on earth was ending. One of those demands is in our Gospel for today when Philip said to Christ, "Lord, show us the Father, and we will be satisfied". Philip, like the others, wanted assurance that they would not be left alone on Christ's leaving, but would continue to have the presence of God with them. He knew, and they all knew, that it could not be like the old days or the Old Testament times when God was separate or hidden from people. God had been with them now in a very personal way, and they knew that life would never be the same again. But they were struggling to understand what to do now that Christ was leaving.

Our readings during these past weeks have been organized to give us some of Christ's words of instruction to his disciples before his ascension to heaven (which we observed two weeks ago). These words of instruction are usually found in the gospel reading. The other readings have given us descriptions of the events that followed Christ's ascension and how the disciples handled the situations in which they found themselves. This way we can see the *connection* between Christ's words of instruction or promise and what actually happened as Christ's followers began to build his church in the world. And, in all of this, we continue to learn more about how the world was changed by Christ's coming and how those changes continue to affect us today.

The change in the relationship between God and human beings that we remember at Pentecost completed the great reformation accomplished by God through His son, Jesus Christ. *Pentecost for Christians is all about the coming of God the Holy Spirit to earth to live in the bodies and souls of normal everyday human beings.* Now God is manifested in the world in *us*! God is no longer in the world in the life of *one* human being. He is in the world in the lives of *all* the human beings that believe in Him.

This is what Jesus was talking about in last week's gospel when he said "I ask (that) those who believe in me . . . may all be one (because) the glory that you have given me, I have given them" (John 17:20). Jesus was saying, *the Father and I are one being. What He has given me I will give to anyone who believes in me and, as a result, we all become one being.*

In the gospel for today, Jesus responds to Philip's demand to see the Father by saying, in effect, "you are looking at him – I and the Father are one." Then he gives Philip an even more comforting message. "Look, don't worry about me leaving, God will still be here – in you. And the way this will happen is that God will send His Spirit and His Spirit will fill you and will teach you everything that you have to know."

The word in the gospel that we translate as "advocate" is sometimes translated as "counselor". In other places, it is translated "helper". It is important for us to grasp what this word is intending to portray. This word in the original text is naming the Holy Spirit and defining him at the same time. In English, we might call this an adjectival noun. All the English words come close to the original meaning, but there is no single English word that can give its full meaning. The Spirit that will come to fill the lives of all that believe in him is *the one who will help you become what you were meant to be*. And what each of us was meant to be from the very moment of our creation is *a child of God*.

This is what our second reading for today (Romans 8:14-17) is telling us: "For all who are led by the Spirit of God are children of God . . . and if children, then heirs, heirs of God and joint heirs of Christ . . .".

When God created people, they were one with Him, filled with Him, innocent and immortal. The fall into sin left people separated from God, filled with selfishness, guilty and mortal. The work of God since the fall has been to bring his people back to Him – to be one with Him and filled with Him, innocent and immortal.

What we have witnessed from Christ's birth to the coming of the Holy Spirit is the process of recovery and healing that changes the world. The world is now filled with God's presence. God exists in the lives of all those who believe in Him.

But though we are God in the world through the power of the Holy Spirit, we still live in the world in human form, subject to all the trouble and weakness of our humanity. So the Holy Spirit, as the expression of God in us, helps us to overcome our weaknesses and speaks for us when we need guidance and forgiveness. Even Christ in his human form was battered by the troubles of life and experienced doubt and weakness. He turned to God, his Father, and God sent His Spirit to help Christ fulfill his ministry. It is this same help that the Holy Spirit gives to us. He is our Advocate. He is the one who makes us *all that we were meant to be* so that we can love God and keep His commandments.

On that Pentecost Day so long ago, the coming of the Holy Spirit to be in the world was announced with visible signs and extraordinary happenings. Those who were present in Jerusalem heard a sound like a wind, saw a sign like a tongue of fire resting on Peter and the disciples, and everyone understood the message that was being spoken in their own language – no simultaneous translation needed. This was a great day. The prophecy of the prophet Joel was fulfilled and the promise of Jesus to Philip was kept. We are not alone. God is with us.

John W. Ekstedt

In our Psalm for today (Psalm 104:30), the refrain says "Send forth your Spirit and renew the face of the earth". Pentecost is our memory of the fulfillment of the prayer of David that all the earth might be filled with God's Spirit and everything might be renewed. The world *is* filled with His Spirit and everything *has* been renewed. This Spirit and this renewal are available to everyone. But, alas, some choose to remain in the world without that spirit – separated from God, selfish, guilty and mortal.

As Jesus said to Philip, *This is the Spirit of truth, whom the world cannot receive, because it neither sees him nor knows him. You know him, because he abides with you, and he will be in you.*

On this day of Pentecost, let us rejoice that this Spirit has been given to us and that because of it we are one with God.

The Life of a Good Person

But the wisdom from above is first pure, then peaceable, gentle, willing to yield, full of mercy and good fruits, without a trace of partiality or hypocrisy . . . submit yourselves therefore to God. Resist the devil, and he will flee from you. Draw near to God, and he will draw near to you (James 3:17 – 4:7-8a).

Our lessons for today are about good persons. First, we hear about the wife who is a great joy to her husband. This reading from Proverbs comes from a male perspective and, in some ways, is like a personal advertisement seeking the perfect woman. But this is also the word of God, and as such it is God speaking to remind men about the power and capacity of women. To have such a person in your life is a truly remarkable thing.

In the Psalm we learn more about the good person. Here, such a person is referred to as "righteous" and we read that "they are like trees planted by streams of water".

The Second Reading, from which our text is taken, is an appeal for people to seek the wisdom of God over the wisdom of the world, and in this way righteousness or goodness will grow and take over their lives.

The Gospel describes a very troubling time for Jesus and his disciples. Jesus was trying to prepare them for his betrayal and death and give them hope by predicting his resurrection. This must have been an agonizing time for Christ. But instead of responding with sympathy and comradeship to him, the disciples began quarreling among themselves and, worse, quarreling *about* themselves. They were worrying about "who was the greatest". It's here that we have the famous admonition that the "first must be last" and the advise that they would do far better by paying less attention to themselves and more to the children among them. And so we see here another lesson about what makes for a good person – *a humble life properly focused.*

If we pay close attention to all of these readings, we see that goodness is always defined against its opposite. The woman who is excellent is seen aside the one who tries to control others with her charm or impress through acts of vanity. The wisdom of the righteous person is set against the wisdom of the unrighteous. Selflessness is placed alongside self-seeking.

I think that we all want to be better people. As some of you know, I worked with prisoners much of my adult life. I had the opportunity to work or correspond with people who committed terrible crimes and were considered by many to be beyond redemption. Within the sciences of psychology and psychiatry there is much speculation about the point beyond which a person cannot be redeemed, when evil in whatever form has progressed so far in a life that it cannot be saved. I have met people who appear to have reached that point in their lives. Other people have given up on them or, as we sometimes say, the "system" has given up on them. By this we usually mean systems of justice or mental health.

But even these people almost invariably claim that they wish they were better. There may even be an appeal from them in which they want to make you believe that they can be better if only given the chance.

As in the Gospel for today, Jesus must have had moments of deep despair over the condition of people in the world – even his own disciples. It is interesting that after Jesus' first attempt to talk to his disciples about his coming capture and death, he seems to stop talking to them about that. Instead, he uses much of his remaining time with them trying to teach them the lessons of faith and righteousness, *how to be a believing people and how to be good people.* It is as though he realized that they weren't ready yet for the message of the crucifixion – that first they had to learn more about him, and about themselves.

But Jesus did not and would not give up on them. He might change his strategy, he might change his emphasis, and he might wait a little longer for them to grow in their faith. But he would not quit.

This is the way I feel about prisoners – those who seem the farthest removed from righteousness, those who often seem impossible to save. If Jesus had felt this way about any of the people he encountered in this world, even his own disciples, the message of salvation would have been lost to all of us.

We are all worth saving. We can all *be* saved. Maybe some of us can never again be set free in this earthly life, but we can all receive the freedom that comes from Christ's sacrifice for us and we can all learn what it means to be good.

Being good presents some interesting problems. We may all want to do it or at least be better at it. We encourage our children constantly to be good. Yet sometimes being good presents an image that we don't like. So we have phrases like "goody two shoes" that refer to the person whose goodness annoys us. And we know that, throughout history, people who have tried to be truly good have often ended up, like Jesus, as martyrs.

We understand that this reaction to goodness often arises out of our own inadequacies, our inability to be good ourselves. And in our lack of goodness, we react negatively to those who seem to be showing us up with their goodness.

There is also the problem that doing the right thing, or being "good", often gets in the way of other things we desire. Throughout our lives, we find ourselves in the position of deciding between the right thing to do and the desired thing to do or have. As is pointed out in our Second Reading for today, this is because our desires are worldly and create envy and selfish ambition in us. This results in conflicts and disputes as we saw happening in the Gospel even with Jesus' disciples. The effort to try and be good when we don't quite have the capacity for it can lead to such difficulty that sometimes people just want to give up and say "what's the use, I just can't do this". I met many prisoners who had taken that attitude, and even the apostle Paul said "I try to do the right thing and I end up doing something else. The spirit is willing, but the flesh is weak".

So what are we to do? Well, here is where our text gives us some guidance by outlining how we approach the problem of being good.

The first thing we need is an understanding about what goodness is, and the second thing is to develop the ability to do it.

In our weakness and sin, understanding goodness is a lifelong task. Because we face so many challenges in knowing how to choose the right things or make correct decisions, the finding of good almost seems to become a matter of trial and error. This is because we are often forced to choose between evils and what we want to find is the lesser evil, the thing that has the most potential to produce something good. This is just a fact in our imperfect world and in our imperfect lives. We can't always do the good or ideal thing and this is sometimes very frustrating for us.

But we can prepare ourselves to make the best decisions possible. We just need to learn the characteristics of goodness and how good comes to us. This is what our text offers to us.

We learn that there are two kinds of wisdom or ways of knowing about anything: the wisdom that is of the world and the wisdom from above. The wisdom that is of the world has to do with fulfilling *our* desires. The wisdom from above is about reflecting the goodness or righteousness of God. In order to know what good is, we must have the "wisdom from above". This may seem a simple thing, but it is not. Even Jesus found it difficult to impart the wisdom from above to his disciples. The many demands and troubles of this world get in the way of understanding or even hearing the wisdom from above. We know that *the wisdom from above is the Word of God*. We need to listen to this word, study it and practice it in order to prepare ourselves to know what goodness is.

Our text provides some guidance about how to define goodness. Notice that *most of the attributes of goodness are not acts but attitudes*. Goodness is about what *kind* of person you are. It is not a list of things that you have done right. Jesus talks about this all the time. You cannot become good by doing good works. This is one of the most profound lessons of scripture and one of our deepest theologies. You must somehow become a good person first and then you can do good things. We do not have the power to make ourselves good persons. Only the One who created us can do that. We are saved and made righteous through God's grace, not through our works.

But having found the source of goodness, we *can* do good things. We can also demonstrate goodness by the way we lead our lives. And our text tells us what that looks like. The wisdom from above informs us about the gifts of purity, peacefulness, gentleness, willingness to yield, mercifulness and good fruits or good actions. Notice that only the last of those has to do with specific behavior. And we are to cloak all of it in being true to ourselves and to others. We are to be impartial and without hypocrisy.

So the lesson is, if we want to live the life of a good person, we need to strive to be a certain *kind* of person. And that starts with being a person receptive to God's grace and the promise of salvation, made a child of God through His sacrifice, and nurtured in heavenly wisdom through the word and sacraments. Like the Pharisees of old, we may think that somehow we can generate goodness from a life of piety and good works. But it is only through God's love and promise that there is any goodness at all in this world. Any piety and good works that we manage are an expression of the goodness of God in us.

Our text says, "submit yourselves therefore to God. Resist the devil, and he will flee from you. Draw near to God, and He will draw near to you". If we seek God first, a good life in service to God and others will follow.

Enhancing the Flavor of Life

Have salt in yourselves and be at peace with one another (Mark 9:50b).

Today's readings are about people who add something significant to the community in which they live. In Matthew 5:13, they are referred to as "the salt of the earth" and here again, in our gospel for today (Mark 9), we find the reference to salt as a metaphor for a good and worthwhile person. Of course, in the context of Christ's teaching, it is also a metaphor for the character of a *Christian* person – a follower of Christ.

Salt is an interesting substance. It is necessary for human life but toxic to most plants. For much of human history, its importance rivaled that of gold, and a lot of human industry was organized to find and produce salt. It is said that the first factory for producing salt was developed in China in about 6000 BC. In the ancient world and well into the modern era, any people who had access to salt in abundance were able to control the economy and politics of their region.

So it would have made all kinds of sense for Jesus to use the image of salt in discussing the type of person Christians should be in this world. It is likely that anyone in his time could understand the point he was trying to make.

Three types or conditions of "saltiness" are discussed in our readings for today:

1. The *person* who uses the gifts they have been given for the glory of God regardless of the disadvantage or danger to them. This is the story of Esther (Esther 7 and 9).
2. The *community* where people support each other in sickness and health – both physically and spiritually. This is James (James 5) talking to the Christians who have suffered under Roman rule and who have been dispersed or scattered throughout the empire in order to reduce their influence or perceived threat. James is trying to encourage them to live as a community and to keep each other safe and in the faith.
3. The *stranger* or anyone new to the faith who may not know all the traditions or come from the same background as most other Christians in the community, but who still seeks to be a follower of Jesus and do good works in his name. This is the message of our gospel (Mark 9) where Jesus is warning his

An Arcadian Vision

disciples not to be protective of their status as his disciples or exclusive in their views about who is worthy of membership in the community of believers. He warns them not to hinder others in their exercise of faith.

Esther

Let's consider Esther, who is the example of our first kind of saltiness. She is a person who found herself in a position to be of great help to her people. But, in order to do so, she had to take the risk that she might lose everything in the process.

The story of Esther tells of one of the great moments in Jewish history. King Nebuchadnezzar of Babylon had enslaved the Hebrew people. Esther, who was Hebrew, had grown up as a Babylonian slave. Through a series of unusual circumstances she was given opportunity to present herself to King Ahasuerus (Xerxes) who had become the king of the Persian Empire of which Babylon was a part. Her beauty and intelligence won over the king and he made her his queen. This is where we come to the events recorded in our first reading (Esther 7:1-6, 9-10, 9:20-22). Esther has pleased the King and he is feeling generous so he asks Esther to request anything that she might desire.

We have to remember here that this was a king who had severe expectations of his women. He had exiled his first wife because she had refused to attend a grand banquet he held to demonstrate his great power and wealth. As a result of his wife's disobedience, he made a law that all women in the kingdom had to give honor to their husbands. This law was made part of the legal system of the Medes and the Persians and was inviolable. The penalty for breaking it would be death.

So Esther was dealing with someone who had both the temperament and the ability to inflict severe punishment on anyone who displeased him – and who also had a certain attitude about women.

The "saltiness" of Easter in this case was that she acted from a pure life devoted to God. She was not overwhelmed by the power of the King because she knew a greater power. But she also used her gift of intelligence to speak to the king with respect to his position and in a way that would turn her request into something that he, himself, would desire.

Esther asked for a favor on behalf of her people, not herself. She asked for salvation or freedom for them. But they were slaves and an asset to the king. Ahaseurus loved his assets. He was always showing them off to demonstrate his power. Now she was asking him to give some of that up – for her.

But Esther was wise. She knew that there was something even more important to Ahaseurus than possessions. Above all, he wanted respect. So Esther said, in effect, how can people respect you if the people of your Queen remain slaves? The king responded to Esther by agreeing to provide relief to the Jews by giving them power to administer their own affairs, including the creation of their own military.

Christians give flavor to the world through knowledge of God, use of intelligence and faithfulness in service to others. Esther demonstrated all of that in the service of her people.

The Christian community

From the book of James we learn of another kind of saltiness. It is the power of a community where the individual members care for each other on a continuing basis. This is like finding a salt quarry. The salt is always there to be used when necessary.

James is trying to bring encouragement to communities where the individual members have been uprooted and separated from each other. He is reminding them that their circumstances will require extra effort if they are to keep their sense of community and provide the physical and spiritual services each member might need. He reminds them that they must always pray for each other.

This teaches us of two ways that we add spice to the lives of others: *the use of prayer*, both as petition and praise; and *dedication to helping each other* stay strong in the faith.

We are reminded here that, just as salt is necessary for physical existence, the truth of God's word shared between persons is necessary for spiritual existence. "You should know that whoever brings back a sinner from wandering will save the sinners soul . . ."(v.20).

The stranger in the faith

The Gospel gives us our last glimpse for today of saltiness in the Christian life. This may be the hardest lesson in some ways. The disciples are worried that they have encountered people who are not part of their group and who are acting and speaking in Christ's name. They are wary of these strangers and have even tried to stop them.

Jesus is almost fierce in his response to this. He actually threatens his disciples with dire consequences if they get in the way of others who are trying to follow him – even if those persons don't seem to be doing the right things.

This is a hard lesson in a world where Christendom is so divided and various churches become jealous of their way of following Christ. We can even see this within church denominations where various factions become extremely critical of others in their own church for the way they choose to exercise their faith.

In today's gospel, Jesus warns us that interfering with someone else's expression of faith in Christ is a very serious and hurtful thing and, if you are going to do that, it would be better to put a millstone about your neck and cast yourself into the sea.

I think that this passage (Mark 9:42-49) is often misinterpreted. We often think that it is talking about individual sins that get in the way of *our* salvation. So sometimes we interpret it to mean that if you have a bad habit or if you can't overcome some passion that gets in the way of your faith, you should get rid of it for your own sake.

But this text is about what our "wrongheadedness" can do to *others*. What Jesus is illustrating here is how salt can lose its saltiness. Salt gives life and pleasure to those who receive it or use it. If we are like salt, then we exist to give life and flavor to others. If we are not like salt, it means we are also in danger of losing our salvation. But the way we lose our saltiness is by failing to give our time and energy to the physical and spiritual welfare of others as Christ has commanded us and as he has done for us.

In order to be "the salt of the earth" we must be willing to take risks on behalf of others as Esther did. We must constantly offer our prayers for those in our community who are in need of physical or spiritual healing. And we must support the stranger, or those with other traditions and practices, who may seek to serve Christ in a different way.

I have one last thought on this subject. Even though salt is necessary for life, we know that too much can harm us. This is also true about helping others. We need to intervene in moderation and not overwhelm people. This is part of being "at peace with one another".

"Have salt in yourselves and be at peace with one another" are two things that must go together. Christians have a responsibility to make things better in this world, to enhance the flavor of life. Let us be the "salt of the earth". It is what our Lord desires of us.

7. Lessons in Ordinary Time

In western Christian tradition, the time when the church is not celebrating a high (some say "strong") festival or season may be called "ordinary time". Ordinary time is the period between Epiphany and Pentecost and between Pentecost and Advent. The total is about 33 or 34 weeks and makes up the bulk of the liturgical year. This is a time when many churches develop worship themes in areas of church life not addressed directly by themes in the high festivals, such as stewardship, evangelism, religious education, etc.

Some consider ordinary time to be a return to a more practical theology after many weeks of worship and meditation on the deepest mysteries of the Christian religion. However, ordinary time for those who express their faith through regular worship is not a release from the contemplation of God's mysteries. If we follow the formalities of the church year, we find that our first Sunday in ordinary time is a direct encounter with the mystery of the definition of God Himself.

We can say, though, that our reflection on these things is now more ordinary in that our focus is not on the great events of God's grace that we remember and eulogize during the seasons of Advent, Christmas, Lent and Easter. The spectacles of these wondrous happenings have been replaced by a reflection on the meaning of these things in the course of our ordinary existence. We now concentrate less on what God has done and more on what we are doing.

Still, a human being that has by faith received the salvation earned through these amazing works, so spectacularly remembered, can live no ordinary life. Even in ordinary time with the demands of our mundane

An Arcadian Vision

existence upon us, we are aware of the wonders of God's grace and how the mysteries of His work among us affects everything we do.

To Know the Mind of God

Does not wisdom call, and does not understanding raise her voice? The Lord created me at the beginning of his work, the first of his acts of long ago . . . I was daily his delight, rejoicing before him always, rejoicing in his inhabited world and delighting in the human race (Proverbs 8: 1,22,31).

Today is the Day of the Holy Trinity or Trinity Sunday. It is one of the few feasts of the Christian year that does not celebrate an event or a person. Instead, it is the celebration of a reality or a doctrine. Last Sunday we observed the Day of Pentecost. Pentecost is the commemoration of an event. We also remember events at high festivals such as Christmas and Easter.

When we review the history of the church year we find that there really isn't a clear reason why we observe a festival called Holy Trinity at this time or even why we do it at all. It is unique to western Christendom and is not part of eastern orthodox Christianity. The theologians of the Eastern Orthodox Church have decided that they should not have any ritual or observance that, even symbolically, tries to define God or fix Him in time and space. They believe that any attempt to define God or give Him boundaries will immediately result in heresy because human beings are too limited to give God definition. For similar reasons, the Hebrew people refused to name God either in speaking or writing.

In western Christianity, most of us do not hold to this view, especially given the events that are described in the New Testament and the teachings about God that flow from those events. The central events, of course, are the birth, death and resurrection of Christ, and the central teaching is that because God became man and accomplished the work of overcoming death our sins are forgiven and we are one with God forever. As a result, we now have a relationship with God that seems to both demand definition and allow for it.

Most of our church doctrine is built on the great events described in the Bible. But again, we usually set days aside to remember the events themselves. It is unusual to establish a festival for explaining or discussing a doctrine.

So this is a unique day. We are concentrating on the doctrine of the Holy Trinity. This doctrine is derived from an interpretation of the meaning of various events described in scripture and the teachings related to them. There are a variety of views on these things. As a result, explaining the Holy Trinity or determining its meaning is difficult and somewhat controversial. There are numerous disputes within Christendom about how to state this doctrine – or even if it should be a doctrine at all. These difficulties arise, again, because this doctrine attempts to define God and, as we all know, human beings have not had much success defining God.

As a result, most statements of doctrine about the Holy Trinity begin by declaring it to be about a mystery. However, someone has pointed out that a mystery is not a wall to run up against but an ocean in which to swim. I guess this means that we should not view mysteries as standing between us and knowledge but as knowledge itself, and we must learn to live fully and happily with the mysteries of life just as we do with any other kind of knowledge. We just need to remember that *mysteries are a form of knowledge that is spiritual rather than intellectual. We can know a mystery without being able to fully understand it or define it.*

Not being able to fully understand the doctrine of the Holy Trinity doesn't mean that it is useless to us. If studying it and thinking about it can give us a little more insight or understanding about God, then it has been worth the effort. We can always seek to increase our knowledge of God even though we accept that we cannot completely understand God this side of heaven.

Whether or not we know all the reasons why our church has chosen to establish a festival of the Holy Trinity in the church year, it does make some sense coming where it does. The doctrine of the Holy Trinity states that God is three persons: Father, Son and Holy Spirit. The word "person" in Greek doesn't mean "being", so we are not to understand God as three beings. God is only one being. The word for person in Greek means "that which stands alone" or "individual reality". We might say that God is one being with three manifestations or individual realities, or that He has expressed himself in three ways. When, for example, He expresses himself as God the Son, His form is distinct and unmistakable and in this form He has accomplished specific work that human beings can understand and describe. Much of our understanding of God comes from the life and work of Jesus, one of the three manifestations of God as a Trinity.

Just last week, we celebrated the coming of the Holy Spirit to be among and in the people of the earth. When God expresses himself as the Holy Spirit, He is specifically that. That is his reality in that moment. When God works to create faith in the life of a believer, He does it as the Holy Spirit.

An Arcadian Vision

But you can see how difficult it is to try and talk about God in this way or to try to come up with a coherent statement about how God can be One and Three at the same time. Great theologians have struggled to find a way to do this but, in the end, it really is like trying to determine how many angels can stand on the head of a pin.

Given that, I find the selection of the first reading for today (Proverbs 8:1-4,22-31) to be very interesting. I have decided to take our meditation sentences from that reading rather than some of the more common readings used for Trinity Sunday.

The book of Proverbs is about wisdom. The primary author is Solomon, the Son of David, who is considered the Biblical example of human wisdom. The book begins by saying that it was written "for learning about wisdom" and its chapters include "the call of wisdom", "the value of wisdom", wisdom as "true wealth", "God's wisdom in creation" wisdom as "true security", "parental wisdom" and many more. Our reading includes portions of sections entitled "the gifts of wisdom" and "wisdom's part in creation".

But why on Trinity Sunday do we have a reading about wisdom? What does this reading tell us about God or the definition of God as a Trinity?

Solomon is trying to do two things in the book of Proverbs. The first is to provide *practical advice about living a good and proper life*. He does this by making every lesson an exercise in wisdom. We live well and we live properly if we know how to exercise wisdom. But, of course, *we have to know what wisdom is. We have to define it.* And that is the second thing Solomon is trying to do.

And it's here that we find the connection to the idea of defining God. It turns out that wisdom was the first thing established by God in creation. It came before anything else. Wisdom was present before any other created thing came into being.

When we read the book of Proverbs, we are helped not only with the problems of daily living, but we also begin to understand how our lives are part of an order where certain behaviors give us strength and life while other behaviors make us weak and threaten death. And we see that these observations about daily living are not random or situational. That is, the path of wisdom does not change depending on circumstances. Wisdom is the same whether we are at war or peace, are rich or poor. Wisdom is constant if we live in a democracy or in a dictatorship, have high education or no formal education, great knowledge or little knowledge, are male or female, or are liberal or conservative.

We learn from Proverbs that the way of wisdom is the way of God and God is not dependent on any of the things that I have just mentioned. God does not change. God is the one certainty, the one absolute in our lives. All else changes, including our knowledge of things, but God does not change and wisdom does not change.

Let's try to imagine this if we can. God, the first of all things, sets out to bring everything else into being. In order to do that there must be an order within which everything fits. We can't imagine a universe where the planets and stars are not kept in place or, if we do imagine it, as in a science fiction novel; what we imagine is chaos, terror and destruction.

We cannot imagine a world where seeds are unable to grow predictably or animals are unable to keep their form or human beings don't know what to expect at the birth of a child. Even though, again, we sometimes try to imagine these things in works of horror fiction or by telling tales of science run amok.

In other words, we cannot accept or tolerate a world that we cannot explain even though we may struggle to explain it. We have to know that the world has order, otherwise we imagine only chaos and terror. This applies to human behavior as well. How can we raise up a child in the way that he or she should go if there is no way of knowing what that way is? And what happens to a child when there is no parental wisdom to guide her?

Before all things came into being, God created wisdom. Wisdom, in the Biblical sense, is order, the right thing, the correct way and the ability to know these things. Wisdom, if you like, was the plan, the blueprint, for everything that followed. Wisdom was made by God and is an expression of God. Without the wisdom that comes from God, nothing exists. Without God in our lives, we don't have wisdom or know what it is. And without wisdom, we can't understand God's creation or live well in it.

The thing this teaches us about God is that He is the order of things and He creates this order and maintains it by expressing Himself in different ways. We know that God's order was damaged by the fall into sin, and so we see God manifest Himself in various ways to restore the order of His plan and His creation. He manifests himself as Jesus, a man, to live the perfect life and die for our sins. He manifests Himself as the Holy Spirit to live in our lives and give us the ability to live according to the way He has determined things should be.

But in all of this, He is God the Father, the force of creation, the source of all life and the preserver of all things until He finishes His work in this world.

It *remains a mystery* how to define God or imagine Him, including the awkwardness of human language and the anthropomorphic use of masculine terms. The doctrine of the Trinity is a way of understanding God in relation to the creation of the world and His work in it. Today we learn that we know God not only by the various ways that He presents His person to us, but also by understanding the attributes or characteristics of each manifestation of His being. And we see one of these attributes beautifully presented in the book of Proverbs.

God is many things. We can say that He is *all* things. But in relation to His created world, He is the wisdom of it and the wisdom in it, and from this wisdom every other aspect of His being is made known to us. His wisdom is a living, breathing thing that fills the world and makes it possible for the world to exist and for us to live well in it.

The book of Proverbs exhorts us in various ways to seek wisdom. Seeking wisdom is to seek God, and through wisdom we can know God, who is the source of all wisdom. We might not be able to define God in some academic sense or explain all His aspects, but we can and do know Him. As our first reading declares so beautifully, wisdom lives and breathes and delights in God and all the things that He has done. When wisdom lives in us, we can also delight in God and all that He has done. Perhaps this is the best lesson that can emerge from our observance of a day called Holy Trinity.

Swimming in the Ocean of God's Mystery

For I want you to know, brothers and sisters, that the gospel that was proclaimed by me is not of human origin, for I did not receive it from a human source, nor was I taught it, but I received it through a revelation of Jesus Christ (Galatians 1:11,12).

Those of you who were present for last week's sermon, or who had a chance to read it on our website, will remember a discussion of the idea that mystery is a form of spiritual knowledge. We said that mysteries should not be viewed as barriers to knowledge, like a wall we run into, but as an ocean of possibilities in which we can swim. We tried to define mysteries as things we cannot understand or explain using normal human language or references from our own experience.

Our topic last week was the doctrine of the Holy Trinity, the church's teachings regarding the definition of God. We said that this might be the grandest mystery of them all – knowing how to define God or even speak of such a being.

Spiritual knowledge is mysterious because we cannot contain it in our physical and intellectual world of boundaries and limits. We often don't know how such knowledge comes to us, and when it does come to us we usually can't explain it in a way other people can understand. Spiritual knowledge is "other worldly". It transcends time and space.

This is why the Bible is full of passages where the words and images seem strange or fantastic to us. This is especially true when the writer is trying to describe God or the spiritual dimension within which God exists (that "place" we sometimes call heaven). An example of this is found in the first chapter of Ezekiel. Ezekiel starts out by saying, "the heavens were opened, and I saw visions of God". The words that follow seem to make no sense at all (read some of this for yourself). And, of course, the book of Revelation in the New Testament is famous for its difficult images and apparently obscure messages. The book of Revelation starts out with these words, "the revelation of Jesus Christ, which God gave him to show his servants . . .". What follows are words of mystery that learned people struggle to translate and interpret. One might wonder if this revelation is the same revelation that Paul is talking about in the Second Reading for today (Galatians 1:11-24) and especially the verses that we have selected for our meditation.

When people first encounter books of the Bible like Ezekiel and Revelation they cannot be blamed for feeling that they have run into a wall. But it isn't just the difficult parts of the Bible that can make people feel that way. Many of us consider passages like John 3:16 to be a simple and straightforward summary of the message of the gospel. This verse says that God loved the world and gave His only Son so that anyone who believes in Him will not perish but have eternal life.

However, many people that hear this message, even in its simplest form, react as though they have run into a wall. This is spiritual knowledge and must be received spiritually. If people receive it intellectually or try to "figure it out" they just get frustrated and, often, angry. The only way this message makes sense is if people release themselves to God's will, listen to *His* word instead of their own, accept that God and His ways are mysterious to us as sinful beings in the natural world, and start *swimming in the ocean of God's mystery.*

All of our readings for today are about mystery. That is, they are about things we cannot explain. Though they are mysteries or miracles of different types, they all present the same truth: *some things happen through spiritual power and they are understood with spiritual knowledge.* This is exactly what Paul means when he says "I want you to know . . . the gospel that was proclaimed by me is not of human origin . . .".

Some of God's miracles and mysteries are discussed in our readings for today. In the First Reading (1 Kings 1:8-16, 17-24) we have a miracle of food or provisions and a miracle of resurrection. In the Gospel (Luke 7:11-17), we have a miracle of resurrection. In the Second Reading, we have a miracle of conversion. And in the Psalm (146), David sings a poem of praise to God for *all* His wonderful acts and mysteries.

The reason we are using the image of an ocean to think about God's mysteries is because to mere mortals the ocean is a limitless expanse within which to swim, and we can't possibly know or touch all of its dimensions. We can see to the limits of our vision. We can touch to the limits of our feeling. We can hear to the limits of our hearing. We can never experience it all as human beings, but we can experience as much of it as our strength allows. We can never learn everything, but we can learn some things, and anything we learn brings us closer to God. While we are in the ocean of God's mystery we are surrounded by His presence and He brings us wave after wave of new knowledge. But as with any swimmer we must give ourselves over to the experience, and part of that is to keep working on our swimming skills.

When we are confronted with God's mysteries, it helps us to at least try to describe them. This is what we were trying to do last Sunday when we were confronted with the problem of the definition of God. The doctrine of the Holy Trinity is an attempt to describe God so that we can at least speak of Him. We don't need to be able to "prove" God in the scientific sense – as a phenomenon you can test or replicate in some way. We just need to say what we know about how God presents Himself in the world.

The same is true of what we might call "lesser mysteries" – though these are no less difficult for us to understand. We find some of these lesser mysteries recorded in our readings for today. But regardless of their magnitude, all these mysteries are things that are not of human origin and we struggle to understand how they can happen.

In our Old Testament reading, God acts through a man to sustain the life of a mother and son through the miraculous provision of food. There are many instances of this type of miracle recorded in the Bible. These miracles are demonstrations of the mystery that God is the source of everything that sustains us. It is no more miraculous for God to guarantee that a jar of meal will never empty than for Him to cause a giant tree to grow from a small, dormant seed. These are miracles of the same order, but we think that we can explain one of them while not being able to explain the other. The limitation is ours, not God's; but even as lesser beings (lower than the angels) our lives become interesting, exciting and fulfilling as we grow closer to God with new knowledge every day.

Twice in our readings, once in the Old Testament and once in the New Testament, God acts through a person to raise someone from the dead. We do not know in a scientific way what changes happened in the bodies of these persons to cause them to function again as full and complete human beings. We just know that God, who is the source of life, chooses in these instances to give life back after it has been taken away. This is another miracle in the ocean of mystery that we can't explain but that we can, in some limited way, describe.

But there is one more miracle in our readings for today that is greater then all of the others. It is the one described in our Second Reading and which Paul uses to illustrate that the gospel he preaches could not possibly be of human origin. This is the miracle of conversion.

Here, Paul is describing the miracle of his own conversion. He is reminding the Galatians that his life was totally changed by an act of God. He had been a man dedicated to the extermination of God's people and now he has become one of those people. He also understands that he was chosen to be a child of God before he was born. He cannot explain that. It is beyond explanation. It is a miracle in the ocean of God's mystery.

But Paul also understands that his conversion is not just about attitude or about those with whom he wishes to associate, but it is about the very nature of his life. He has been born again. He has regained immortality. He has received spiritual power and spiritual knowledge. He has moved into an entirely different dimension. He cannot properly explain it but he knows it, he can feel it and he can act on it.

It was said of Jesus at his resurrection that "he was once dead and yet now he lives". This was a reference to the physical resurrection of a specific person but it was also a symbol of the spiritual resurrection of all of us. In our spiritual resurrection, we are converted from a life in opposition to God to a life that is at one with God. God is the source of life, and those that are separated from him will die. If we are one with him we will live – forever.

This is the greatest of all of God's miracles. The other miracles are symbolic of this great one. We deserve death, yet we are given life. We were mortal and now we are immortal. When God chooses to extend the life of someone who is dying or who has died He shows us the power that gives us life forever. When He chooses to improve the lot of those who are living by making food available to them or sustaining them in other ways, He shows us the power that gave us life in the first place.

But when He forgives us for the sins that separated us from Him and makes us His child once again, He shows us the greatest of all the miracles in the ocean of His mystery. This is the miracle of *love* that transforms everything and that allows us to live in His world with confidence and joy knowing that one day all will be revealed and the miracles will be mysteries no more.

Parabolic Teaching

(*parabolic*: of or expressed in a parable; *parable*: allegory or comparison)

Many of the lessons of scripture come to us in the form of parables. We are told that Jesus always used parables when teaching to the uninitiated or people who could not hear with the ears of faith (Mark 4:34). This may explain why those of us who have been with the church a long time are likely to think of parables as being for children. We relate them to our Sunday school years and to religious books written for children. Parables were good for us when our understanding was limited and great religious truths were too much of a mystery to ponder. We might even think of them as being simple explanations for simple or unsophisticated people.

But maybe we don't give parables enough credit. Maybe the reason they seem simple is that they start with something we already know. The images put before us in parables usually don't have to be learned, even by children. They are what we might call "common knowledge".

The parable of Christ about "the sower" (Mark 4:1-20) is a good example of that. Every child in an agricultural community knows about seeds. I remember the feeling of excitement that I had as a child when my father announced that it was planting time. Of course, I already knew when it was time to sow because the activities involved in getting ready for planting were obvious and, as the years passed, involved more and more of my personal time – even as a child.

Which field would be plowed and which field would lie fallow? What crops would be planted and in what proportion? I often heard these matters discussed anytime we were all together for a meal or driving somewhere in the car. Getting ready for planting involved time in the field turning and harrowing soil and time in town choosing the seeds for the big crops and, more importantly, the individual packages of seeds for the small gardens tended by my siblings and myself. And, of course, there were the flowers disdained by those of us who grew "real" things but carefully tended by my mother and one of my sisters. These flowers grew – to the eventual amazement of all those who visited us as well as to the appreciation of the county fair judges who almost always chose something from among them for an award.

Yes, even a child knows about seeds and about the "time lapse" that occurs in their growing. I'm sure that we have all seen pictures resulting from time lapse photography. The little green knob poking its way out of the soil; the coiled stem writhing upward; the spreading leaves; the budding flower; the shadow of something growing inside; the burgeoning fruit. Or, with root vegetables, the lifted lacy or leafy greens forming little trees or bushes that indicate a vegetable forming underground. And the impatient pulling of a plant to see "how big they are now" – always too soon.

Children and adults wander the plots and fields in the morning light looking for the first sign of the miracle of the seeds. So if you want to teach such a child something about God you might say, "the kingdom of God is as if someone would scatter seed on the ground; and would sleep and rise night and day; and the seed would sprout and grow; he does not know how". Immediately we identify, not just with the words of it, but with the feeling of it. We have been subjected to a method of teaching that not only touches us in our minds, but also in our bodies and our souls.

This is the genius of the parable as a method of teaching. It starts where people are and takes them to a new place. The parable does this by providing us with an opportunity to compare what we know with something we do not yet know or which we may have a hard time understanding. Parables engage us with our lives and help to bring together our thoughts and our feelings. Parables provide us with the opportunity to transcend what we know by using what we know as a springboard to increased awareness and new insights.

But, in spite of all this, we are reminded that parables are not enough to fully and completely know the things of God. Yes, it is true that parables are a unique and effective teaching tool. But they are a human creation, designed by human beings to assist in the learning experience. Jesus used them because the technique was familiar to many people of his time and because it was a very effective way to get their attention in the hope that some would seek more knowledge as a result. *That is really all that we can ask of our teaching, isn't it, that students will be stimulated to know more and ask more questions.* The parable helps us to know what questions to ask.

Why did Jesus speak to the crowds in parables but explained everything in greater depth to His disciples (Mark 4:34)? *Because they were ready to ask the questions and had the faith to hear the answers.* Parables were still useful to them but they were ready for more.

This is the time in the church year when we celebrate the completeness of God and the various ways in which He comes to us. Two Sundays ago we celebrated Pentecost and the coming of the Holy Spirit to be with us after Jesus ascended into heaven. Last week we saw the completeness of God in the Holy Trinity – Father, Son and Holy Spirit. We have learned that it is through the Holy Spirit that everything is now brought together. The Holy Spirit is the power through which we can understand all of the lessons of scripture and especially the teachings of Jesus. It is the Holy Spirit that allows us to transcend our earthly knowledge and learn to know the mysteries of God. It is the Holy Spirit that completes the lessons for us that were begun in the speaking of the parables.

Jesus talks about this very thing in John, chapter fourteen. In this passage, one of Christ's disciples actually asks him why he doesn't explain things to all people in the way he explains things to them. His answer is that the people of the world are unable to understand these deeper truths because they lack faith, they do not believe in him and therefore cannot love him. All these things are necessary to understand the meaning of God's Word, including the meanings of the parables (read John 14: 12-27).

So what we learn here is that it is not enough to have knowledge, it is also necessary to have faith. Faith comes by the Holy Spirit. By faith we are able to love God. We may be able to know what God commands through the exercise of our minds, but we can do what God commands only through love of Him. That is why love is greater than knowledge or even faith (faith, hope and love, these three, but the greatest of these is love – 1 Corinthians 13).

It is interesting that after Jesus talks to his disciples about the necessity of faith and love in order to know God and understand His Word, he immediately begins again to teach them using a parable. This was the parable of the vine and the branches that we discussed several Sundays ago. Parables are a great teaching devise that can take us deeper into the meaning of scripture but it is only through faith and love that we can apply that meaning in our own lives and live it to the glory of God.

John W. Ekstedt

A New Curtain

(A message about the objects and symbols used in worship)

Therefore, my friends, since we have confidence to enter the sanctuary by the blood of Jesus, by the new and living way that he opened for us through the curtain (that is, through his flesh), and since we have a great priest over the house of God, let us approach with a true heart in full assurance of faith, with our hearts sprinkled clean from an evil conscience and our bodies washed with pure water. Let us hold fast to the confession of our hope without wavering, for he who has promised is faithful. And let us consider how to provoke one another to love and good deeds, not neglecting to meet together, as is the habit of some, but encouraging one another, and all the more as you see the Day approaching (Hebrews 10: 19-25).

Today we will be taking a moment to dedicate some new chancel adornments. We received a new piano this year and last Sunday we worshipped before new chancel curtains. We have recently received a new music stand and guitar holder for use in the chancel. Each of these objects has come to us as a result of the dedicated work of our members. Some of our members have actually traveled great distances to obtain these objects and transport them back to our church.

It would be possible, I suppose, for us to acknowledge these things briefly and move on. I know that many of us have commented on these various adornments and, in the case of the piano, our summer pulpit program and the French school program have allowed for a variety of persons to enjoy this instrument.

But while, in the course of ordinary events, these things would be noted and received gratefully, I would like to suggest that there is nothing at all ordinary about these objects. Each of them involves gifts of our money, our time and considerable attention on the part of individual church members.

Yet even that isn't enough to make these gifts worthy of too much more than a word of appreciation and a promise to care for them in the spirit in which they were given. One of the things that may make these objects seem a little bit more special than they otherwise might is that we all can rightly feel that these objects are gifts given to us as individual persons. Those of us who have faithfully worshipped here and who have lived with transient and temporary instruments, however appreciated, or old and fading curtains, however loved, can look on these new things and feel, in all sincerity, that this is something for us. Something of which each of us can be individually proud. And so we say, "have you heard *our* new piano

An Arcadian Vision

or seen *our* new curtains" or "did you notice *our* new music stand today?" These are *our* things and we know the story behind them that, in some cases, goes back many, many years.

But while our feeling about these things makes them more than a little special, we know that this is not the reason why we would stop for a minute or two in the middle of a formal worship service to dedicate them. There is something here that goes beyond our personal interests, and as it happens that thing is the focus of our readings for today, especially the Second Reading (Hebrews 10:11-14 [15-18] 19-25) from which the text for our meditation is taken.

On several occasions, we have discussed the importance of places of worship in the history of humankind. As we follow God's people through the sagas of the Old Testament, we see how often the tabernacle or temple was the place where great things transpired or notable moments occurred. Last Sunday, we observed one of these moments as we remembered how the poor widow gave all that she had as an offering to God in the temple and how this became an object lesson used by God Himself to instruct on the ways of a Christian life.

Today, our first reading and the responsive reading (I Sam. 2:1-10) are both taken from incidents occurring in the temple at Shiloh. In the first incident, Hannah, who is barren, pleads with God to be given a son. It was the custom that women were to remain in the background in the temple. This moment was notable because Hannah pushed herself forward and stood before the Lord for all to see. But she remained modest and prayed silently. However, even this made her more noticeable because the custom was to pray out loud with singing and chanting. These actions brought her to the attention of Eli, the priest, who intervened with God on her behalf.

The second incident recorded in our responsive reading for today is the prayer of Hannah as she brings her son Samuel forward in the same temple and dedicates him to the service of the Lord.

These are moments in the temple. Over and over again we see how God guides his people and provides for their future through things that happen in the temple. Samuel became a great prophet and judge of Israel. His mother's appeal that day in the Shiloh temple set the course for the future of Israel.

We remember how God instructed his people as they were wandering in the wilderness to construct a tabernacle and keep it. The last fifteen chapters of the Book of Exodus are about the details for making and furnishing the tabernacle. This included every ornament, table, chair, vestment, parament and curtain. Instructions were given on how these things should be placed and what they represented.

The temple was to be *the* place for meeting God. God could be found everywhere, of course. But His promise was that He would always be in the temple and He would hear the prayers of His people there because it was a place prepared for offering sacrifice and hearing God's word. It was a place where people could be reminded of God's promises and see evidence of His mysteries. It was a place that, by design, shut out the distractions of the world so that prayers, like the prayer of Hannah, could find voice and reach the ear of God.

What our text for today assures us is that the temple is still here for us. The priests still make offering and the curtain still hangs as a symbol of the veil that hides from us the Holy of Holies where God rests and awaits our prayers and offerings. We still prepare this place and give it the order He prescribed. We build furniture for it and stock it with instruments of music.

But now, while we honor the old ways and mimic many of the original implements, we learn that we have a temple with a difference. We are done with the old sacrifices. There is now a new sacrifice that has opened the veil for us and given the curtain a new meaning. Because Christ became the "single sacrifice for our sins" the veil is opened. The curtain no longer hides God from us but becomes a door through which we can approach God directly. In the old temple, only a priest could enter the sanctuary. Now we can all enter the sanctuary. The people who built the original tabernacle lived in the days of the Old Testament. We live in the days of the New Testament. We have seen God's salvation in the sacrifice of His Son, Jesus Christ. Our salvation is no longer a promise, it is a reality.

But the temple remains. It is still the place where we come to meet with God. The symbols reflect both the promise and the reality of God's salvation. The curtain that was a veil has become a door. Christ has accomplished this. We see the curtain in a new way but are reminded of what it was for God's original people. It is a place of the past in that it holds the memories of God's relationship with His people throughout human history. But while we are reminded of the past, we know that the temple is a place of the present. It gives us power through the Holy Spirit to live in the world of today. The temple is also a place of the future in that it gives us a glimpse of the heavenly kingdom to come.

The day will come when temples of stone will no longer be necessary.

This is the message of the gospel for today. When the end times come and we are taken to be with God forever, the purpose of the temple will cease and it will fall away as do all earthly things.

But while we live in this world, we are to use the temple and care for it. The last verse in our text says:

And let us consider how to provoke one another to love and good deeds, not neglecting to meet together, as is the habit of some, but encouraging one another, and all the more as you see the Day approaching (Hebrews 10:25).

So let us dedicate these things that we have brought to the temple to the glory of God for the edification of all the people who come here. These are offerings fit for God and reminders to us of His great love for us, and of our duty to God and to each other.

The Power of a Woman and the Love of a Mother

The Lord opened her heart . . . she and the members of her household were baptized (Acts 16:14b-15a).

Today is another of those days when secular and religious themes merge or overlap. It has been my practice to mention this when it happens and to try to find some way to develop a common theme for the day. With some observances, such as Christmas and Easter, it is not difficult to explain why a religious observance might evolve into some type of secular celebration as well (or vice versa). With other celebrations, such as Valentine's Day, the connection may be more obscure. Still, it is possible to see how something that started in a religious context could become a more general observance, crossing religious boundaries and even taking on a commercial tone or purpose. And how a secular observance, such as Memorial Day or Mother's Day might evolve with some religious significance.

Today *is* Mother's Day. The connection, if any exists, between Mother's Day and any religious observance is minimal, perhaps even non-existent. But in our churches we tend to want to do something with Mother's Day – as though it were a religious observance. In this case we have a secular observance that we might choose to include in our worship because we approve of it and think it is worthy of recognition in the context of our religious experience and worship life.

One of the frustrations that I have experienced in my preaching is that there is usually not any obvious connection between the scripture readings for a day like today (Sixth Sunday of Easter) and the fact that this day has also been set aside as Mother's Day.

However this year, either accidentally or on purpose, we do have a scripture assigned to the sixth Sunday of Easter that is also appropriate for Mother's Day. This scripture is our first reading from the book of Acts (16:9-15) which is the story of Lydia.

I have often thought of Lydia when debates have been underway about the role of women in the church or even when the role of women in society as a whole has been at issue.

In my lifetime, many changes in attitude have evolved concerning the role relationship between men and women. Numerous studies exploring social and political attitudes about the status of women have been undertaken. Most of these have resulted in demands for political action and social change. Many topics have been addressed including equal pay for equal work; the politics and scholarship of the feminist movement; the stay at home Mom; the working Mom; women in management; and, in the case of the church, women as clergy. We have all heard of the desire of many women – even the demand – to "have it all": social status, career, economic freedom, sexual freedom and motherhood.

And it all seems so right. Whether or not men in the modern world realize all their aspirations or are treated fairly in every circumstance, it remains the case that, in general, men are the more privileged class in the vast majority of the cultures of the world. Women have been discriminated against and have suffered many liabilities not common to men. How can we not support any attempt to fix that? What fool would accept any social behavior that would put his mother at a disadvantage; or his sister, or his wife?

But these are not usually the things that are talked about on Mother's Day. Mother's Day, it seems, is not a day for political rhetoric or rebel action. It is a day for each of us, male and female, to remember the woman in our life who is, or was, our mother – or who has been a mother *to* us (sometimes this is someone other than our biological mother). It is a day, it seems, when we hope to recover fond memories and express loving appreciation – if we can.

And if our Mother seemed to work harder than the rest of us or was at a greater disadvantage than we seem to be, we remember that too, with appreciation and love. And those of us who had a Christian Mother, and understand her influence in the formation of our lives as servants of God and members of the church, may be especially happy to remember her *in church* with a prayer and with a song.

All of this brings us to our scriptural Mother of today – Lydia.

First of all, how do we know that she was a mother? The scripture does

An Arcadian Vision

not seem to say that. Well, as is often the case in understanding the Bible, we take its meaning from the context and the way words were used at the time of the writing. In English, we read that Lydia had a "household". In Greek, the word used means a family, including offspring. We also are pretty sure that Lydia was a widow because it was always the practice in New Testament times to name the husband when identifying a woman. If no husband is mentioned, it is usually assumed that the woman is a widow. We have previously noted that widowhood was a common state of women because the life and work of men was dangerous and the mortality rate was high.

One of the reasons that Lydia is so fascinating is because she seems very modern, even in our terms. She was obviously a businesswoman and was probably quite wealthy for her time. She was a dealer in purple cloth and lived in a city (Thyatira) that was famous for its production of purple dye. Purple clothes and drapes were very expensive and generally were reserved for royalty or those of great wealth. In order to trade in this product, Lydia would have had to consort with people of wealth and importance.

We also know that Lydia was a gentile. How do we know that? We know that because in our scripture reading she is called a "worshipper of God". In those days, there were some gentiles who had accepted the God of the Jews (Yahweh). They were not believers in Christ, just as many of the Jews were not believers in Christ as the Messiah. But they had accepted the Jewish faith. The Jews had a term for such people and that term is translated "worshipper of God".

So we are reasonably sure that Lydia was a mother; that she was a widow; that she was a successful businesswoman; and, that she was a religious person in the same way that most Jews were.

The story of Lydia has become part of the scriptural record because she was an early convert to Christianity and impressed the Apostle Paul very much. She was obviously a great encouragement to him in the early days of his ministry. She was the type of woman who could be an example to others, and he wanted others to know about her. She is an example for both men and women in several ways.

First of all, she belies the proposition that Christianity is the "opiate of the masses" or a useful religion only for those who are oppressed or poor or disadvantaged. Even in her time and culture, Lydia was no such thing.

Secondly, Lydia was an archetype of femininity. While she was successful at mundane or material things, she was committed to the spiritual side, to the higher things of human existence. She sought answers to the questions of life and she practiced what she learned in her daily life.

Thirdly, Lydia made sure that her family was included and instructed in her beliefs. When she was baptized, her children were baptized. It would not have occurred to her to separate her life goals and desires from those of her children. If belief in Christ as Lord was important for her, it was important for her children as well and would be made available to them. Her children would never have reason to doubt her values or be left alone without a reference point to guide their lives. As they grew they might move on to other things, but as members of her family they would know that they lived in a Christian household, and they would know what that meant.

Lastly, for all of her success and all of her certainty of faith, Lydia knew humility. She said "if you have judged me to be faithful to the Lord, come and stay at my house". She did not flaunt any of it: her riches, her family or her faith. She humbly asked these men of faith to confirm for her that she was really demonstrating a true faith. She did not think that she had attained or completed anything. She knew that she was a work in progress and that was okay with her. She was inquisitive and unafraid – characteristics that some say are more likely to belong to women than to men.

So on this Mother's Day we are fortunate to have the story of Lydia to give us a reference point for thinking about the importance of the women in our lives – especially our mothers. Very often in my ministry I have seen mothers struggling to get their children to church, often without the help of their men who had to work, who were gone for other reasons, or who just didn't care. And when men do care, when they lift the spiritual banner, when they are inquisitive and unafraid, when they watch out for their spiritual welfare and the welfare of their children, it is often because of the women in their lives – including the guiding influence of their mothers.

So we honor our mothers as we reflect on the story of Lydia today and we honor all those other women in our lives who are mothers *of* others or *to* others in one way or another. We *do* take them for granted and I suppose that has as much to do with their nature as with ours. They ask for so little.

But we should not take them for granted. Instead, we should give thanks to God for this blessing in our lives and be as much like them as we possibly can.

On Being Spiritual

The glory that you have given me I have given them, so that they may be one, as we are one, I in them and you in me, that they may become completely one... (John 17:22-23a).

To the uninitiated, much of scripture appears, on first reading, to be obscure, even nonsensical. Many of us feel that the Bible is too difficult for us to cipher and that, at best, we can get something out of it only if we have a qualified teacher to guide us.

Those who feel this way should not worry. The written word has always seemed an exclusive domain, still accessible to most people only in its simplest of forms – even considering the various methods of universal education that have emerged in the world over the last few centuries. For most of modern human history, the written word was literally inaccessible to the vast majority of people. Learning to read and write was a luxury available only to the wealthy and privileged. We have learned to equate reading and writing with being educated, and it is often felt that only the *most* educated can handle difficult writing – such as is found in the Bible.

There are other reasons why people sometimes shy away from the Bible. The writing in it is very old and has gone through many translations to get to us. When it appears before us in English, it is a mixture of antiquated forms with modern forms. Consequently, the writing often appears awkward to us.

But even if the syntax and grammar are tolerable, the Bible doesn't seem to be the kind of book that can just be read – like a novel. As the ancient Rabbis often said about the Torah (the first five books of the Bible), the Bible is a book that must be studied. We might say that the Bible is "high" literature concerned with the deepest meanings that a human being can encounter. Even its simplest parables are full of profound philosophies and lofty ideals. Much of it seems beyond us. It is all very nice but of little practical value. Who has time for it?

Probably the thing that seems to make the Bible the most difficult is that it is not just about ethics or philosophy. In fact, it turns out that it is not really philosophy at all. The Bible is not, first of all, about people – or their views of things. It is about God and God's view of things. It is not a philosophical book. It is a *spiritual* book. It requires us to transcend our bodies and our minds and move to another dimension. It is a thing of the Spirit and from it we are to learn how to be spiritual – not physical, not intellectual, not emotional – but *spiritual*.

John W. Ekstedt

It is no wonder that we need help with it.

And help we get. We learn from the Bible that we can know its meaning because it will be *revealed* to us. It is God's Word and it is God's spirit that will inform us of its meaning. And in the process, we too will be filled with God's spirit and will learn to be *spiritual*.

During the Easter season, we talked about how Christ's resurrection has affected our spiritual lives. You remember how we discussed the influence of Christ's life, death and resurrection on our total existence. How we understand God (theological), how we understand the future (teleological), how we understand ourselves as individuals (spiritual) and how we live together with others (cultural).

Today it is our *spiritual* side that we want to talk about a little bit more. There are things about the spirit that we need to know.

First of all, we need to understand that to have spirit or to be spiritual means *to have God in us*. We are children of God through faith. God is our spiritual parent and, as we do with our earthly parents, we might say that we share His DNA. This is what our gospel for today (John 17:20-26) is about. Jesus is saying to His Father that the glory (spirit, power, life) of God has been passed on, first to Jesus and then through Jesus to all others who believe or who accept Jesus as the Christ, the Messiah, the Son of God. In several places in scripture, we are told that we have "inherited" His glory.

Secondly, we need to understand that *to be spiritual* (that is, to have God in us) *is to have power*. When we are one with God, we have the power of God available to us. For example, it is well known that when people of God pray, they are able to accomplish great things. This is why we talk about the power of prayer. But spiritual power may show itself in other ways. One of those ways is described for us in the first reading for today (Acts 16:16-34).

One of the things that we have been talking about since we celebrated Christ's resurrection is how the new Christian church began to develop and, with that, the idea of ministry involving pastors and teachers. We have discussed how Peter received his call to become the first pastor and then how Saul, who became Paul, was called as the first evangelist and teacher. We saw two weeks ago how Peter was able to bring someone back to life, and last week how Paul brought an important local businesswoman to the faith. These are both examples of the *spiritual power* that these men had received through their faith in Christ.

Today we see another example of this power at work. As is often the

An Arcadian Vision

case with the exercise of spiritual power, the outcome seems miraculous to us. We sometimes say that Christ "works through us in miraculous ways, his wonders to perform". Paul certainly must have felt that way in the account recorded in our first reading.

There are several points in this reading that are worth noting. The first is that people sometimes try to take advantage of the trouble and human defects that have resulted from the fall into sin. In this case, some people were abusing a girl who was obsessed with a "negative spirit" (we might say that she was mentally or emotionally disturbed). They saw that they could make money by having her tell fortunes. In other words, by presenting her as a freak able to do mysterious things. (Much in the way of the modern carnival or freak show.) Paul, through the power of the Holy Spirit, was able to heal her of this misfortune and, as a result, her value as a fortune-teller was lost to her owners.

We learn from this that spiritual power can heal the mind as well as the body. We also learn from this that spiritual power can be used for both good and evil, that there is a devil or an evil force in the world. People whose lives are not filled with the spirit of God are in danger of being filled with the spirit of Satan.

Paul, in the name of Jesus, was able to heal this unfortunate girl of her malady but the struggle between good and evil is not so easily won. The girl's owners were furious and began a campaign to discredit Paul and his companion Silas. They managed to get Paul and Silas thrown in jail as political insurgents, accused of promoting practices that were against Roman law.

It is while they are in jail that we see another example of what spiritual power is. Something happens that neither Paul nor Silas had intended. But it happened because they had spiritual power and were expressing it in the best way they knew how.

They had accepted their imprisonment. They were not trying to escape. They were full of the spirit and were praying and singing hymns. We are told that the other prisoners were listening.

Sometimes all we can do with our spiritual power is worship. But we need to remember how powerful worship is when it comes from a heart filled with God and devoted to His service. God wanted to show what people of faith are able to do without even intending it. All they have to do is be faithful in their worship.

And so God sent an earthquake to break open the doors of the prison and loosen the chains of the prisoners.

The reaction of Paul and Silas, and even the rest of the prisoners, is an illustration of the difference between lives filled with God's spirit and lives that are not. The prisoners did not run or try to find some other way to take advantage of this situation for their own benefit. The person who was guarding them assumed that is what they would do. He knew that, if his prisoners escaped, he might as well kill himself. Paul quickly alerted him that the prisoners were still there. And, of course, the guard was amazed and could see immediately that these people had a different spirit from the prisoners he was used to guarding. He knew right away that he wanted to have what they had.

When people are filled with the spirit of God and become spiritual themselves, their essence changes, and God is able to accomplish great things through them. This happens to us too. We don't always know the way in which our life of faith will affect others, but we need to keep living it and demonstrating it any way we can.

I imagine that missionaries like Peter, Paul and Silas were only beginning to realize the extent of the power that was in them as they went from place to place during these early days in the development of Christ's church on earth. They were probably as amazed as anyone else at what was happening.

While at one level these things are difficult to understand, at another level it is quite simple. There is a God who is the creator of heaven and earth. His power and glory were brought into the world through the birth of His Son, Jesus Christ. As a result of Christ's death and resurrection we are made children of God and have been filled with the same power and glory. So now what ever we do is an expression of God's power in the world. And mostly we should do what we know how to do, and that is to live our lives in worship and praise to Him. We don't know how God will use our lives of worship and we don't need to worry about that. What needs to be done will be done as long as we are faithful in God's service.

In our second reading for today (Revelation 22:12-14, 16-17, 20-21) God promises us that, if we are faithful, we shall see His Son again and be rewarded by him. This is the promise for our future (or teleology) that has been confirmed by Christ's work here on earth. Jesus promises that in the future he will come back and reward all believers according to *their* work in this world. That work, interestingly, is described as " those who wash their robes". This means those who keep their faith well and tend to it are those who have the right to the tree of life. God, through Christ, gives us the ability to keep our faith well. But we must attend to it and not let our robes fray or get dirty. This is what we do when we worship and pray. We "wash our robes" so that on Christ's return we will be ready to enter the gates of the holy city with him.

Scripture gives us much to ponder. It sometimes seems difficult, but in the end the message is clear. Believe in Jesus as Lord and you will be filled with God's spirit. We grow in this Spirit through worship and prayer – by "washing our robes". As we grow in Spirit, God works through us to do great things. God's spirit is eternal and with it in us we have eternal life.

The greatest wisdom is to make the complex simple. This is really what the Bible does. It is not obscure or inaccessible. But we do need to pay attention.

Identity Theft

Today also my complaint is bitter . . . if only I could vanish in darkness, and thick darkness would cover my face (Job 23:1 and 17b). You lack one thing; go, sell what you own . . . then come, follow me (Mark 10:21).

The problem of identity theft has become a popular theme in news reporting. Almost everyone is now aware of the dangers resulting from the conveniences of our technological age. These conveniences include an ability to pay debts on machines located in public places as well as by computer in the apparent privacy of our homes. However, the ability to do these things may place us in positions of high vulnerability where someone may steal the number on our card or the password for access to our account. Because this new age of information technology is so efficient in storing and linking information, the access to one account may lead to the access of other accounts or other information particular to the identity of a person. With this access, an unscrupulous person may actually assume the identity of another person – at least in a commercial sense. When someone else is spending your money without authorization, destroying your credit or impersonating you, it may become evident that you are a victim of identity theft.

I am interested in the responses of people who have been the subject of identity theft. The sense of violation seems quite severe. I suppose that this is because this thing we call identity theft is not just about money, it is about reputation and character. I watched a television newscast of a victim of identity theft describing his feelings and his deepest concern was that "people now think I am a bad person and there seems to be nothing that I can do to fix it". He lamented his discovery that, in Canada as least, identity theft is not defined as a crime and that other avenues for pursuing and making claims against perpetrators appear limited and difficult.

This is a serious problem and we must not treat it lightly. As consumers in a consumer society, we need to take every precaution to prevent such violations of our personal lives.

But what is really at issue here? What is our identity anyway? And is it possible to steal it?

I think that we all understand that the term "identity theft" with reference to theft of the ability to spend your own money does not refer to the loss of a person's identity in the strictest or most meaningful sense. Certainly we are more than the accumulation of our possessions. We don't cease to be a person because someone has taken our money from us. And even the loss of reputation, if it results from false claims, while hugely difficult and unfair, cannot destroy a person's sense of self. Can it?

It could be said that our readings for today are about identity. At least that's one theme that can be taken from them.

We once again hear Job crying out in his afflictions. His pain and suffering have become so great that he just wants to shrivel up and die. His faith in God is profound and famous and has sustained him through so much. But, in his suffering, he searches for God and cannot find Him. He has endured all for God. His service to God is his identity. What does he do now?

In the Psalm (22) David cries out the great lament that was repeated by Christ on the cross "My God, my God, why have you forsaken me?" He, too, seems discouraged beyond redemption. He is being laughed at and scorned, like Job and like the modern person suffering identity theft.

We find some hope in the second reading (Hebrews 4:12-16) but even here we learn that the word of God is a two-edged sword. On the one edge, it lays bare the soul and brings judgment on our thoughts and actions. On the other edge it gives us the message of hope that Christ, God's son, has shared our life and sympathizes with our weaknesses and has experienced the sorrow and hopelessness that we all feel.

But it's in our gospel, from which we get our text for today, that it all seems to come together. And by that I mean this business of trying to reconcile who we are (our identity) with what we have (our possessions) and the related question "if they take everything that I have, then what is left?"

The gospel for today is well known to most of us. It is about the rich man who wants to inherit eternal life. Here is someone who has acquired wealth and who is well established in the community. He has a good reputation and is seeking spiritual things. He is not superficial and all indications are that he has acquired his wealth honestly.

This man appears to be in an entirely different position than Job or David, in that he is not being crushed by his enemies, laughed at by strangers or tormented at the hand of Satan. But in at least one respect he is in a similar position. He is seeking God and doesn't know how to find Him. Like Job and David, something is getting in the way and he doesn't know what it is.

The encounter between the rich man and Jesus is another of those moments when both parties turn away from each other in sorrow. We have talked before about all the occasions when Jesus responded to the questions of those who were with him on the way to the cross and how many times Jesus was left saddened by their inability to understand his message.

The rich man was a good man. He did not want eternal life as just another possession. He recognized Jesus as a true messenger of God and he was sure that he could get the answer he wanted from Him. And he did. Only he couldn't deal with it.

Why was this? It was because *he was confused about his identity*. I don't think that the rich man was opposed to giving money to the poor. He probably did it all the time. But his identity was based on his *ability* to give money to the poor, on having riches to dispose of, on bearing the authority that money brings to influence decisions and work for the common good. He was not a bad man but he was a rich man, and now Christ was asking him to give up his identity.

So when Jesus heard the response of the rich man, he saw an opportunity to give his disciples another lesson. See, he said, how hard it is to give up your identity, especially if it is based on wealth and power. It is the need to hang on to your identity, that is, to hang on to yourself that keeps you from inheriting the kingdom of heaven.

It's interesting that the disciples got the point this time. They realized that, in human terms, if a good rich man could not enter the kingdom of heaven, then no one has a chance. "Then *who can be saved?*" they asked. And Jesus said, *"For mortals it is impossible, but . . . for God all things are possible".*

Identity is at the heart of it all. There are all kinds of reasons to be upset about identity theft even if it's only of the kind that involves someone stealing your money and destroying your reputation. Identity is the heart of who we are. And we will fight to preserve our identity to the day we die.

That is why it is so hard, nay impossible, to enter the kingdom of heaven on our own accord. It is always our own self-centeredness that gets in the way, even if we are good and decent people.

Look at David and Job. They are heroes of our faith. We read their words with wonder and admonish each other to try to be more like they were. But in our lessons for today they, for all their goodness, cannot find God. And it is their identities that are getting in the way.

Look at David's words. The reason we like him so much is that he speaks for all of us. Look at how many of the pronouns I, me and my are in the Psalm. David is saying "God, look at me. I pray to you. I honor you. I follow my ancestors who trusted you and yet I am scorned and despised. I look for you and you are nowhere to be found."

Job does the same thing. "His hand is heavy despite my groaning . . . I would lay my case before him, and fill my mouth with arguments. (But) if I go forward, he is not there; or backward, I cannot perceive him . . . . "

When I read the lessons for today, I was immediately reminded of the victim on television complaining about his inability to get help after his identity theft. He was so frustrated and disappointed. And, indeed, like David, like Job and like the rich man, it is a good thing to appeal for help. It's just that help may not always be in the form you expect.

David and Job both used images of death to describe how troubled they were. The rich man went away shocked and grieving. The disciples were perplexed and astounded. It is a hard thing to realize that in order to enter the kingdom of heaven you have to give up your identity, yourself.

But, of course, as we are told over and over in scripture, what you get back when you have given your identity over to God is so much more than you had before. This can even mean that you end up with more in the earthly, or material, sense. Giving our lives to God is a blessing. Fighting to hang on to our own lives without God is a curse.

We cannot give up our worldly identity on our own. We just cannot. It is all we have and, in our sin, we can see no alternative but to hang on to it. It is only through the power of the Holy Spirit that we can release our identity to the will of God and receive back the benefits that result from that.

So we might say to David, Job, the rich man and the disciples, "Relax. Put your trust in God. Don't always be asking what you can do and why God doesn't seem to be responding to what *you* are doing. Instead wait on God, trust in His Spirit, and He will give you His salvation with a new

An Arcadian Vision

identity more complete and more satisfying than anything you could have built on your own".

We know that Satan will work hard to steal the identity that you have received through the grace of God. He will want you back again in the throes of worldly pleasure and the search for selfish-identity that consumes all of us. But God has sent His son to give us new life and He has done this by sharing our earthly life with us and overcoming the temptations we all experience. We need only trust in Him.

As is written in our Second Reading for today:

Therefore, since we have a great high priest who has gone through the heavens, Jesus the Son of God, let us hold firmly to the faith we profess.

Let us then approach the throne of grace with confidence, so that we may receive mercy and find grace to help us in our time of need (Hebrews 4:14,16).

Sacrifice: What Is it?

Truly I tell you, this poor widow has put in more than all those who are contributing to the treasury. For all of them have contributed out of their abundance; but she out of her poverty has put in everything she had, all she had to live on (Mark 12:43-44).

We tend to be thinking about sacrifice these days. Remembrance Day in Canada falls in the middle of this week. In the secular world, the observance of Remembrance Day is calculated to focus our attention on the sacrifice of persons who engage in armed conflict on behalf of a nation or a country. We normally refer to such conflicts as "war" although we may try to tone down such incidents by calling them "police actions" or "occupations" or even "peacekeeping". But we all know that conflict involving the use of lethal force creates the potential for terrifying consequences and that those who engage in it may pay the ultimate price, the loss of their lives. War can be so terrible that even those who live through it may find their remaining life not worth living and, in a real sense, they have lost it.

So is this what sacrifice is? Do soldiers give us our best example of the meaning of sacrifice?

War certainly provides one context for understanding the meaning of sacrifice. However, our scriptures for today seem to take the idea of sacrifice in a different direction. It is true that there are moments in war, as well as in other activities of life, when individuals act genuinely and selflessly on behalf of others. *We understand sacrifice to mean that a person engages in an action intending to give up something for the benefit of someone else and that they expect no return whatsoever for doing it.*

Many warriors are mercenaries and expect gain for what they do, if not in material wealth then in some other form of recognition. Only the mentally disordered go to war to get killed. This may not at all take away from the possibility that most warriors enter into their profession honorably and with high motives. But it might be better to say that most soldiers teach us about sacrifice not because of *their* intentions but because of the intentions of the presidents, prime ministers, kings, and tribal warlords who seek to achieve their personal and political ends by using soldiers to act for them. It is probably more accurate to say that soldiers are *sacrificed by others* than to say that they sacrifice themselves or that they even know what the meaning of sacrifice is. In my mind, this is the most terrible outcome of war – so many people lose their lives and may not even know why.

In order for an action to be a true sacrifice it requires volition. It needs to be a deliberate act emerging from the knowledge of what you are doing. Death that is accidental or occurs without intention is every bit as tragic as one entered into willingly – perhaps more so, but it is not a sacrifice.

Now this may just be semantics, an unimportant discussion about the meaning of a word. But the idea of sacrifice is so central to our faith we should at least be clear about what we mean by it.

Our readings for today give us a look at the character of sacrifice, including a lesson about what sacrifice is not.

In the first part of our gospel lesson for today we see the antithesis of sacrifice. Jesus is talking here about the scribes and is warning his disciples about using them as an example. Elsewhere in the New Testament, Christ also refers to the church leaders of his day as not truly representing the character of people who faithfully serve God. In some of these places he calls them hypocrites – even liars.

It is worth remembering that it was very important for the Jewish temple leaders to maintain control over the Jewish community, especially while the Hebrew people were under Roman occupation. One of the ways that they sought to do this was by presenting an image of piety and self-sacrifice so that the people would admire them and follow them. Consequently they dressed to be seen and spent hours engaging in public prayers and other visible acts of piety. And while it has to be acknowledged that they led disciplined lives in making their religiosity known to others, it was no sacrifice for them. They were seeking gain for themselves on almost every imaginable level. They wanted power and control even to the point of preying on widows.

The reading today from Ruth (3:1-5, 4:13-17) gives us a look at the attitude of true sacrifice. I think that the story of Ruth has even more profound meaning today than it had in her time or in Christ's time. This is because the actions of Ruth would be considered much more unusual or sacrificial in the developed societies of today's world. Ruth engaged in a sacrifice on behalf of her mother-in-law that might even seem inconceivable today.

Ruth and her mother-in-law, Naomi, were both widows. Being a widow was a frightening prospect for women in Ruth's time. Not only could a widow end up poor and destitute but also left without descendents. In the culture of Ruth's time and place, women in this condition would live in a state of shame and humiliation. Basically what Ruth did was to give up the independence of her own life to assure that her mother-in-law would not live in destitution or without the prospect of an heir. She gave herself up to a stranger on the encouragement of her mother-in-law and, as a result, both she and her mother-in-law were blessed to become the ancestors of King David. God obviously had a plan in all of this but it depended on the sacrifice of Ruth.

The attitudes of sacrifice that Ruth demonstrated were *love* and *obedience*. She made a deliberate decision that she would never leave Naomi and would do whatever she could to keep Naomi safe in her state as a widow. Because of her love for Naomi, she trusted her implicitly, and when she was asked by Naomi to do something, she obeyed. She gave up any other options she might have had to carry out the wishes of her mother-in-law, with no way of knowing where it would take her. This is the definition of sacrifice.

We often point to stories like this from the Old Testament as being precursors of the work of Christ. In this case, Ruth's sacrifice helps us to understand Christ's sacrifice, which is the central feature of our second reading (Hebrews 9:24-28). Christ offered himself up on our behalf with the same attitudes of sacrifice demonstrated by Ruth – love and obedience. He loved us, of course, but first of all he loved his father and for the sake of that love obeyed his father and carried out his father's will – even as Ruth did. Christ's sacrifice took him to his death. Yet the sacrifice was *not* a decision to die, it was a decision to give himself up in obedience to his father. The sacrifice Christ made was to take on human mortality and thus create the *possibility* that he could die. (Perhaps this is not so unlike the warrior who chooses to go to battle for his country thus creating the possibility that he could be seriously injured or killed.)

It is interesting how often in scripture the lessons about a life in service to God come to us in the examples of widows. We started today with the story of the widows Naomi and Ruth, struggling to figure out how to make their way in the world. Now we end with a lesson from another widow who seems oblivious to her needs in this world.

The imagery of the widow in our gospel for today somehow seems more poignant to me than the story of Ruth and Naomi. In some ways it even seems a more instructive lesson on the nature of sacrifice in Christian living.

Maybe the reason for this is that the story of the widow in the temple seems simpler – more straightforward. The story of Ruth is about an important event in the lineage of Christ. Christ's sacrifice for our sins is so powerful and central to our faith that we study it constantly and remind ourselves of its meaning over and over again. These are the things of books and prayers, and study groups and curricula for teaching.

But the story of the widow in the temple is more like a painting. We have the impression that we are not required to study it or write books about it. It is enough just to look at it.

When I read the gospel for today (Mark 12:38-44), I see two postures standing in comparison to one another. The first is the posture of the scribe, haughty and adorned. The second is the posture of the widow, withdrawn and humble.

When the scribes and the rich people presented themselves in the temple, they often did so to gain attention or to do service to themselves. I cannot believe that the widow could have imagined getting anything out of what she was doing and, if Jesus hadn't been there, she might not have been noticed at all. It is very likely that most of the time she *was* invisible to those around her – not wanting to be noticed nor believing that she deserved any recognition in her culture – because she was a widow.

This widow gives us another attitude of sacrifice – *selflessness* or *self-denial*. Her own needs were not important when she made her offering in the temple. If they had been, she would have kept at least one of the copper coins. But she gave it all up, "everything she had". Ruth got something out of her sacrifice – a husband and a future. But the sacrifice of the widow in the temple seems to have no earthly place to go. What can come back to her? This widow is sacrificing in secret. Jesus is there to point out her sacrifice but he notices her because he is the Son of God and can see what she is doing, and he can know her heart. And even He, God in her presence, seems to offer her nothing. He gives her no guarantees of a good meal or a roof over her head or the possibility of any further income. She comes, makes her sacrifice, and leaves more destitute than when she arrived.

It is interesting that church leaders, even today, encourage people to make material sacrifices on the grounds that God will give back to us more than we give to Him. Indeed, scripture also offers that possibility to us. But we must not dare to give tithes or sacrifices to God on the assumption that He will make us richer or materially better off than we were before. This is the way of the scribe. True sacrifice is the way of the widow.

Sacrifice, what is it? It is the giving of something entirely for the sake of another, not knowing what might come of it or if those who benefit from it will appreciate the sacrifice. It is an act of love and obedience accomplished without regard to self.

Soldiers can make sacrifices and often do so to the point of losing their own lives. Religious leaders can make sacrifices that are not self-seeking and that bring blessing to the people they serve. Widows, its seems, make sacrifices almost by definition. We learn the character of sacrifice from all those who enter into it with the attributes of a true sacrifice. We use these lessons to help us understand the great work of God in Christ for us. We also use these lessons to help us know how to live in this world – with love, obedience and selflessness.

A Pioneer of Salvation

It was fitting that God, for whom and through whom all things exist, in bringing many children to glory, should make the pioneer of their salvation perfect through sufferings (Hebrews 2:10).

I have always had a fascination with pioneers. I suppose this is because I have lived most of my life in places that have been newly developed or at least retain a sense of newness in comparison to much of the rest of the world. I was born and raised in a very rural part of a land which many people call the "new-world" (the Americas). As children, we were able to tell tales of the first person who lived in such and such a house. We even knew where the first house was that was built in our county. We were very close to the modern beginnings of the place where we lived and so it was easy to have a sense of the drama and difficulties people encounter when they come to a new place and try to make it ready for living.

My great-grandmother was the first white woman in our county. She was a schoolteacher and all her students, until her own child started school, were members of a tribe of aboriginal people. My great-grandfather established the first abattoir or slaughterhouse in the county to prepare wild and domestic meats for public consumption. He later became the meat inspector for the county. So even as a child, I had a sense of the spirit of pioneering and a feeling for what it meant to be such a person.

When I first visited Europe, I was struck with its oldness. And I remember wondering if anybody could remember who had started things where they lived. It was such a different feeling for me to be in a place so far from its beginnings.

When we came to Canada in the mid-twentieth century, we knew that we were in a place of pioneers and very close to its beginnings. In my explorations across the parish to which I was assigned, I soon began to find out who the pioneers were and what they had accomplished. I was able to visit James Shand Harvey (d. 1967) on several occasions at his cabin near Entrance, Alberta – just up the road from here. I met some of the Moberlys who lived in the area of Grand Cache before that town was built and learned of their ancestor whose cabin still exists just outside of the town of Jasper, Alberta. These were important pioneers who did much to prepare the way for those of us who now enjoy the fruits of their labors. They were also people that suffered from numerous setbacks and difficulties especially, in this case, the Moberlys and others of their community who were forced to uproot after the area they settled was proclaimed a national park.

One of the aspects of pioneering is suffering. We all talk about it. In our conversations we occasionally remember our own immediate ancestors and wonder at their way of life. We think that it must have been hard for them not to have the conveniences we enjoy or that they had to scratch out a basic existence from a land that is sometimes harsh and unforgiving.

Our text for today speaks about Christ in an unusual way. He is called a pioneer. Now it is true that some translations of this passage use the word "author". But if you look up the words "author" and "pioneer", you see that they both have the same primary meaning: originator or initiator. Pioneers and authors are people of beginnings and, it can be said, both originate or create through their suffering.

In this context, I like the word pioneer better than author. Especially given the way that we use the word author these days. Author for us is usually used with reference to the arts – the creation of literature, music or drama. When we use the word pioneer we tend to mean "the first one", the "trailblazer" or the one who was here before us. This is more of the tone of the word used in our text.

An Arcadian Vision

The reading from which our text is taken starts out talking about the ancestors of the Hebrew people who were surely pioneers in their own right. We remember much about them. How they suffered various forms of exile and enslavement almost from the first days of their existence. How they made the great escape from Egypt and suffered for an entire generation under the most primitive of conditions while they made their way to the Promised Land. How they worked to form a nation and build a great religion only to have their lives torn apart, time and time again.

This is the stuff of pioneers: great striving and numerous setbacks. But there is a quality to true pioneers that enables them to survive the difficulties and trials of their leaps into the unknown, and that quality is *vision*. I don't think it is possible for pioneers to succeed without a vision of the thing that they are striving to achieve. It is this vision that sustains the pioneer through the suffering that is sure to follow the first steps on any new journey. And, for the people of Israel, it was the vision of their Promised Land and the hope of the coming Messiah that sustained them through such difficult times.

The real pioneers, in any situation, are those who have the vision. Others may follow them but it is the visionaries who keep the dream alive and have the strength of spirit to get past the doubts and obstacles. In our reading, these people are called prophets and it is they who sustained the people of Israel through their darkest hours. Moses, Joshua, Aaron, Isaiah, Ezekiel, Hosea, Joel, Amos – these are just some of the names of those with prophetic vision who were pioneers of the people of God.

Even Job, who is the character of note in our first reading for today (Job 1:1, 2:1-10) and who gives us one of the great lessons of the meaning of suffering, teaches us much about the attributes necessary to sustain a pioneer.

Suffering will destroy anyone who loses vision and can no longer see the grace of God in all things. We do not know why some people suffer more than others do. But the lesson of Job is that those who do suffer and retain their faith in God offer a great gift of truth and love to anyone that observes their suffering. As we see from Job, suffering occurs at the juncture between good and evil. Suffering is possible because we live in a world of sin where Satan *does* have power and where, because of their sins, human beings must constantly live in the struggle between good and evil. Job's example is extreme because he sought good all of his life and, as a consequence, evil sought him out. It was a great test in the struggle between the love of God and the power of evil in the world. Job kept his vision and was a real pioneer in teaching the lessons of suffering.

Our text comes from the Second Reading where we are told how God speaks to us and teaches us to maintain our vision through His Son, Jesus Christ. The pioneering vision of the prophets has brought us to the moment of the coming of the Messiah. This Messiah is the pioneer who will confirm our salvation and do it as all pioneers do, through his suffering.

One of the questions asked by all pioneers as they struggle to find or achieve new things, especially as difficulties mount, is "is it worth it?" For the entire history of the Hebrew people, the prophets, priests and kings who lived and worked for the purpose of keeping God's people together in the faith struggled with doubt and were constantly disappointed by the rebelliousness and resistance of the people they were leading. All the prophets and religious leaders that I named earlier fill their writings with expressions of self-doubt. In the words of the reading just preceding our text this problem of self-doubt and accompanying sense of unworthiness is addressed again.

Paul, in writing to the Hebrews, reminds them that God did not prepare a "new world" or heavenly kingdom for His angels who serve Him perfectly and in spirit. Instead, He created a new world for human beings, those of his creation who occupy a position lower than the angels but who, in spite of this, are the crowning glory of God's creation.

It seems a paradox that we, as lesser beings, should be considered the most glorious of God's created beings. But this is because we are made in God's image. Part of the image of God is the power of free will. Because of this, human beings must endure the struggle between good and evil and use their free will to decide which to choose. The outcome of this struggle is that human beings do not serve God perfectly. They do not always choose correctly. And because they do not serve God perfectly they must learn to live with suffering. Maybe it can be said that beings who transcend evil and are unaffected by it are greater beings. But what is more glorious than winning a battle that you have the ability to lose?

With free will come all the oppositions arising from the coexistence of good and evil. Among these opposites – of which we could list many – are hope and despair. The constant encounter of God's pioneers in this world with the despair of suffering is countered by the hope of salvation, the promise of the Messiah. The Messiah came, we are told, as a pioneer for our salvation, leading the way through his suffering, including the suffering of death. And as a true pioneer, our Lord kept the vision of his

Father and overcame all the consequences of all the suffering that anyone can experience – even death.

This is the hope for those who suffer and keep their vision. We will overcome through the sacrifice of Christ and the grace of God, his father. It is also the hope of the prophets and all those who accept the call of God to lead the people on to new things and a new life. Jesus became a human being, one of those creatures lower than the angels, to bring hope and salvation to all that believe in him. It is not within the power of angels to believe. They can only obey or disobey. But it is within our power to believe and through the exercise of our will become one with God. We then become greater than the angels for all of our suffering. We might even say that we are greater than the angels are *because* of our suffering.

So, when we remember our earthly pioneers, let us not forget to think of our Lord and Savior who was the pioneer of our salvation and whose vision for eternity gives us the courage and power to sustain us through the suffering and turmoil of this life. This was the hope of Job. It is an even greater hope for us because we have seen the Messiah come and know the truth of his salvation.

Finding Peace in the Whirlwind

Then the Lord answered Job out of the whirlwind . . . (Job 38:34).

Once again, our meditation for today is taken from the book of Job. The book of Job requires us to address the problem of suffering. It offers us many lessons about the struggles of human beings in this world, especially those persons who seek to do good or make meaning of their lives. We have learned already that Job would not have experienced so much trouble if he had just given up on his desire to be a good and righteous man – a man of integrity. He wanted meaning in his life and he believed that such meaning could be found only in serving God faithfully. He would not give up on this quest and, as a result, he suffered in the most profound ways (read Job 27:2-6).

In one of our earlier meditations, we called Job a "pioneer of suffering" and suggested that he has blazed a trail for all of us to follow in dealing with the pain, confusion and apparent injustice of trouble in this world. In another meditation we compared Job's dilemma to persons in our modern era that experience identity theft or loss of self. We learned how Job's greatest suffering was his feeling of separation from God, the source of his identity and his reason for being.

Today, the lesson of Job is a little bit different. In the earlier lessons we encountered Job complaining to his friends and crying out to God for relief. And we saw that Job was unable to find satisfaction. There was no explanation for what he was going through. God seemed nowhere to be found.

But in our lesson today it is God talking. Up to this point most of the dialogue in the book of Job has been between Job and his three friends Eliphaz, Bildad and Zophar. These friends had stayed with him through all of his suffering and self-searching and had tried to counsel him. As it turned out, they didn't help that much, mainly because they tried to find ways to dissuade Job from what they regarded as his persistent and reckless stubbornness. They tried to convince him that his difficulties were his fault and that if he would just quit protesting his innocence and repent of the sins that he had obviously committed, he would feel better and stop suffering so much.

But while Job knew that suffering existed in the world because of sin, he was not at all ready to concede that in his case this was caused by something specific that he had done – that he deserved it for some reason. He knew that he had done everything he could to act with integrity and serve his God faithfully. He was sure that his suffering was not of his doing. Over and over he cried, "if I could just find God and make my case then surely He would see that what is happening to me is unjust." Job protested with the question that all of us ask from time to time, "why me?"

His friends, and even his wife, seemed to be saying, "if you think God is being unfair about all this, why not just curse Him?" But Job would not do that. He kept beating back the advice and counsel of his friends and refusing to give in to the idea that his suffering was his own doing. He just wanted an explanation from God as to why this should be happening to him. And in the end, of course, Job was right. At the end of the book of Job, God berated Job's friends for their false advice, but he also forgave them on behalf of Job because they were genuinely trying to help. They just didn't know how to help Job and they should have kept their advice to themselves.

So what does God say when He finally comes to Job and speaks to him?

First, it is worth noting that He seems to appear without warning, without notice. Job is in the middle of a dialogue with another friend, named Elihu, not one of the original three counselors, when God seems to suddenly appear. Elihu, interestingly, didn't agree with the tact taken by the other three nor is he in total agreement with Job. He seems to bring a different perspective to these arguments about Job's trouble.

An Arcadian Vision

But finally, out of it all, God speaks. And this is where our first reading for today begins.

I think that we should take note of the first line of that reading, *"then the Lord answered Job out of the whirlwind."* Some translations use the word storm instead of whirlwind.

We quite often see drawings or paintings that portray God speaking out of some kind of storm or visible disturbance. We explain this by saying that this is a way God makes Himself evident to His people. For example, God may create a phenomenon like a burning bush to draw attention to His presence.

But I'm not sure that is the type of thing happening here. There is no indication up to this moment that any physical disturbance is taking place, like a storm or whirlwind. However, in the previous chapter, Elihu is trying to comfort Job by pointing out that everything that happens in this world is an expression of God's power and will. And when speaking of this, Elihu used images such as storms being the thunder of God's voice or snow and ice coming from the breath of God.

But even though these images are used throughout the book of Job to describe God's presence, it probably makes more sense here to interpret the whirlwind as something that signifies Job's own agony and searching. It is as though Job has experienced a kind of spiritual hurricane. God comes to Job when his suffering and his search for answers have become like a storm in his soul. The word used for storm or whirlwind in this text can also be translated to read *personal turmoil* or *torment*.

However, regardless of how we take it, God has finally appeared to Job to give him the answers that he has been seeking for so long.

We note that God does not give Job any new information. God's answer for Job is not to explain away his suffering but to remind Job that God is the maker and ruler of all things, that He is present with Job and always has been, and that He will take care of Job in his troubles. It is God's *presence* that comforts Job, not some elaborate explanation about why suffering happens in the world. And God is present to Job, as He is to us, through His *word*. This is why it is important for us to keep ourselves in the presence of God through His word and sacraments. This is the great teaching of our church.

In the end, Job could only say (Job 42:1-3), "look, I know God can do all things and no plan of His can be thwarted . . . surely, I spoke of things I did not understand, things too wonderful for me to know". And with that Job was able to relax and put his whole trust in God again. We read that God blessed the last part of Job's life more than the first (Job 42:12) and he was able to live a hundred and forty years (Job 42:16).

As is usual, the other readings for today follow this theme about suffering, followed by anxiety, and finally the healing power of God's grace.

The second lesson (Hebrews 5:1-10) is about those who have been chosen to be priests or spiritual leaders and how they must acknowledge their own suffering and weakness. When leaders deal with their own suffering and uncertainty they can have the humility to deal gently with others. In this reading, Jesus is presented as the example of a high priest that, out of his suffering, offers up prayers and supplications to God, his Father. As with Job, God heard Jesus and blessed him in his suffering. We are told that Jesus "learned obedience through what he suffered," as Job before him had learned obedience, and just as we all must.

The Gospel for today takes us to a different place. Two of Jesus' disciples, James and John, sincerely express a desire to serve Christ and to be his chief disciples, one sitting on his left and one sitting on his right. This causes some dissent among the other disciples, and Jesus has to remind them that they are all equal before God and should remain humble and serve each other.

But the main lesson that Jesus wants to give to James and John is that they should be careful what they ask for. He reminds them that his is the cup of suffering and that if they want to remain close to him, they will have to drink from that cup as well.

Our sin and separation from God has brought suffering into the world. Now we must live with it. This is the lesson of Job, the burden of the priest, and the cup from which Jesus, and all that follow him, must drink. We can deal with our suffering by recognizing that God is present in the world, and it is His presence that covers us with comfort and strength. He is the ruler of all things, even suffering, and is able to bring us through our suffering (as with Job and Christ) better than we were before.

In the midst of our suffering, it is sometimes hard to find God through the pain and frustration. But since Christ has accomplished the ultimate suffering for us, we can come to God assured that the consequences of sin cannot destroy us. We need, like Job, to keep the faith and search honestly and persistently for God in His word and sacraments.

The Psalm for today gives us the words of praise that we can use to keep God before us when the whirlwind of our suffering and confusion gets too great:

An Arcadian Vision

"Bless the Lord, O my soul: O Lord my God, you are very great! You lay the beams . . . you make the winds . . . you set the earth upon its foundations . . . how manifold are your works . . . Bless the Lord, O my soul."

Watch Your Mouth!

(No) man can tame the tongue. It is a restless evil, full of deadly poison. With the tongue we praise our Lord and Father, and with it we curse men, who have been made in God's likeness. Out of the same mouth come praise and cursing. My brothers, this should not be (James 3:8b-10).

The text for our sermon today comes from the Second Reading for this Sunday as assigned in our Lectionary. (First Reading: Proverbs 1:20-33. Second Reading: James 3:1-12.)

The idea of second readings has been intriguing me lately. I am working on a book now that I have chosen to call "Second Reading". In the introduction to it, I play with the idea that in many activities of life, there is something called a First Reading where an idea or proposal is introduced. This happens in government with the introduction of bills for new legislation. Formal committees in government and business often use first readings of proposals to determine if they want to proceed with them. If they do, they often request a more thorough examination of the subject presented to the committee in a second reading. In universities, proposals for dissertations at the Masters and Doctoral levels take the form of consecutive readings where an idea for research is presented in a first reading. If the research is approved, the student develops the idea further, creating objectives and methods for researching the topic. When these are completed, they are presented for approval in a second reading.

And, of course, each Sunday morning our worship is centered on readings. In the formal organization of these readings (the Lectionary), the church has created a lesson plan where the First Reading sets the tone, is embellished by the Psalm, expanded on in the Second Reading, and given context in the Gospel.

Sometimes it is not easy for us to see the connection between all these readings, but usually the flow between the first and second reading is pretty clear. I think this is true of our readings for today. If you wanted to use homely or somewhat crude language to summarize the two readings, you might say that the First Reading exhorts us to "smarten up" and the Second Reading advises us to "watch our mouth". It is pretty clear that one flows from the other. We are, first of all, to seek wisdom, and it is only through acquiring wisdom that we can control our speech and use words for good instead of evil.

Linguistics is an interesting academic discipline. Linguists set out, in a general sense, to study languages – how they have evolved and are structured. Linguists are curious about the differences between languages including trying to determine what is lost when a language dies. We see this concern expressed as the languages of aboriginal people fall into disuse. Is culture determined by language or is it the other way around? What happens to a people when their ability to express themselves in their own language declines, and they begin to falter in their speech because they are using unfamiliar words representing concepts or even objects with which they have little or no experience?

Language is important. Words are important. Their meaning must be taught, and children must grow up knowing how to use them correctly and with a proper awareness of their power. How they can be used both to help and to hurt others.

Having said this, it is also very important to note that language and the knowledge that comes with it are unique characteristics of human beings. This is part of what is meant when we are told that "we are made in the likeness of God". We have the power of the word and it matters what we do with it.

It is interesting that the Second Reading starts by cautioning us that there aren't many of us who should become teachers. You would think that the scathing criticism of the ignorant in the First Reading would result in an appeal for as many teachers as possible. Ignorance means lack of knowledge or behaving uncouthly because of lack of knowledge. That's what the First Reading is all about. Think about it. A teacher has to know how to impart knowledge correctly and assist people to overcome the bad habits learned because of lack of knowledge. People who choose to become teachers are therefore, according to the Second Reading, "judged with greater strictness". Their mistakes take on greater significance, especially when other people are relying on them for the knowledge that can help them build a better life. Teaching is a high calling and not everyone can do it. It is through teaching that we can learn how to keep our behaviors in check and use our words in ways that do not inflame negative passions or cause shame and humiliation in the lives of others.

Perhaps we should review some of the ways in which words are destructive. While these may seem obvious, it doesn't hurt to occasionally be reminded of these things – to think about our behavior and its effect on others.

Living the lie – There is, of course, the misuse of words in the effort to intentionally deceive. There are many reasons why we do this. But underlying most of it is our fear of dealing with the unknown. We do not know what people will do or how they will respond if they know the truth about us.

It is an interesting characteristic of sinfulness that we always want to cover it up. We wouldn't need to try and deliberately deceive anyone if we were comfortable with the truth about ourselves. We lie to cover up the truth. Think about children who lie to their parents. Often, this happens because they have been criticized so much for their behavior that they become ashamed to expose it. So they misbehave and cover it up. Here we have a two-sided problem. The parent's tongue is harmful in its criticism and the child's tongue is harmful in its lying. Both lack knowledge about how to speak to each other, and as our reading says, "how great a forest is set ablaze by a small fire". I have spoken to children in houses of detention who have become wards of the state because neither they nor their parents knew how to talk to each other.

There is another form of lying, of course. This is the lying which people often describe as unintentional. It occurs when people offer advise or give counsel when they are uninformed and lack the expertise to be of assistance. This happens when someone is trying to be a teacher and they are unprepared or otherwise unable to dispense knowledge truthfully. People who give advice concerning things they don't know about are liars, and anyone who believes them or acts on their advice or instruction can be seriously misled.

Then, of course, there is the lie that is deliberate but is intended to help, not harm. Sometimes we call this "the white lie". We do this because we believe the listener cannot accept the truth or that the truth will make the person's condition worse. There may be times when a white lie is the least harmful thing to do in the moment but, if that is so, it may be better not to speak at all.

Telling the truth – As in the problem of the white lie, we sometimes find that insisting on telling the truth can also be a misuse of the tongue. One way of thinking about this is to remember our mother's admonition: "if you can't think of something nice to say, don't say anything at all". There are moments when saying what we think about someone to his face, even if we're sure we're right, can be harmful and self-defeating.

But beyond this, there is the problem of truth itself. What is it? This is the question that Pilate asked Jesus, and it was a good question.

Scientists often avoid the use of the word "truth". They do this on the grounds that human beings can never know the whole truth about anything. Scientists learn over and over again that things they were once sure of turn out not to be so. And so they always treat knowledge as a search that never ends. Instead of talking about the truth, they talk about what works, what results can be reproduced, or what can be verified by someone else.

In our relationships with others, we would do well to take this attitude, especially if our idea of the truth results in making judgments about someone else. We can rarely know enough about another human being and what they are going through to be judgmental. Sometimes telling people the truth as we see it can be very hurtful because we may be wrong and our truth may be a lie.

However we must not think that the truth is beyond our knowing or that we can never tell it. The answer to Pilate's question, "what is the truth?" was standing right in front of him. "I am the way, the truth and the life", Jesus said. Knowing Jesus and hearing his word is to know the truth. We can and must share that with others.

Sometimes knowing God's Word and exercising the knowledge of the world that comes from God's revelation to us requires that we comment on the affairs of human beings and point out when human beings are acting contrary to God's will, thus doing harm to the people who are God's creation. But we must be careful that we speak God's truth and not our own because, as the Second Reading for today points out to us, we all make mistakes. We see through a glass darkly and, while we live in this world, our vision of the truth will always be flawed. So sometimes we must hold our tongue even if we think we are telling God's truth.

There is a reason why we all have a hard time liking people who act like "they know it all". Those of us for whom television is a recreation are probably familiar with the situation comedy Cheers. Cliff, one of the characters in that series, was a "know it all". He attempted to cover up his obvious failings by expounding on any and every topic. In this way, he was able to stay in control, and his comments were usually so outrageous or obscure that no one could dispute them. Of course, he became a laughing stock.

Regardless of what we know or don't know, it is always better to hold our tongue especially if no one has asked for our opinion. I am often reminded of Reinhold Niebuhr's suggestion that it is "harmful to throw answers like stones at the heads of those who have not yet asked the question".

Sometimes the best use of the tongue is to not use it at all. Knowing when to be silent and simply be present with others in times of trouble is a great skill.

There are many ways that the tongue can be hurtful, but it is most hurtful when we are not being true to ourselves or when we are acting with an improper motive. This is why the First and Second Readings for today go so well together. Both of these readings are harsh and seem to focus on the worst aspects of our humanity. The Gospel lesson for today continues this tone by warning us to focus on Christ and his word, rather than selfishly seeking the things of this world. But we also learn that even when we try to seek the things of God we can do it with a wrong motive. The biblical accounts of the actions of the Pharisees in Christ's time serve as a constant reminder of this. In the Gospel for today we learned that even the apostle Peter, among the most beloved of Christ's disciples, sometimes tried to gain favor with God for selfish or self-serving motives.

We cannot be someone or something that we are not. This is why we are advised that not many of us can become teachers. In the words of the reading, "we cannot grow olives if we are a fig tree". And it is through our speech that we reflect who we are. Even if we don't know who we are or what we are good at, others can know us through our speech. This is why it's important to listen to the "feedback" that others give us, as well as watching the words we speak to others. Speech reflects who we are, what we know and how seriously we have sought knowledge or been attentive to God's Word.

Like all sinfulness, this problem is resolved for us by giving ourselves over to the will of God and applying Christ's teachings in our lives. We can exercise discipline in what we do and how we use language. But we must be serious about seeking knowledge so that we reflect a right relationship with God and a proper knowledge of the world. We need to learn to be loving and not critical or judgmental in our disposition with regard to the speech and actions of others. The love of God in our lives helps us to understand that we are all sinners, that we have all been forgiven and that we all need help to live well in this world. With this spirit we are less likely to misuse our tongues and more likely to be among those who can be good teachers – by word and example.

John W. Ekstedt

On Politics

Such knowledge is too wonderful for me; it is so high that I cannot attain to it (Psalm 139:6).

This is the week of the presidential inauguration in the United States. Barack Obama, a man of African and Irish descent, has been elected to serve as the administrative leader of, arguably, the most powerful nation on earth. I suppose that if there were ever a time for someone performing the functions of a priest in a house of worship to talk about politics, it would be now. After all, every inquisitive and thoughtful person in North America and, indeed, in most of the rest of the world, is interested in the outcome of the recent election and the reaction of people to it, as might be reflected in this ritual event of inauguration.

Some have said that these election results signal a change in paradigm. What they mean is that they see something happening that is so profound it could change the face of everything. They believe that decisions will be made differently and that priorities will be reordered. Some hope that particular values, seen as being uniquely American, will be restated and given renewed authority and ideas which have been devalued will be revalued and made new again.

Of course, some remain skeptical about the possibility of any change of real significance. Others fear the possibility of any change at all. The world is in too much trouble. The economy is too bad. It would be foolish to expect too much. But even these people do not deny the significance of this inauguration as symbolic of a new era in American politics. A man has become president who clearly symbolizes the breaking of another link in the chain of racial strife and inequality in the United States. And no one can fail to notice the rising power of women in the political culture.

I recently wrote a piece for the local newspaper discussing the importance of ceremony and ritual in our community life. Part of the purpose of ceremony is to give honor and recognition where it is due. When we recognize others who have accomplished rare or unusual things, it gives us hope that we, too, can be part of something grand or transcendent. In the church, we often talk about the importance of recognizing, through rituals and ceremonies, events in the life of Christ and the church that give us hope and are examples of possibilities for our own lives.

At the very least, the event of a presidential inauguration gives us opportunity to consider our own place in world affairs. The rising to power of a black man in a society established, in part, on the backs of Negro slaves gives a great many people hope for the future of their own lives.

It's an interesting time, to be sure, but should a pastor or priest talk about politics and world affairs from the pulpit? Isn't there supposed to be a separation of church and state? Doesn't the church do better to concentrate on the message of love and the gospel of salvation and leave civil affairs to the officers of the state, appointed or elected? Shouldn't we "render unto Caesar the things that are Caesar's and unto God the things that are God's"?

This is not an easy question, and most clergy with whom I have associated struggle to find the best way to address political matters in the context of church life and worship experience.

It is clear that it is better for clergy in their official capacity and for the church as an institution not to be involved with what we call "party politics". It would probably be wrong of me to use the pulpit to promote or support a specific candidate in an election. Of course, we know that in some churches this does happen and the line between civic and religious mandates becomes blurred. When this happens, we begin to identify such churches as much by their political ideology as their theology. Politics and theology merge into each other and can become indistinguishable. We tend to call societies where this type of merger has been fully realized theocracies. In North America, most people believe that a political democracy cannot survive under such circumstances.

Yes, we do believe that the separation of church and state is an important principle. The state should not dictate our doctrines or beliefs as a church and the church should not try to control the civil order or seek to have power over it. But this is such a tenuous balance that we can all identify occasions and circumstances when both the church and the state have violated this principle.

The word politics means "of public affairs". If officials or members of the church were to avoid talking about politics in that sense, they would have to set aside many of the teachings of the Old and New Testaments. Those who give first allegiance to God are to co-exist with non-believers in a civil and positive manner. We learn from scripture that the function of prophets, and the purpose of prophecy, is to speak God's word to human power and authority. Those who are chosen or called by God to speak for Him have as one of their primary duties to bring God's word to the whole world including those responsible for civil welfare.

Preachers of the Gospel talk about politics every time they apply God's word to the problems of living. This includes lessons on human values, community life, Christian living, evangelism, stewardship, the raising of children, the purpose of marriage, the needs of the poor or imprisoned as well as any of the other personal and social responsibilities that apply to any human being in this world. Politics is about civil order, and ministers of the gospel speak to that all the time.

In politics, the difference for Christians is not the issues, but the motivation for engaging in them. We are interested in the politics of the world because our duty is to do God's will and communicate God's message. We are not interested in accumulating personal power or promoting any particular political party or ideology. (It is possible for a government or political party to promote an ideology that allows or promotes actions contrary to the teachings of God's word and the welfare of human beings. When that happens, the church must reject such actions or political doctrines through a persistent proclamation of the Law and Gospel.)

Christians need to be concerned about the character and beliefs of their political leaders. So we do our civic duty by observing their behavior and listening to their message. We pray for them because they have power in this world and we are affected by what they do. We need to be wise and not allow ourselves to be fooled by false or misleading messages. We have a duty to support policies that contribute as much as possible to the welfare of all people. The salvation of the world is our business and we need to be aware of how the civic world works and how people in power think. We are not of this world, but we are in it and we must understand how to carry out the responsibilities assigned to us both as citizens of the world and members of the body of Christ.

As much as anything else, we need to understand ourselves and know what our gifts are so that our message to people with political power will be consistent and effective. We wish this as well for our political leaders: that they will learn the will of God as well as the desires and needs of the people they serve.

The activities of politics are about influence – about obtaining power and keeping it. In the most positive sense, politics is about using that power for the welfare of the people governed. This requires that people in power have access to knowledge and the wisdom to use that power properly. Politics requires prudent action and judicious behavior in order for people to be governed well. When politicians are scheming and crafty, the welfare of the people is usually not served.

Christians understand that there is a relationship between faith and power. Faith is about power – about the source of all power – and through

An Arcadian Vision

both faith and reason we understand the attitudes and skills necessary to be wise leaders or supportive followers.

If we walk our way through the lessons for today, we see, as always, a theme emerging. All of the readings speak to the attributes or behaviors of people who live a successful Christian life and who, as a result, make good citizens and leaders.

The Psalm (139), from which our meditation verse is taken, reminds us that, while much is required of us, human beings struggle to summon up sufficient knowledge or wisdom. God is the source of all wisdom and often his "knowledge is too wonderful" for us to comprehend. The Psalm reminds us that we cannot trust in our own wisdom; we need the guidance of God who made us. Citizens and their leaders need to understand the need for humility in their quest for wisdom and right political action. They need to realize where the source of wisdom is to be found.

The first reading (I Samuel 3:1-21) is a reminder that, however powerful we might be, we must keep our own house in order. We are constantly exposed to reports of the antics of public officials who use their power for personal gain and pleasure seeking. In this reading three important lessons are emphasized. The first is that the prophets or ministers of God have a responsibility to speak to the wrongdoing of powerful people as soon as it is found out. The second is that a leader must take action against wrongdoing no matter how close to home it might be. The third is that there is an unforgivable sin. We commit this sin when we blaspheme God by ignoring His word and refusing to accept His Holy Spirit. Without His Spirit we cannot receive His gift of salvation or offer it to others.

All civic leaders and the messengers of God who seek to counsel them are reminded to attend to their own lives and the lives of those closest to them if they are to retain their earthly power. Again, you don't have to search far in this modern world to find examples of those who have learned this lesson the hard way.

The second reading (I Corinthians 6:12-20) further emphasizes that the friends we choose make a difference. Wrong associations are contaminating and drag us down. Paul reminds us that, all things considered, human beings can pretty much do what they want to do. "All things are lawful for me", he says. But some things are good for us and serve the welfare of others. Some things are not. And whatever we decide to do, we have to remember that we are the place where the spirit of God dwells. We must act accordingly or the spirit of God will be driven from us and our decisions will become negative and hurtful. If we are people with civil power, we may diminish or destroy the lives of untold numbers of people.

The Gospel (John 1:43-51) speaks about the relationship between leaders and followers. The lessons are practical and seem obvious but are so often ignored. First, talent and good leadership can come from anywhere and we should not let prejudice inhibit our ability to see this. "Can anything good come out of Nazareth?" Second, we should see leaders for who they are and not be fooled by the glamour of their presentations or the passion of their rhetoric. Jesus cautions Nathaniel about becoming a follower of him just because he thinks Jesus can do magic or is capable of supernatural acts. Jesus reminds him that great things, supernatural or not, can come only from God. Jesus does not want Nathaniel or anyone else to follow him because they think he is an impressive *man*.

So as we think a little bit about politics this week and watch the presidential inauguration with all its pomp and circumstance, let us remember these lessons. After all, no matter who the political leaders are, our faith is the same and our salvation is assured. Nevertheless, we wish the best for our leaders and we pray for the welfare of all people in a troubled world.

Faith and Food – Life in Two Dimensions

(This sermon was written for the Ecumenical Advocacy Alliance as part of their Food for Life Campaign 2010-2011. The Alliance is based in Geneva, Switzerland.)

And if you spend yourselves in behalf of the hungry and satisfy the needs of the oppressed, then your light will rise in the darkness, and your night become like the noonday (Isaiah 58:10).

We are here today, at least in part, because of the challenge that has come to be known as the "global food crisis". We share an interest in this issue because of our common identity as members of the church that is the body of Christ in the world. We have an interest in applying ourselves to this challenge as a matter of our religion. We are a community of faith and, as such, we continually strive to understand what our faith is and what it requires us to do. We are here to learn how we may express our faith through good work. We are moved by the many admonitions of our Lord that compel us to care for the hungry and the afflicted.

We note that others are concerned about the social and political effects of food scarcity. Increasing food prices and reduced food availability coupled with an expanding population and global climate change are resulting in some dire predictions for global hunger in this century. And, of course, the recent global financial meltdown has elevated all resource issues to a new level of dialogue and concern. The food issue is high on the agenda of agencies like the G20, the European Union and the United Nations. For those who have been fighting the food battle in various locations in the world and have observed the inefficiency resulting from fragmentation and competition, this may seem a good thing. But there are serious dangers emerging from the current tendency to treat food shortages and emergency aid as matters of cooperation between governments, rather than as concerns of private philanthropy or other non-government agencies. When issues of social benevolence become elements of government policy, cooperation may evolve into competition and benevolence into regulation and control. In competitive environments, as we know, someone usually loses and it is likely those who need assistance the most who will be the losers.

While this is not the place for a discussion on the economy and politics of food production, it is enough to say that faith communities with an interest in this problem should try to understand the world within which they seek to do their work. In Matthew's gospel (10:16), we are warned of the dangers waiting for us in the world and advised that we "be as shrewd as snakes and as innocent as doves". We would do well to keep such counsel.

As a community of faith, we know that motive matters. We are reminded in the book of Colossians that "Whatever you do, work at it with all your heart, as working for the Lord, not for men" (Col. 3:23). We are here, at least in part, to act from this motive with regard to the food needs of all people.

We are not unlike Noah or Isaiah or Jeremiah or Ezekiel, who were among those who were given a vision of the physical and spiritual waves of destruction coming and who were charged with responding either by issuing a warning or preparing a solution. And, in every case, they asked 'why me?' 'What attributes do I have that can in any way stem the tide of such destructive forces?' And in each case the answer was 'because you have a motive for action that gives you the power. You do it for a reason that will work. You do it for the love of God. You do it because God has asked it of you and not as a matter of self-interest, no matter how altruistic that self-interest may appear.' We are always and forever in memory of the promise "Come . . . take your inheritance . . . for I was hungry and you gave me something to eat" (Matt. 25:34-35).

So let us consider for a moment this issue of the relationship between the faith that establishes our motive and the activity of providing food for a world growing increasingly hungry.

When the two words "faith" and "food" are written or spoken together, it is sometimes in the context of a ritual acknowledgement of food as a gift of life and the giver of food as the source of life. All of the world's faith traditions imbed in their literature and their practices an acknowledgment of the power of the relationship between faith and food. The Holy Scripture of the Christian faith offers numerous illustrations of the way in which these two words or concepts are conjoined. God, the Author of faith and the Source of all life informs us in so many ways that food is not just a need – it is a gift, an offering, and a blessing that either feeds our spiritual life of faith or emanates from it. Food is both the source of *physical* wellbeing and an expression of *spiritual* wellbeing.

Since the beginning of recorded history, it has been taught that food cannot be rightly offered or received without recognizing its connection to our spirituality. That is why we learn to either offer a blessing or ask for one when we are about to partake of food. This is a formal acknowledgment of the connection between our faith and our food.

In the activity of offering food to the hungry, the motivation of faith may be especially important when those in need are living in dire and threatening circumstances or when they are in competition with each other for scarce resources. The great need that is generated by hunger makes people vulnerable to manipulation and threat and drives communities into political disorder. In Christ's ministry we find many examples of the danger that results when someone acts in the name of God to address the problems of people in need. He lived, as we do, in a world reeking of political intrigue and uncertainty. In the lives of people like Dietrich Bonhoeffer, we also observe the consequences of acting from the motive of faith. His life, as we remember, was a testament to the power of faith when political forces threaten the physical and spiritual welfare of people. We learn from such lives that those who wish to follow Christ's example in service to others should at least be aware of the possible consequences.

With regard to the challenge before us, it might be helpful to note that faith and food are the same things happening in different dimensions. Both are about sowing and planting, birthing to new life, growing and nurturing to maturity. The dimension of food is physical or temporal. The dimension of faith is spiritual or mystical. Both are about life and living.

Given this understanding, we might ask if it is possible for faith and food to even exist without each other. Is spiritual existence necessary for physical existence? Would God continue to provide food in a world where no faith exists or, like the destruction of Sodom and Gomorrah, would the rivers run dry, the soil turn to ash and human beings disappear from the face of the earth? The world seems to be diminishing in so many ways. But many strive in hope that the earth can be renewed or the damage to it at least contained. The world continues to exist though people are made mean and low by the toxins emitting from it, and many die from lack of available nourishment. Part of the lesson of Sodom and Gomorrah is the assurance from God that He will stay His wrath, even if only a few people of faith are found (Gen. 18 and 19). So while people of faith remain in this world there is still hope for the hungry and oppressed. Food may be produced and distributed for those who are hungry. The poisons with which we litter our world can be removed from the soil and filtered from the water. These things are possible because people of faith remain to answer the call to Isaiah, "who will go for us" (Isaiah 6:8). If we count ourselves among these people, we must remain steadfast, for we are also told, again in Isaiah, that "if you do not stand firm in your faith, you will not stand at all" (Isaiah 7:9).

Let us ask the question in reverse. Is our physical existence necessary to our spiritual existence? This question is profound, for it addresses the very nature of human purpose. Is it necessary for human beings to exist in physical form to know God? And in the same way, was it necessary for God to exist in physical form for human beings to know spiritual fulfillment? If human beings desecrate the world to the extent that the production of food is no longer possible and people can no longer continue to live, can faith survive? We are told that man cannot live by bread alone, but is bread required to seek and maintain the faith from which salvation comes?

God became man in order to show human beings the secrets of finding immortality in a temporal, mortal world. He demonstrated that, through faith, we are able to overcome the limitations of our human condition. Yet even He was careful to nurture His body and provide for the physical nurturing of others. The great lessons of faith come to us because we have received the gift of life on the physical plane. Our temporary and limited lives are a gift of God that we are to appreciate and use in His service. The opportunity to find God and receive His grace in a world that is broken and unclean is possible only if a person has the ability to receive God's word and act on it. Giving food to those who need it is not just an altruistic act of mercy. It is an offering of the hope of salvation itself. For spiritual existence to be maintained, the physical existence of human beings must be nurtured. It is from the dimension of our physical being that we enter the dimension of the spirit and return to a relationship with God. Gifts of food and water thus become the greatest of all gifts from one human being to another. The ability to produce food and make it available to others is among the highest of all skills and the most worthy of occupations, for these things give people the opportunity to know God.

Is this what faith and food have to do with one another? Does the temporary nature of our physical existence, supported and sustained by food, really have a direct connection to the eternal nature of our spiritual existence, supported and sustained by faith? And will the answer to these questions assist in affirming our resolve to distribute food to the hungry?

Sometimes when people like us organize to do work in the world, we think of our work as "faith-based". We would like others to know that what we do is work of faith. Work of faith, we are told, is "good work". It seems clear that if we want to understand the relationship between faith and food, we must also understand the relationship between faith and work. For this, our battle cry is found in James 2:14-17 wherein we learn that faith is dead without work. And giving food and clothing to the needy is the example James uses to teach how work can make faith complete and alive.

Regardless of the reference one uses for the source of wisdom on this matter, it is clear that we are here to live and to advance our lives both physically and spiritually. Life is a thing of grand dimension. It can flower and bloom into great works of art and intellect. It was never meant to be the sweaty groveling for sustenance of a life mired in ignorance and poverty. Life was given to us to be beautiful and fulfilling. Our life in this world is certainly less than it was meant to be for all of us, faithful or not. For many in the throes of poverty and disease, it doesn't even come close.

Life is a gift that requires reciprocation to have meaning. We have life and we give life. That is why we exist. The message of God's intervention in this world through the life, death and resurrection of His son is that "you might have life and have it more abundantly" (John 10:10). Human beings have discarded or ruined much of what life was meant to be. As a result, numerous exhortations in scripture encourage us to grow in the knowledge of life and in its practice and to offer that knowledge and those skills as a gift of love to others (Proverbs 22:9, 1 John 3:17, etc.).

It seems a paradox that the gift of life may sometimes come at the risk of death. Like Christ, we must sometimes face down the threats and ugliness of a world bent on self-destruction in order to offer even the most

An Arcadian Vision

essential or basic elements of life to another person. There is no greater love than to risk one's own life so another might live (John 15:13). But receiving life and giving it back really is reciprocal and we are promised that "he who is willing to give up his life for my sake will save it" (Matt. 10:39, Luke 9:24, Mark 8:35).

The activity of living with faith in the temporal world is given meaning through its danger and difficulty. There is no higher work of faith than to risk one's life for another. Because life is both a physical and spiritual pursuit, sometimes the risk to a physical life in the service of God is a genuine advancement in a spiritual life.

Supporting the physical lives of others through the gift of food or food production can indeed be a difficult and dangerous pursuit. This may be especially true in circumstances that are volatile or politically threatening. But we are bound to do it. It is our calling. It is the reason we are here. It is our ministry, and only those who have life in both dimensions can be consistent and effective in this ministry. We are people who not only have food – we have faith.

We may feel that we have burdened ourselves with a difficult task carrying forward this concern for the hungry and the oppressed. But what choice do we have? What charge has been given to us other than the command that we who have received life offer it without reservation to others? A cup of water to one who is thirsty, a serving of food to one who is hungry, a cloak to one who is naked, given with the blessing of God and the promise of His salvation. There is nothing else for us to do.

Is Freedom Just Another Word?

Now the Lord is the Spirit, and where the Spirit of the Lord is, there is freedom (2 Corinthians 3:17).

I have often wondered about freedom as an idea or ideal; as a state of being; as a state of mind; or as a real physical thing that we can touch, feel or experience. What is freedom? What does it mean to be free?

We are all shaped by our experiences. When we talk about the things that make us who we are, we usually think of specific people, the place where we were born or live, and our way of life.

The people we remember are often, or perhaps always, parents, other family members, important mentors or teachers and heroic figures.

Let's consider heroic figures for a moment. In recent years, there have been interesting studies on the importance of heroes to all the cultures that have recorded their history and ideas. The great stories and myths of every civilization are about heroes and how people seek them out to hear their words and bask in the glory of their presence. Much of the literature of antiquity is about heroes and the lessons they teach about courage, overcoming flaws and weaknesses, perseverance in the search for reward, greatness in the face of tragedy, and agony in the search for truth.

Discussing the heroes of mythology would take much more time than we have here today. For our purposes, we will remind ourselves of only some of them. There are the heroes and heroines of classical Greece such as Achilles, Hercules, Pandora and Midas. We remember the Titans of Greece and Rome such as Atlas and Prometheus and the heroic messengers of Hebrew and Arabic tradition such as Moses and Abraham. As children we learned of the heroes of English and Welsh mythology such as Bran the Blessed, Branwen, Arthur, and Robin Hood. We may even know of the Seven Heroes and Five Gallants of China led by the famous Lord Bao who strove to bring his people out of servitude and oppression. There are many more of these. I have named some to remind us of who they are or have been in the epic tales of human beings. Today, some people might list Obama or Mandela as people approaching heroic stature. We might well ask ourselves: who are our heroes today?

Heroic figures may be real or invented. They may come to us as people with special talents and insights or we may create them out of our own desires and aspirations. They arise out of things that matter to us as a people. And so our heroes take on the look and feel of our place and culture. They reflect the values to which we aspire. They are like us, only much better, much wiser, much stronger, much more fulfilled. They seem more capable than we are in the struggle to deal with the disabilities that we all share.

While the look and language of our heroes may be different in time and place, there is something consistent about them. In one way or another, they all strive to be free. They present their struggle for freedom in different ways and always with some liability or weakness that they have to overcome. They may have a physical weakness such as Achilles, they may be constrained in the way of Prometheus, they may be naïve as was Arthur, or they may be foolish as was Pandora. Their heroism is found in their attempt to rise above their weaknesses or act courageously in the face of them. That is why they are heroes to us. We admire them because they seek to be free of the limitations that are imposed upon them and, in so doing, they give us a glimpse into the meaning of freedom itself.

In a similar way, I have wondered how North American Christians understand the language of scripture since scripture is so full of images of comfort for people who, in this life, had little chance of ever experiencing freedom. Freedom, as we know it in an affluent democratic society, was simply unknown and even unimaginable to the majority of people in Biblical times. They knew about servitude and enslavement. They knew about the constant threat of occupation by others. They knew almost nothing about property ownership or personal rights.

When these people were warned about becoming enslaved to sin they knew what that meant because their whole lives were lived with the threat of enslavement in one form or another. In the scripture, and for these people, the message of salvation was almost always couched in the language of freedom. For them, freedom was the greatest desire because it was the thing most often denied. So it was not difficult for them to equate sin with slavery and personal salvation with freedom.

There are many people in today's world able to receive the message of salvation in a manner similar to that of the people who are addressed in our scripture readings for today. But I sometimes wonder about those of us who have the enormous privilege of having been born into freedom, at least of an earthly kind. Could it be that we are the living illustration of Christ's warning that "it is easier for a camel to go through the eye of a needle than for a rich man to enter the kingdom of heaven"?

And who are our heroes? Do we admire people who seek to overcome their flaws and limitations in the search for freedom and truth? Are we enthralled by the tragic lives of those that lose everything but remain true to themselves and their beliefs? Or are our heroes different people now? Do we instead admire those who are acquisitive and grasping? Who succeed when others fail? Or worse, succeed *because* others fail? Has the place where we live and the way of life we have forged for ourselves made it harder to receive the message of the Gospel with understanding? Are our freedoms false and our wealth a mirage? Do these things actually get in our way when we seek to know the message of God for us? Have we fooled ourselves into thinking we have achieved those things sought so valiantly by the heroes of our mythology only to find that we remain chained like Prometheus or that, like Pandora, we have only managed to unleash trouble into the world. And in the end, seeking the golden touch of Midas only serves to diminish our lives.

In the final analysis, of course, the heroes of our making, both real and imagined, fail us. Even revered leaders such as Moses or Abraham were not able to achieve freedom for themselves, and both died still in the hope of it. They were great heroes and they did great things but like all our heroes they were too much like us to succeed in their godlike aspirations. But at least, in the case of heroes like Moses and Abraham, they were able to accept their weaknesses and failures in the light of God's promise to them. Their heroism was flawed but their hope was real and perfect.

So what is this hope? *It is the promise of freedom.* And the lesson is that this freedom is not necessarily freedom from servitude to others but, instead, *freedom from servitude or enslavement to self.* It is to be free in spirit, and we learn from our scriptures for today that you must be *born* into it. You cannot achieve it through a heroic act or acquire it by virtue of wealth. It is a birthright. This is something everyone in Biblical times could easily understand. As slaves they knew they were *not* born to freedom in this world. The message that they could achieve freedom by the right of a second birth was a wondrous message of salvation to them.

The Gospel message for today talks about two births: one of water and one of spirit. We are told that if we are to enter the kingdom of God we must experience both births. We sometimes use the phrase "you must be born again" in recognition of this truth.

The important message here is that the circumstances of our birth by water do not give us the freedom that saves us from the consequences of our weaknesses and disabilities regardless of the place and time in which we live. Whether you are born into this world slave or free you have no hope of salvation unless you are born again from above. We have all been born of human parents. It is also necessary to be born as a child of God. This is accomplished when we receive the Spirit of God in us just as through natural birth we have received the characteristics of the earthly parents who formed us.

Our earthly parents have given us much, but they cannot give us freedom. And as we see in the struggles of all our heroes, it is freedom that is our greatest hope and our greatest desire. Freedom, as we learn in the text for this meditation, is where the Spirit of the Lord is. *"Now the Lord is the Spirit, and where the Spirit of the Lord is, there is freedom."*

We receive the Spirit of the Lord in faith. Faith comes to us through the word and sacraments. We receive the promise of God's Spirit in our baptism and we nurture it through attention to His Word and attendance at His Holy table. *We are not just made wise or holy by these things – we are made free.* Freedom is a birthright given to us by God through His grace and mercy. Our earthly birth brings us trouble and we find or invent heroes in the hope that they can transcend this trouble and, at least, teach us how to cope with it ("man that is born of a woman is born of sorrow"). But God, through Christ, has released us from the need to make heroes of men. Through our second birth, we are free of that.

You don't have to be a slave to appreciate freedom. You don't have to be a hero to achieve freedom. What we need is a second birth where we are filled with the Spirit of the Lord and are finally and forever born into freedom.

We Are All Together in This!

Can anyone withhold the water for baptizing these people who have received the Holy Spirit just as we have? (Acts 10:47)

Christians who follow the traditional church year and who are interested in deriving meaning from the various observances associated with it have an opportunity for a very rich worship life. The themes, the colors, the artifacts, the music and the symbols all create an atmosphere of meditation and expression that is uplifting to the spirit and stimulating to the mind. These things can bring out the best in us and motivate us to create even more of the beauty that surrounds us in worship. We can give back to the worship experience by developing our talents in music, painting, writing and speaking. Worship done at a high level results in the creation of great art, profound words and ageless music. Wood and stone are turned into images of wonder and they, too, are made to tell stories. A rich worship life lifts us up to be better than we are and moves us to learn more, say more, sing more and make more of life in this world.

All throughout scripture we are encouraged and admonished to praise the Lord with music, singing, art and architecture. We are to build houses of praise and fill them with music, fine wood, worked stone and other beautiful things. It is possible to live an entire lifetime moving from one great worship experience or worship place to another without doing the same thing or seeing the same one twice. The highest level of human endeavor throughout history has been reflected in its places of gathering and worship. The recovery of ancient artifacts through applied sciences such as anthropology and archeology continually reinforces the centrality of worship in the lives of people. Scientists often deliberately focus on the discovery of places of worship in ancient cultures. These places teach us much about the characteristics and culture of people long vanished from the face of the earth. The practice of religion has been the great central feature of all people throughout history. At its best, these practices reflect an honest recognition of the spirit of God working in the world and a desire to acknowledge and portray that spirit through human action.

But there is another side to this. At its worst the construction of great houses of worship or other religious monuments and artifacts can become a narcissistic and self-centered attempt to glorify an individual human personality or elevate the status of a particular community. Religious practices can be used to enforce the ways of a dominant culture at the expense and exclusion of others. Many of the great monuments of history, both religious and secular, have been built on the backs and with the blood of the oppressed – and all this often for the glorification of an elite family, tribe or individual.

We see evidence of such monuments in the Valley of the Kings in Egypt and read about the human catastrophe resulting from the building of the Tower of Babel in Babylon. We see considerable evidence of personality and family cults in the excavations of Mayan and Aztec cultures in the Americas and of the human sacrifice that kept these cults alive. All such cultures were maintained through the use of religion to deliberately subjugate the people through fear and ignorance.

The Christian church has not escaped the human tendency to use religion as a means to control the masses. Our Lutheran church exists as a result of a rebellion against the misuse by the church of its authority over its members including a misuse of its rituals and symbols to subjugate people and maintain control over them. This was done, in part, by withholding from the people the very source of their religion – the scriptures on which the doctrines of the church are based.

Worship rituals and the corresponding places of art and beauty that arise from them can be great and enduring in their elevation of the human spirit when people enter into them in a right relationship with God and with their fellow human beings. But when these things are done only in an effort to give praise to men or to advance the interests of a particular group or culture, they become an abomination and evil flows from them. The very places designed to reflect the magnificence and enduring love of God become places where innocents are persecuted in the name of holiness and from whence holy wars are waged.

So why talk about this? Why should our thoughts drift to the problems that arise in the world when the things of worship are misused or places of worship are turned to the service of men rather than the glory of God?

For me, these thoughts have been triggered by the general tone of our readings for today. These readings seem to address the elements of "right worship" in a world and during times when worship had become a distorted and abused practice.

The tone of right worship is set in the Psalm (98) that exhorts us to "shout with joy" and "sing a new song". Worshippers are encouraged to elevate or amplify their voices with harps, trumpets and the sound of horn. This is an appeal to the transcendent worship discussed earlier in this meditation.

Having set this tone, we are reminded in the Second Reading (1 John 5:1-6) that worship is about "the love of God". We learn, though, that the love of God flows two ways in worship – to God and from God. God loves us and extends His love to us through the sacrifice of His Son and the gift of His spirit. In worship, we are reminded of this through the word and sacraments. We love God back by recognizing Him in praise for His gifts of life and love and through the offerings that are the works of our hands and the fruits of our labor.

But even beyond that, and as an essential element of our worship, we love God by keeping His commandments. The Gospel reminds us that His commandment is that "you love one another as I have loved you". The love of God in the world is demonstrated to others in the way God's children love each other and gather together to share that love in unselfish lives of worship. We do not offer up our hymns, or play our instruments, or raise our crosses, or build our altars, or carve our candlesticks or sew our banners to give glory to ourselves but rather to demonstrate our love to God and to each other. We can do this because God first loved us.

This love that binds us together affects everyone and everything. The sacrifice of our Lord Jesus Christ for us and the gift of the Holy Spirit to us have changed everything. The great change in the relationship between God and humankind and within humankind itself that has resulted from Christ's sacrifice is at the center of the great festivals of our church and in the content of every aspect of our worship experience. Even the non-human parts of God's creation recognize this change. The Psalm tells us that "the seas roar", "the rivers clap their hands" and "the hills ring out with joy".

But perhaps the most important point here is that the love of God and the gift of the Holy Spirit and all the change resulting from that are for everyone. The blessings that we recognize in worship are not just for those who have special status. The Hebrew people struggled throughout scripture with the meaning of their history as the "chosen people". Christ's message of freedom and salvation for everyone was difficult for them. Yet that was the change that Christ brought to the world.

John W. Ekstedt

The blessings of worship are not earned by doing good works or the keeping of particular practices – even if those practices are intended as worship. These gifts are not won by war. These gifts are not reserved for those with earthly power or status. Instead, these gifts are freely given to all those who believe. The scripture makes clear that "whatever is born of God conquers the world. And this is the victory that conquers the world – our faith. Who is it that conquers the world but the one who believes that Jesus is the Son of God."

From our scriptures for today we learn that it is through the gift of the Holy Sprit that the world will be one again. This gift is received in worship and fed by worship. We are made one together as we nurture our faith together. We are able to do this through the work God has completed for us, especially His own death as a human being.

That great monument of human ego, the Tower of Babel, tore us apart. According to scripture, prior to the Tower of Babel the people of the world spoke with one voice. But the building of this monument for their own glory was an indication that the people had lost touch with the God of their creation and were intent on becoming gods themselves. So, we are told, God interfered with their intent by confusing their language and scattering them over the face of the earth. Numerous tongues or languages dividing people into many tribes and nations resulted. It was from here that the story of God's redemption began as He chose one of these nations to be the people from whom the work would be done to bring all His people together again.

So, in the second reading (Acts 10), we learn that God did send His Son as the promised redeemer who would bring the people together again. We read that the "good news" of this is to be preached to the *whole world* by people like Peter.

Admittedly, all of this comes as a surprise to the chosen people or "the circumcised" as they are called. After all, the people of the world had been separated for so long. It was hard to imagine that anything could happen to bring them together again. In Acts (10:45) we read, "the circumcised believers . . . were astounded that the gift of the Holy Spirit had been poured out even on the Gentiles for they heard them speaking in tongues" (that is, even though they were speaking in a different language, the "circumcised" *understood* them).

Because of the work of Christ, we have come full circle back to the place of the Tower of Babel when the people pulled away from God and each other to "speak in tongues" or separate languages. Now, although we remain stuck in this thing of our own doing and remain people separated by language and culture, something has happened that can bring us all back together again – that will give us common knowledge, common language and common culture. Through Christ we are able to unite in a spirit of cooperation and with a single purpose. We *can* keep his commandment to love each other as he has loved us.

When we started this meditation, our thoughts were taken with ideas of worship. We remembered how we organize ourselves to express our faith and join together with our fellow believers to give the best of our talents for the praise of God who has done such great things for us. What a magnificent thing to imagine: the whole world united in faith, worshiping God with the beauty and grandeur of our music, our art and our intellect. We *can* overcome the problems of language and culture, and all the other things that separate us, to find common ground in the love of God.

Jesus said, "I am giving you these commands so that you may love one another" (John 15:19). When everything we do is an act of love in the name of Jesus, then everything we do is an act of worship. The world can unite again in one great voice to worship God and, when it does, the world will know that it is healed.

Now That's What I'm Talking About!

(The last sermon)

We have come to believe in Christ Jesus, so that we might be justified by faith in Christ, and not by doing the works of the law . . . (Galatians 2:16).

Therefore, I tell you, her sins, which were many, have been forgiven; hence she has shown great love (Luke 7:47).

This is the last sermon that I will preach for awhile – maybe ever. Of course, I also felt the same way some years ago when I found myself moving on from parish life to academic life and, eventually, to retirement. As you all know, I have been glad to have the opportunity to preach again – not so much for you as for me. I cannot begin to explain what it has meant to be back in the routine of thinking and writing required in the life of a pastor. The search for spiritual knowledge and finding ways to communicate that knowledge involves a lot of wrestling with both devils and angels. No true preacher ever feels worthy of this life. Inadequacy seems to be our strongest attribute. We muddle along trying to sound confident in the process.

I don't think that pastors who feel this way are being falsely modest. I know that occasionally a sermon can be pretty good. Sometimes the stars align just right or the topic touches someone's life just as it is needed.

John W. Ekstedt

Sometimes the energy of the preacher is very positive and the mind is clear and bright with useful illustrations and proper distinctions. Sometimes it all just works.

Of course, when we talk about preaching this way, we are evaluating it from a human perspective. What God does with His word is well beyond the ability of the preacher to know. Even the most muddled sermons can bring peace and salvation to the heart that is open. The important thing is not how good the preacher is but whether or not God's word is present in the preaching. Directing people to God and the message of God's word is supposed to be what preaching is about.

When I began thinking about this "last" sermon, my goal was to try and come up with something that would serve as a summary of the time we have spent here together. Of course, it was then necessary to ask "summary of what"? Would it be to sum up how we have felt about the church, the people and the town or would it be an attempt to encapsulate the teachings from God's word that we have tried so hard to learn and understand during the time that we have been together?

And there is another related matter. I have often wished that I could find a way to effectively explain or describe the life of the spirit. We have been talking about that a little bit these past few weeks. We have discussed God as mystery and the concept of spiritual knowledge. But somehow our attempts, once again, seem inadequate and even unworthy of our calling. Surely we can do better than this.

I thought for a while that, just for this Sunday, I might leave the routine of our church year and find a scripture and a topic that would speak more directly to some of these issues. And then I read the lessons that are provided for this day and was reminded again that it is God's word that is important, not mine. God's word for today speaks very directly to the life of the spirit as well as to some of the theology that makes our own church so important to us. These readings seem just right for today. So I picked a verse from both the Gospel and the Second Reading for today as the basis for our meditation.

The verse from our second reading (Galatians 2:15-21) comes from the passage which so profoundly changed Luther's life and became the central feature of his reform theology. Luther's struggle to define and declare the meaning of these words not only helped to change the nature of the church on earth but also influenced the direction of modern government or civil order. To understand the religious, cultural and political struggles of Luther's time is to understand the foundation of the Lutheran church

An Arcadian Vision

everywhere, including our church here in Jasper. The emphasis that we have placed on the words written in the second chapter of Galatians has rooted our church for almost five hundred years. Our task, as we know, is to keep this message relevant in the modern world. This is the general theme of the most recent edition of our church periodical (Rocky Mountain Rose, Vol. 2, No. 1).

We know that Lutherans are not the only ones that speak the truth of God's word. It's just that we do it with a specific emphasis and from a specific history. Our emphasis is "justification by faith, not works" – this is the idea that we can do nothing to work out our own salvation because it is a free gift of God. Luther was a Roman Catholic priest who was struggling with these issues because his church had fallen into disrepute. It had mixed its theology with politics. It had sought to gain the favor of kings and princes and in so doing had perverted itself. Its message was no longer freely given; even kings had to pay for it and peasants often couldn't. But the worst perversion was that it was not only the church's services that were being sold or given as rewards for work done, it was salvation itself. People were being led to believe that they could buy God's love and forgiveness or, said another way, that they could buy their way into heaven. The revelation to Luther from Galatians and elsewhere that salvation is freely given and freely received gave him the courage to stand up to both priests and kings against the heresies and excesses of his time. This is our heritage. This is why there is a Lutheran church. We receive this heritage with thanksgiving.

But I must tell you that it is the message of the Gospel for today that is the most pleasing to me and that best summarizes what I think we have been about these past two years. It is the same truth but somehow made more personal and human in the story of the woman who had "lived a sinful life".

There could have been several reasons why this woman was described in this way. A common interpretation is that she was a prostitute. And she may very well have been one. But I think it is just as likely that she was an independent woman, one who didn't keep her place or follow the rules – especially in the ultra-orthodox world of the Pharisees. If she was living as an unmarried woman and having any relationships with men that were not chaperoned she would have been considered a prostitute. Expressing sexual freedom in this way might have been one way that she expressed her independence, but the context of her sinfulness seems to be bigger than that. She had obviously offended the church leaders in a significant way and even Jesus acknowledged that she had gotten herself into a lot of trouble.

The thing about this passage that says so much about the essence of Christianity, Lutheran or not, and about the virtue of the doctrine of justification by faith, is that the Pharisees, for all their good works, were far less pleasing in the sight of God than this fallen woman. It turns out that she knew how to love – maybe because she knew how to live. The Pharisees thought that they didn't need forgiveness for anything they had done and so forgiveness was not extended to them. The woman had no doubt about her need for forgiveness and, therefore, forgiveness was given to her. The Pharisees may have known how to pray in some formal institutional way. The woman knew how to love – simply, humanly, genuinely. Who is the sinner here?

This is Christianity defined for me. You and I don't have to figure it out. This is spiritual knowledge, not intellectual knowledge. *Love and faith* are the sinful woman washing the feet of Jesus with her tears. *Justification by faith* is Christ forgiving this sinner, not because she had successfully completed a rehabilitation program or had given a sufficient offering to the church, but because she knew right away who he was and believed in him. According to the Pharisees, she had done no good work that allowed her access to God. Christ, in effect, said to them, "you are right about that. You have done the good works, she hasn't. Isn't it interesting that she knows who I am and you don't? Isn't it interesting that she is justified and you're not?"

Justification by faith – that's what we're all about as Christians and as Lutherans. A doctrine forged in the drama of Paul's conversion, renewed in the agony of Luther's struggle with his own church, and typified by the sinful woman bathing Christ's feet with her tears.

Preachers aren't just about preaching. For example, I like basketball. I played it in college as a young man and as an old man with my grandchildren, and have followed it all my adult life. Those of us who are "fans" know that the National Basketball Association finals are now being played. There is a player on one of the teams famous for his shooting skills. Often his mother is sitting in the stands and when her son makes a particularly difficult shot, the television camera swings to where she is sitting and you can see her mouth the words "now that's what I'm talking about".

This is the way I feel today about the doctrine of justification by faith that is so perfectly illustrated by the woman who lived a sinful life. When I read her story I just want to say, "now that's what I'm talking about".

8. Essays

The following were written either for the church periodical (*Rocky Mountain Rose*) or for church magazines such as Canada Lutheran. As with the sermons, most of these were initially directed to the audience comprised of the people of Jasper and the members of Jasper Lutheran Church. However, we were glad to see that, over time, these notes were used as part of a larger mission to Park visitors and various participating churches in the United States and Canada.

The Church in the World

Our focus for this issue of *Rocky Mountain Rose* is "the church in the world". In previous issues we have presented descriptions and opinions about our *specific* church here in Jasper. Along the way, we have discussed how church life has changed over time (both here and elsewhere). We have included commentary on issues related to the worship experience as well as vignettes from the history of our church including some of the programs remembered fondly by various persons who have visited or lived in this area.

The Lutheran church has been a presence in Jasper for nearly sixty years. We celebrate its history starting from the gathering of a few Canadian immigrants in the mid-twentieth century. These people were mostly of Scandinavian and German origin. Along the way, we have acquired a building of historic importance and have experimented with a variety of programs unique to the setting within which we exist. Some of these such as the Summer Pulpit – where pastors from North America register to stay at the church for one week and officiate at one worship service – have become fixtures and are emblematic of our presence here.

But behind the history and fond memories has been the struggle to understand and remain faithful to our roots. We are not the only church or gathering of believers in town. What is our relationship with these others? What makes us different? Our church is a Lutheran church. At least we know that much. But as time has passed, our church, like some of the others around us, has had to revisit its reason for being. We need to not only know and remember how we got here, we need to know who we are now in order to define our place and help others understand how to be with us.

There is no doubt that the energy to maintain a Lutheran presence in Jasper came from the desire of recent immigrants to express themselves in a culture and tradition that was familiar to them. We all understand that Lutheranism is a *specific* way for people to gather and express their faith. It is not the only way, but for some of us it is the preferred way for reasons that may be cultural as well as theological. So we will work hard to preserve those things that make our church unique while at the same time being open to those with different backgrounds who may find our theology and worship experience helpful to them in their Christian living.

Every church seems to struggle with deciding how they should present or "advertise" themselves. To what degree can we or should we adjust our practices or beliefs to accommodate others? Should we concentrate on making a clear statement about our beliefs, so that there can be no doubt about where we stand?

Of course, as soon as we begin struggling with these issues, we realize that we have to understand the difference, if we believe there is any, between our *specific* church and *the* church that many agree is *the body of Christ in the world*. We all realize that the differences between churches are often based on opinions about which specific church best represents or reflects Christ's intentions when he established his mission to the world.

We all know that there is a difference between cultural and historical ways of expressing faith and the definition of faith itself. Faith is often defined in the statements of belief (sometimes called doctrine or dogma) produced by church bodies for the purpose of clarifying the premises on which their faith is founded. Specific churches that organize their beliefs into such statements are usually called "confessional churches". These churches openly confess their beliefs as a way of describing or defining their understanding of the church as the body of Christ and how they believe themselves to be part of that body. The Lutheran church is a confessional church and it has been a priority from its founding that its members should know and remain true to its confessions. The application of the beliefs stated in these confessions to people of every time and place is the task of each Lutheran congregation. These confessions and the scriptures on which they are based are constantly reviewed and discussed so that they may always be reflective of God's Word and Christ's intent when He commissioned us to build His Church in the world.

We Lutherans want to be true to ourselves while open to others who are also members of the body of Christ. When churches gather to consider joint action or talk to each other about principles of faith, we say they are practicing ecumenism or "being ecumenical". While this has become a somewhat controversial movement to some, in its proper form it simply recognizes what we all know to be true: whatever our church is, it cannot be the only one that contains persons who are members of *the* church – the body of Christ. But from a Lutheran perspective, when we talk with others, work with them, worship with them, or in some other way join together, we do it on the basis of our confessions – on a clear declaration of what we believe and how those beliefs are derived.

Sometimes it's important that we think beyond ourselves and our own specific problems and interests. But when we do so, we must do it knowing full well who we are and what we have to give to others. This is the church at work in the world and we are glad to be a part of it.

A Shadow of Plenty in a Diminished World

(This was written as a pastoral statement for the first edition of *Rocky Mountain Rose*)

I now realize that my life as a preteen boy was idyllic in many ways. While my parents were poor and we experienced the tragedies of illness and injury, much of my time was spent drifting in a world where reality exceeded any of the inventions of my imagination.

For several years I lived in a forested area on a hillside rising a few kilometers above a saltwater bay. At one end of the bay nestled a natural harbor and around the harbor a small fishing community had been formed. My father made his living selectively harvesting timber from our property on the high plateau above the bay. He used horses for this activity, and in the fifth and sixth grades I was allowed to ride one of the horses to school. Whenever possible, I would ride the trail down the hillside to the harbor below and while away the hours in the summer sun.

The bay and the larger water that fed the bay supported both recreational and commercial fishing throughout the year. The greater body of water, called a "sound", eventually connected our little bay to the Pacific Ocean. In my youth I was only vaguely aware of these connections. Such insights did grow as I listened to the locals explain how the humpback and killer whales that would occasionally drift into our bay had "come from the ocean".

What I loved most about the village was its wooden pier that extended out into the harbor. Along the pier were attached the iron wharves used to moor the fishing boats and other sea craft that occasionally visited the area. Most of the time the pier was unoccupied except for the infrequent fisherman or a child with a dog. It was the perfect place to take a sack lunch or a bag of shrimp, purchased at the fish store for twenty-five cents, and sit with feet hanging over the end of the pier and watching the sea world below.

In those years I thought the water was for fish. It was their home and they were always there. There was no point to the water except for the fish. My friends and I could catch fish whenever we liked. They swarmed beneath the dock, swirling and dodging as flashes of silver, blue and gray. Or they sat, like thieves in hiding, hugging the pilings that provided the foundation for the pier on which we rested, watching.

What did we know? Our world was fish anytime we wanted them and the trees were so large that they had to be cut in smaller sections so that my father's horses could manage the haul to the loading ramp by the side of the road. We children thought that we had a hard life because we had to do a little work now and then and the house we lived in was made of logs. I was twelve years old, living in paradise, and it was being destroyed as I played in it.

Seven years later, I was living in the suburbs of a city where I had moved to attend a residential school. I was about to leave for university and wanted to show my girlfriend (now my wife) the place where I had played "in the day".

We found the bay and harbor but not the town. We found the road where we loaded the timber but not the house – and not the trees. The plateau above the bay was now a suburb not unlike the one in which I was currently living. Some buildings were left where the town used to be, but it was a shadow of its former self. And the fish were gone, as were the mussels and the shrimp. Some sea worms remained but it would have been a fool's game to try and catch them.

An Arcadian Vision

Looking into that barren water was, to that point, the most shocking experience of my life. I simply could not believe it. And while I was no longer a naïve, preteen boy, I could come up with no reason why the water continued to exist. For me, it had lost its purpose.

Today, I can find very few people who identify with this story. When I share it with others, I often realize that they think I am exaggerating. They have never seen such a thing. Why should they believe that it ever existed? That it was once possible to fish without a line or bait. All you needed was a net or quick hands. Sometimes I feel that when I am gone there will be no one to carry the memory of it.

I am now what some people used to call a Religious. I am a clergyman, a pastor and a theologian. I proclaim my faith and it is not a burden to me. I find comfort in the Gospel and in the doctrines of the church. I do not fear these things and I do not fear to question my understanding of these things. But a world so diminished seems a terrible price to pay for our sin, ignorance and separation from God. Yet we were warned, weren't we? The wages of sin is death. We carry death with us everywhere, when we were told, instead, to be stewards of the earth and to take that responsibility seriously. This includes learning the skills necessary to take care of what God has given us. We hear the admonition, "Who then is the wise and faithful manager . . .? The servant who knows his master's will and does not do it will be punished . . . From everyone who has been given much, much will be demanded . . ." (Luke 12:42ff).

Some efforts are now being made to bring the fish back, and in some places there are signs of progress. This is true as well for buffalo, grizzlies, wolves and many other species. Yet it seems that every move forward is matched by two moves back as the natural world changes around us – and largely because of us.

I remember the churches of my youth and the great sound of hymnody and praise that was uttered from them. As a young adult, I attended one of the great Lutheran churches of New York City. This church occupied a square block of prime real estate in Upper Manhattan. Included in its offerings were a pre-school, a day school for grades one through seven, youth programs, and a variety of social and cultural programs. But most of all it was a place of worship where the preaching of the gospel and the administering of the sacraments were received joyfully by numbers sometimes reaching more than a thousand at a sitting.

I recently learned that this church is selling some of its properties and holdings, that the school no longer exists, and that the permanent membership has fallen to less than one hundred people.

As with the fish in my little bay, the signs of decline in one place help us to predict and understand what is happening everywhere – what the general trend is. Since in my retirement I have returned to service as a pastor for a congregation, the stories of decline in the life of the traditional church have been heaped upon me. I have returned to a place that doesn't look the same anymore. The bay is still there but the fish are gone. So what is the purpose of the water?

Is it the same thing? Do the stewardship of the earth and the stewardship of the spirit rise and fall as one thing? If we take care of one will we also be taking care of the other? How does all of this work?

We know that things change. We cannot always be striving to return to the same place, no matter how idyllic it was or how much it meant in our lives. Sometimes the fish don't come back. They just reassert themselves in another place. Sometimes the people to whom the church must speak have come from a different place and have different needs. They may not respond to the offerings of the church as others once did.

But one thing is sure. The fish need clean, nourishing water and people need the message of salvation proclaimed so that they may hear it and learn from it the things required for their spiritual well being. We cannot make the water into something else no matter what changes occur within it, and we cannot make God's Word something else regardless of the changes happening around it.

Maybe the fish won't come back to my bay the way they once were. Maybe the people won't come back to the New York church the way it once was. But by seeing these changes we learn of our duty to keep the water clean so more fish will not be lost. And we learn to preach the Gospel and offer the Sacraments faithfully so that more people will find their way to God. The two things do go together.

We have a responsibility to teach our children well. What do we teach them about this?

One thing they need to know is that change happens. The things of our youth will sometimes be things to which we cannot return and we have to learn how to let them go. But the only way we can deal with change effectively is to know what is permanent and necessary so that we can be strong in the face of change and have the courage to contend with it.

There are things we must fight for and hold true to ourselves so that our stewardship of the earth and our spiritual stewardship can be examples of "a wise and faithful manager".

We teach our children well when we offer them the knowledge of God through His word and sacraments together with the knowledge of the world in which they live. They need to see that these things are connected, and they need to see the connection in us. They must learn to care for the things that matter in their own lives and in the world around them. This is worship in its truest form. This is water filled with fish and houses of God filled with praise.

Afterward

It seems that so much has changed in recent years. We have all experienced the rush of technological innovation and the difference it has made in every aspect of human endeavor. Every day we are reminded of changes in the natural world often accompanied by expressions of deep concern as to what it all may mean. Words and phrases like global warming, pollution, overcrowding, desertification, endangered species, contamination and natural disaster impose themselves on our conversations and provide the headlines for our news reports. This language coexists with the jargon of human suffering and malice: poverty, hunger, war, rebellion, coup, destruction, disease, revenge, rape and refugee.

For those that have organized their lives in the church and have imagined it as the rock of stability in a sea of change, the transformations taking place in organized religion and the varying attitudes about it have, perhaps, been the most unsettling thing of all.

Where is the place that we can go? How can we find the knowledge and the power that will make all this right again?

We do live in a broken world. But it has been so almost from the beginning of things. The negative conditions affecting the world and those who live in it have been the subject of record since human beings began to speak and learn to write. It has always been about fire, flood and earthquake. It has almost forever been about disagreement, conspiracy, vengeance and murder. The great epics and myths of the people of the earth are about power and the search for it, the fame of the conqueror, the glory of battle, the heroism of the warrior. Where love has tried to intervene or a person has emerged to try and make things right, the scribes want to portray them as gods for attempting to transcend the human condition.

An Arcadian Vision

And such heroes always seem to be brought down either by the wrath of the crowd or by some fatal flaw in their own makeup. We know no other story.

These things are worthy of our concern but they are not new to us. Yes, there was a time in this world of trouble when the church as an institution seemed a different thing that was more relevant and respected. The church was a dominant institutional power and few dared to speak against it. But that is precisely the image of the church so many now rebel against. We should not forget that the little Lutheran church in Jasper is itself a product of historical resistance against the misuse of power by church officials.

Growing numbers of people no longer live in fear of the church. We can only imagine that as a good thing. After all, Jesus drove the moneychangers out of the temple, and the apostles who followed often warned about the many abuses that are possible within the church as it, too, is affected by the things of the world.

But we do lament that, even at its best, the churches are not held in the kind of regard that they used to be. The buildings fall into disrepair and the people speak against them as though they are an enemy. It seems sad and retrogressive that people of faith have somehow lost or are losing the rich cohesiveness that the institutional church has provided for, now, thousands of years.

The theological debates within the church and the utterances about the church by authors, media commentators and other public critics from the secular world are surprising and confusing to a new generation trying to find their "spirituality". However, it is important to remember that the human quest for comfort and happiness has often come with a rejection of those teachings most dependent on the highest levels of faith and reason. The encounter of Jesus with the rich man reminds us of the difficulty people have with the demands of the righteous life. It is simply too uncomfortable. Faith seems to require too much.

In the modern era, there is increasing resistance to the idea of an afterlife, the concepts of heaven and hell, or the belief in an omnipotent and omnipresent God (especially one who "would allow *such* suffering"). These teachings seem counter to human reason and human expectation. They become the reasons why some people can't take the church seriously. Salvation doctrine may be accepted as a harmless or even a psychologically positive teaching, but notions of punishment and damnation are too hurtful to the human psyche and too outrageous to be believed.

It would appear that one of the hardest things for human beings to accept is their own humanity. That difficulty is partially evidenced by the trouble people have in taking responsibility for themselves and their own actions. Confirmation of this is found in our rehabilitation centers, mental health facilities and prisons. In the end, we have to know that no one has done this to us. We are the decisions that we have made both individually and collectively. And our decisions have driven us down rather than elevating us. Like the people of the Tower of Babel, we are sometimes fooled into thinking that we are more than we are. But we are finally crushed by our inability to transcend our own selfish desires. The miser becomes his greed. The murderer gets lost in his violence. This happens because people are free to choose evil just as they are free to seek forgiveness. The erosion of the message of the church adds another dimension to all of this. In their search for meaning, people may accept the problem of evil and the value of not doing it but they may reject ideas about punishment or forgiveness. This was the problem of the Pharisees. They gave up their lives to the task of pious living. They valued good over evil, but they denied the need for forgiveness not only for their specific sins but also for living in a state of sin. They were humanists cloaked in institutional religion, and the idea that they could not earn their own salvation or would be punished for being "wrong" was abhorrent to them.

All persons know that their actions bear consequences and that "the wages of sin is death". For people who will not face this reality, the way of comfort is to assume that any consequences are temporal or temporary and that there is nothing beyond this vale of tears. If there is no lasting consequence, no eternity, then why be concerned about what we believe or do beyond that which provides immediate gratification or contributes to our limited self-interest? The church teaches about loss of self in service to God and about things that have to do with eternity. Denying God and ridiculing the church is a way to be rid of having to think seriously about these things.

Yes, sometimes the institutions of religion deny or misuse their own teachings and become the source of terrible trouble for persons who are seeking God in this world. But we must know how to exercise faith *and* use reason in our search for understanding and truth. As has been discussed in several ways in this book, we must know who we are and what we need and not be deterred either by our own lack of will or by the self-serving preachments of others.

Perhaps the most interesting trend in the modern age is the evolution of humanism or pantheism as religion. Religion, after all, is primarily a system of belief. It is a mistake to equate religion with a *particular* system of belief or only with those systems of belief that have a particular institutional form or that promote a certain idea about God. I have not yet met a person who has openly rejected the idea of God or the institution of the church who is also devoid of religion. It is usually the case that people who describe themselves as atheists or agnostics have well-articulated belief systems with all the characteristics of any other form of religion.

If one is going to deny the existence of God or the possibility of any relationship with such a being, then the religion of that person must be based on some form of worship of humans or the natural world. The oft-repeated claim that "I am spiritual but not religious" is probably a type of non sequitur in that it implies that a person's spirituality can be separate from the things they believe. Normally, people who reject a particular form of organized religion or a belief in God remain committed to some form of religious ideal. These beliefs may emphasize either the spirituality or ideals of human beings (humanism) or the existence of spirit or divinity in all the objects, forces or manifestations of the universe (pantheism). It is interesting that the modern rejection of "church" or "religion" often involves a return to beliefs that are more primitive in character and concept than any of those found in Christianity.

Sometimes it helps to take a practical view of the meaning of faith in the world and the importance of the church in the nurturing of such faith. Religious life as expressed through the church is faith quantified. The quality of faith may wax and wane in the life of an individual or in the life of the church as a whole. The church is the body of Christ in the world. As with Christ himself, while he lived upon this earth, the church suffers all the pangs of humanity, because it is humanity. Various forms of spiritual and psychological distress, hunger, disease, the maladies of aging, and the grind of daily living including its persistent repetitions, all assail the church. Its members must commit considerable energy to maintain minimal health in a world that assails them on every hand.

But for all of this, the church remains. Its numbers are its measure. It is a great army that serves in the trenches of a broken and altered world. Its sores may fester, its sight may dim, its body may weary, but it is the church. It is all of us together in the great wave of humanity washed by the blood of the lamb. "I looked and there before me was a great multitude that no one could count, from every nation, tribe, people and language, standing before the throne" (Rev. 7:9). This is faith quantified crying out in a loud voice "salvation belongs to our God who sits on the throne" (v. 10).

John W. Ekstedt

The world is changed by the existence of the church. Broken and inadequate though it may be, while it exists the world is better. The attributes of faith reach into every aspect of every person's life. Because of faith there is the possibility of tolerance, civility, respect and peacefulness among all people.

In these meditations, much has been said about the nature of faith. The concept of faith and the meaning of it have been discussed in many other forms of literature including, of course, the Holy Bible of Christianity. We learn that faith can be based on many things: power, authority, force, fear or deception. Everyone has had the experience of believing in someone or something and then "losing faith" in that person or idea. When this happens, we know that the faith we held was not properly grounded and turned out to have no meaning at all. When someone violates our trust we say that they have "not been faithful". Even in the modern world where it seems many long-held values are questioned, faithfulness is still held in high regard. It is a primary virtue no matter what else one may believe.

In the Christian church, the communities of faith that make up the body of Christ know that faith has meaning if it is based on love. When faith springs from love, it is life saving and eternal. This is why we are reminded that, of the three great virtues (faith, hope and love), love is the greatest (1 Corinthians 13). People may put their faith in other things and, as a result, may even seem to accomplish great things. But in the end, it becomes clear that any foundation other than love, and especially love *of* God and love *by* God, is sinking sand.

The church exists in particular places. Jasper, Alberta, Canada is such a place. I have heard many people describe Jasper in an Arcadian way. They live their lives in it knowing they would not or could not be anywhere else. Many that don't reside in Jasper visit it regularly to find the peace that it offers. For some, it is a holy place and within it there are places of power where they go to feed their spirit. I have heard it said that if God can't be found in the mountains and river valleys of Jasper National Park, God can't be found anywhere.

These, of course, are sentiments of appreciation for a place in the world that we imagine still retains some of the character of God's original creation. I can tell you that the human condition is the same in Jasper as it is anywhere else and, of course, we would all expect that. Most of us are not fooled into thinking we can find or create a "tower" or a place of utopian wonder where sin no longer exists and our basest instincts are no longer at play. Left to our own devices, we tend to bring the places that we occupy to ruin. Often our places don't elevate us – instead, we seem invariably to bring our places down. Such is the power of sin and the force of evil – unforgiven.

In fact, there may even be better places to see the face of God, or be touched by the spirits that emanate from God (those beings we sometimes call angels) than the few remaining gardens of God's original creation. For example, we might be advised to frequent the prisons, hospitals, soup kitchens and fields of destruction resulting from natural disaster and human conflict. In these places, people often *use* God's power rather than simply observe it. In these places, people may be far more likely to have Arcadian vision.

The Lutheran church that has existed in this Arcadian place for almost sixty years is experiencing its difficulties keeping the ministry going. Ironically, its physical location partially contributes to this malaise with its limited and transient population base and variable economy. However, it also suffers from the modern phenomena affecting many, perhaps all, churches. Many of the historical and cultural reasons for the existence of specific congregations no longer hold. And faith in God is fading as a motivation for living. Like the bay of my childhood, there are some places where the fish are gone or are going. They may come back or they may relocate in another place. That is the way of things in God's world.

But wherever the church is, there is hope. And the church is in Jasper as it is everywhere. The joy of having had these moments of meditation in the mountain village of Jasper, Alberta is clearly the result of experiencing the faithfulness of a small group of people who share the love of Christ and of each other without assuming anything of it. They do not aspire to bigness or greatness in any way. Keeping the church going is sometimes a struggle, but no more than with any of the other struggles of life. They are people who know how to deal with life because they have faith based on love. They would probably deny that their faith could "move mountains" – especially the mountains soaring all around them – but it can and it does.

Postscript

When a project likes this reaches its end, I am almost always left with a sense of foreboding or uneasiness. It's not that I fail to appreciate the work or that I am left unsatisfied with the product. It has more to do with the problem of time and space. It seems that, once I stop, the work will begin to recede into the past and soon become irrelevant – that eventually it will no longer speak to the time in which it exists.

I have written or co-written textbooks and reference materials for use in colleges and universities. I have written some creative non-fiction and a memoir. All of these seem, in one way or another, to be lost in time. This is most noticeable, of course, with the textbooks as they soon become outdated and must either be revised or discarded. But even the others appear stuck in the past and useful mostly for historical reference.

This is not necessarily a bad thing. Everyone can appreciate notes from the past, or expositions from a particular time. But sometimes in my fantasies I just want the thing that I have done to stay in the moment, to be unaffected by time, to always be immediate and relevant. Even as I write this note of self-disclosure, I am aware of time slipping by, and I already feel the need to update the illustrations or at least point out the connection between the material in this book and events post-2010.

Of course, if any of this material meets the criteria for the "true" preaching of the gospel, then it will be relevant in time and space and up-to-date all of the time. Still, the desire remains to keep pointing out the connection.

For example, as this book was entering its final edits in the summer and fall of 2011, serious and troubling events occurred in two cities of the world known for their democracy, affluence and relative peacefulness. At

An Arcadian Vision

various times, these cities have been among those in the world regarded as the most desirable in which to live. The events were riots and they were immensely destructive. They caused considerable damage and shook the confidence of the local inhabitants and their governments. People began to question their long held assumptions about morality and the practices of civility. The cities were Vancouver, Canada and London, England. The world media chattered about these events for days and even weeks as the two cities tried to recover their dignity and achieve retribution. The summation of all the inquiry and analysis seemed to be attempts to get at questions such as "what would cause people to behave like this?" or "even if there are legitimate grievances, why do people appear to have no moral compass or capacity for common civility?"

In the meantime, terrorism continued to stalk the streets of Middle Eastern cities and the faces of starving children stared out at the world from towns and villages in Africa and elsewhere.

So it goes in time and space. The limitations of the temporal world seem to deny us the ability to live together as we know we should. The "fix" would appear to be to develop the ability to transcend our limitations, to be able to act beyond and above our own selfish interests. To know when we have enough and, more importantly, to know what enough is. We can't do it, or it would have been done by now.

Yet the message of this book is that it can be done and it has been done. What we need to do is apply the fix that exists rather than believing we can somehow construct a solution of our own making – while becoming confused and discouraged when we discover that, once again, we can't do it.

I guess this is why I want to keep going or at least why I feel a little uncomfortable about stopping. Yes, if the message is real it won't get stuck in time and space. Yet it is very tempting to try and make sure that it doesn't stop or get lost by continuing to restate these lessons in every moment to every situation – while we are still here.

But that is my job for *my* life. Pastors and priests cannot be trapped by the arrogant assumption that they are responsible for the way anyone else lives life or that they have to try and make meaning of everything.

Still, we know that preachers will preach because that is their work. And so, while this project ends, another will soon begin – by someone, somewhere.